# Tools Useful for Task Achieving

[Ed. Trans.]
**Katsutoshi Ayano**

[Authors]
**Katsutoshi Ayano
Syouzou Iida
Kiyoshi Inoue
Toshifumi Shimoda
Mitsuhiko Fukushima
Takao Yamagami**

**JUSE Press, Ltd.**

Originally printed in Japan as "Kadai Tassei ni Yakudatsu Tool" (Tools useful for task achieving) by Katsutoshi Ayano *et al*. ©Katsutoshi Ayano *et al*. 2010, published by JUSE Press, Ltd.

**Tools Useful for Task Achieving**
Copyright © 2011 by Katsutoshi Ayano
Published by JUSE Press, Ltd.
5-4-2 Sendagaya, Shibuya-ku, Tokyo 151-0051 Japan
All rights reserved. Printed in Japan
ISBN 978-4-8171-9415-2

# Introduction

This book is based on the series of articles titled "Kadai Tassei ni yakudatsu Tool wo Manabou Imakoso Kadai Tasseigata wo koukatekini katsuyo shiyou (Let's Study Tools Useful for Task Achieving - Effectively Utilize Task Achieving Type, Now)", that appeared on the *QC Circle* magazine (published by the Union of Japanese Scientists and Engineers) from July through December 2009, and re-edited and added explanations for better understanding.

The purpose of this book is to make the basics and tools of Task Achieving understood to the people who are going to study Task Achieving from now, including those who are going to enter business world, and to the leaders and members of small group activities like QC Circles, already working as members of society.

As the background for the publishing in the *QC Circle* magazine, it became expected that even the improvement activities at shop floors to cope with the changes in management environment, to contribute to management and to effectively conduct task achieving, to cope with the changes in management environment at an un-experienced scale that were brought about by the global economic recess triggered by the sub prime loan problems in 2008.

Currently, although the global economic recess are becoming weak, led by the economic recoveries in the NIES countries centered around the Southeast Asian countries, it goes without saying that the management environment is changing day by day to the degree we never have experienced before. In these circumstances, it became required to apply Task Achieving approach even in the job shop improvement activities.

It is known worldwide that one of the reasons of Japanese recovery to the World No. 2 economy from the devastation after the World War II was the introduction of participative management in which control and improvement of quality of work centered on customer satisfaction are continually conducted through small group activities like QC Circles.

It is the problem solving procedures called "QC Story" that contributed to the continual improvement activities. However, toward the end of 1980s, increasing number of companies started to apply the "Task Achieving" approach from the recognition that there were issues that could not be approached only by the problem solving approach. Therefore, at the beginning of 1990s, a Task Achieving procedures so called "Task Achieving QC Story" was proposed by QC Circle Keihin District as a core group.

Thereafter, through the series of books summarizing the study results of QC Circle Kanagawa District and the publication of case examples by QC Circle Keihin District. The "Task Achieving" approach came to be used even in QC Circle activities.

In 2000, "Measures Implementing Type QC Story" was proposed. Currently, there are three types of prosedures, "Problem Solving", "Task Achieving", and "Measures Implementing" used for problem solving and improvement at the work shop. In this book, it is explained how to apply these approaches properly.

More than twenty years has passed since the Task Achieving approach was proposed, and there are various concepts and tools proposed on idea generating and organizing (*seiri*) methods used for Task Achieving. Among improvement cases, there are those cases which would have been further improved if they used those tools, and even used, there are not a few cases that cannot be said the tools have necessarily been used properly.

Here, the term "tools" is used to mean, not only techniques, but something convenient and useful, such as tables, concepts, and idea generating methods.

In this book, the tools useful for each step of Task Achieving are explained step by step. We are sure you will get some hints for solving problems that fit to Task Achieving, starting with the ferretting out, selecting prioritized problems and tasks, applying the Task Achieving thinking and idea generation methods.

It is our great pleasure, if this book will become some help for improvement activities with big contribution to management to overcome the change in management environment.

It is acknowledged that Ms. Toshie Sonoda and Mr. Shin Ishida of JUSE Press, Ltd. has been a great help for this publication. We thank them from the bottom of heart.

April 2010

Katsutoshi AYANO

# Tools Useful for Task Achieving
## Contents

Introduction / iii

## Chapter 1 Understand the Task Achieving Procedures / 1

1-1 Kaizen (Improvement) and QC Story —— 2
1-2 Three Approaches Effective for Problem Solving —— 3
1-3 Steps of Task Achieving Type and Implementation Procedures —— 5
1-4 Tools Useful for Task Achieving that are Explained in this Book —— 16
1-5 A Case Example to Learn the Procedures of Task Achieving Type —— 17

## Chapter 2 Tools Effective for "Theme Selection" / 31

Points and Tools for "Theme Selection" —— 32
Tool 2-1 Problems and Tasks Digging up Checklist —— 36
Tool 2-2 Problems and Tasks Selection Sheet —— 40
Tool 2-3 Problems and Tasks Narrowing down Evaluation Table —— 42
Tool 2-4 Improvement Procedures Selection Method —— 46
Tool 2-5 Gantt Chart —— 48

## Chapter 3 Tools Effective for "Clarification of Attack Points and Setting Targets" / 51

Points and Tools for "Clarification of Attack Points and Setting Targets" —— 52
Tool 3-1 Stratification —— 55
Tool 3-2 Investigation Items Selection Table —— 60
Tool 3-3 Benchmarking —— 62
Tool 3-4 Questionnaire Survey —— 66
Tool 3-5 QC 7 Tools and New QC 7 Tools —— 71
Tool 3-6 Attack Points Selection Sheet —— 79
Tool 3-7 SWOT Analysis —— 87

# CONTENTS

## Chapter 4 Tools Effective for "Planning of Measures" / 91

Points and Tools for "Planning of Measures" — 92

**Tool 4-1** Brainstorming Method — 97

**Tool 4-2** Tree Diagram — 102

**Tool 4-3** Brain Writing Method — 107

**Tool 4-4** Wish-Points Listing Method — 111

**Tool 4-5** Defects Listing Method — 115

**Tool 4-6** Checklist Method — 119

**Tool 4-7** Focused Object Technique — 123

**Tool 4-8** Visual Connection Technique — 126

## Chapter 5 Tools Effective for "Pursuit of Success Scenarios" / 131

Points and Tools for "Pursuit of Success Scenarios" — 132

**Tool 5-1** PDPC Method — 135

**Tool 5-2** Obstacles/Side Effects Exclusion Examination Table — 140

**Tool 5-3** Merits/Demerits Table — 143

**Tool 5-4** FMEA — 146

**Tool 5-5** Quality Table — 151

**Tool 5-6** Worksheet for Pursuit of Success Scenarios — 157

# CONTENTS

## Chapter 6 Tools Effective to "Implementation of Success Scenarios" ~ "Standardization and Fixing of Control" / 163

Points and Tools for "Implementation of Success Scenarios" ~ "Standardization and Fixing of Control" —— 164

**Tool 6-1** Gantt Chart —— 166

**Tool 6-2** Arrow Diagram Method —— 169

**Tool 6-3** PDPC Method —— 174

**Tool 6-4** 5W1H Matrix Diagram Method —— 177

**Tool 6-5** QC 7 Tools —— 180

## Chapter 7 To Utilize "Task Achieving" Effectively / 185

**7-1** Let's Become an Expert of Tools —— 186

**7-2** Let's Learn from Case Examples of Task Achieving Activities —— 188

**7-3** Do's and Don'ts of Task Achieving —— 214

References / 225

# Chapter 1

## Understand the Task Achieving Procedures

# Chapter 1

## 1-1

# Kaizen(Improvement) and QC Story

Every work is said to be "to solving problem" or "to Achieve Task." It is also said that improving work continually enhances the value of the products and services provided to customers and through it the continual development of the organization becomes possible. In other words, continual improvement is essential for existence of company and organization.

What is effective for such continual improvement is the problem solving procedures called QC Story.

The QC Story is originally used as the plots or steps to report or present the results of kaizen (improvement) activities by small groups at workplace. But soon after, it became known as the problem solving procedures with QC approach, for if kaizen activities are conducted along with the Pro-blem Solving Procedures, the problem solving can be done with certainty.

Currently, various kinds of summarizing the steps of QC Story are proposed, but if simply one says "QC Story", it means this Problem Solving Procedures with QC Approach. Typical QC Story is shown in Fig. 1.1.

Step 1, 2 and 10 in the Fig. 1.1 are necessary for reporting or presentation, and the steps from 3 to 9 are the Problem Solving Procedures with QC Approach. Because the effectiveness of the Problem Solving Procedures with QC Approach is not limited to QC activities, in this book, we call it as the Problem Solving Procedures omitting the phrase "with QC Approach".

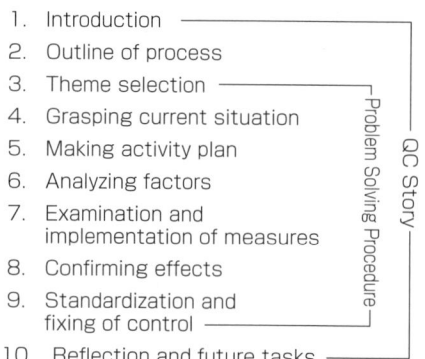

1. Introduction
2. Outline of process
3. Theme selection
4. Grasping current situation
5. Making activity plan
6. Analyzing factors
7. Examination and implementation of measures
8. Confirming effects
9. Standardization and fixing of control
10. Reflection and future tasks

Fig.1.1  Relationship between QC Story and Problem Solving Procedure

## 1-2
# Three Approaches Effective for Problem Solving

The Problem Solving Procedures based on the QC Story worked effectively for the recovery of Japanese Economy after the War through the continual improvement activities. However, toward the end of 1980s, recognizing that there are those problems that cannot be approached only by the problem solving methodology used by that time, number of companies that tackled with the "Task Achieving" approach increased. Therefore, entering 1990s, centered around QC Circle Keihin District, the task achieving procedures called "Task Achieving type QC Story" was proposed.

Thereafter, through the publication of a series of books that summarized the results of study by QC Circle Kanagawa District and a case book by QC Circle Keihin District, the "Task Achieving" approach came to be widely used even in QC Circle Activities.

Entering the year 2000, "Measures Implementing QC Story" was proposed, and currently it is said that there are three approaches, of "Problem Solving", "Task Achieving" and "Measures Implementing".

"Problem" is the issue that needs solution for the management and shop operations, and the approach to solve the problems that are visible because the work has been done so far is the Procedures of Problem Solving Type.

The Task Achieving Approach is developed to tackle with the kind of the following cases:
① New tasks that have not been experienced so far.
② The cases where new method of work is to be introduced.
③ The cases where the problem solving with partial changes is not sufficient.

On the other hand, when the factors or points of measures for a problem is clear and the direction of the measures to achieve the target is also clear, the

# Chapter 1

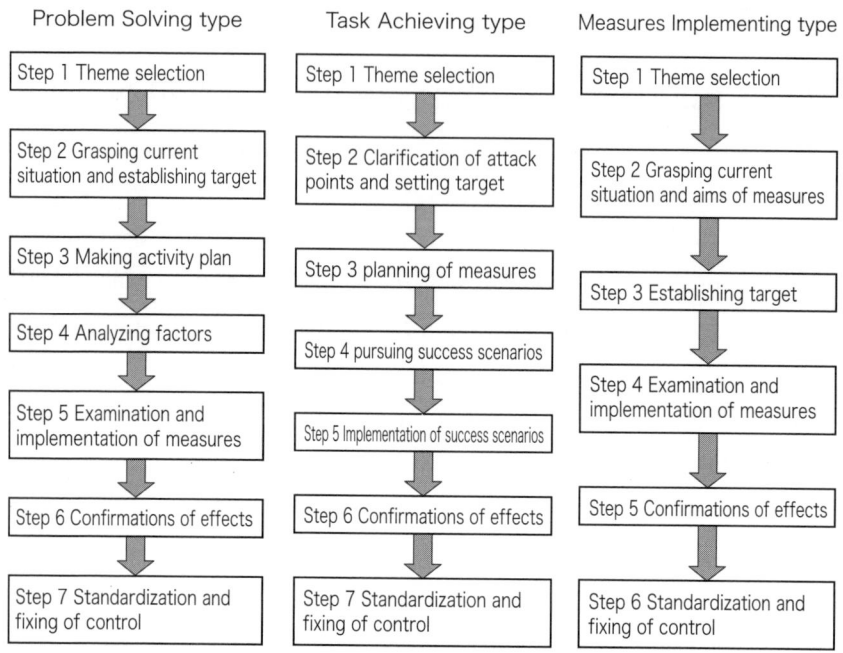

Fig.1.2 Comparison of "Problem Solving Procedures"

Measures Implementing Type of procedures is used. When the procedures of Problem Solving type, Task Achieving type and the Measures Implementation type are compared, it looks like Fig. 1.2.

It is necessary to understand the features of each of the types well. You should not adopt problem sol-ving type because it is a "problem", nor task achieving type because it is a "task"., without When selecting the improvement procedure, you are recommended to utilize the "improvement procedures selection method".

Especially, as to the task achieving type, it is recommended to tackle with after acummulating experiences on problem solving type.

Understand the Task Achieving Procedures

# Steps of Task Achieving Type and Implementation Procedures

In this section, for those who want to study task achieving type a more in detail, each steps and implementation procedures are explained easy to understand way along with notes to take care.

## Step 1　Theme Selection

This step is composed of implementation procedures of 5 steps and there is not much difference from problem solving type. It is necessary to choose a theme that fit to Task Achieving Type after examining as many theme candidates.

Step1 Mainflow of "Theme Selection"

### Implementation Step 1　Ferreting out (Examine completely) Problems and Tasks

Ferret out problems and tasks from various angles and aspects.

### ONE POINT

◆Examine those things that you have in mind from everyday and surroundings to company level broadly. You can hold examination meeting of problems and tasks with relevant persons. Sometimes, your boss may suggest some.

### Implementation Step 2　Narrowing down the Problems and Tasks

① Decide on evaluation items and narrow them down to those that you want to select as the theme based on the evaluation.

5

# Chapter 1

② Discuss with your boss on the narrowed down theme and get consensus that it is the priority item and decide the theme.

## Implementation Step 3  Choosing the Improvement Procedures

As to the theme selected, judge which improvement procedures is effective and efficient to tackle with.

## Implementation Step 4  Clarification of the Reason of Theme Selection

① Clarify the necessity, the degree of importance and aims to tackle with the theme concretely.

② Set the "theme title" expressing the requirements (aim, function) to be solved simply and understandabley.

## Implementation Step 5  Establishing the Overall Activity Plan

① So that the project can be promoted with certainty, make overall activity plan on the overall schedule and the role allocation for each step through to the theme completion.

② Summarize the overall plan documents and confirm with all the members with advices from your boss.

## Step 2  Clarification of Attack Points and Setting Targets

Step 2 is composed of implementation procedures of 2 steps. The first is the "Clarification of attack points" and it is a step to break down the task into various approaches of analysis (investigation items) for analyzing the theme, and to think over attack points to examine the measures, and to narrow them

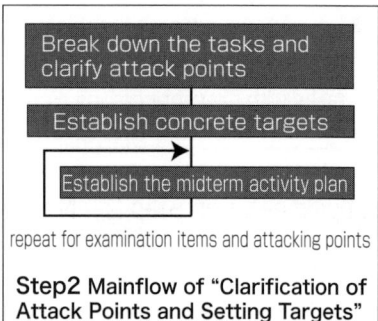

repeat for examination items and attacking points

**Step2 Mainflow of "Clarification of Attack Points and Setting Targets"**

down. The second is the "setting targets" to set the practical targets based on the clarification of the attack points.

## Implementation Step 1  Clarification of Attack Points

① Confirm the characteristic that reflect the overall theme (overall characteristic) that you are attacking and the level. Then, grasp the "desired level" and "current level" of the characteristic. Next, decide on the approaches of analysis (investigation items), and for each investigation item, grasp the "desired level" and "current level" (Note). Based on the investigation, clarify the gaps and consider the attack points to examine the measures focused on priority items.

(Note) There is not much problems which sequence to take to investigate the "desired level" and the "current level".

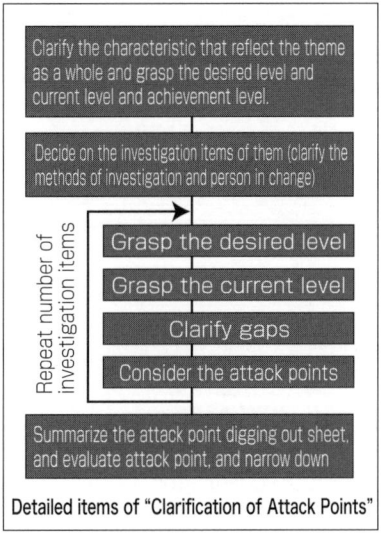

Detailed items of "Clarification of Attack Points"

② The above activity should be summarized on the "Attack Points Selection Sheet" and narrow them down. This procedure is divided in to 7 implementation items. The flow is shown on the figure above.

### Implementation item ①  Grasping Overall Characteristic

Clarify the characteristic that reflect the theme as a whole (overall characteristic), and grasp the desired level and current level and confirm the achievement level. The achievement level is the level you want to achieve, and is linked to the target setting. Depending on the theme it may be the desired level itself, or may be set considering desired level or the gap between the desired level and current level.

> **ONE POINT**
> 
> ◆The "overall characteristic" is the object for examining itself as the task and it can be expressed by the results index. Concretely, they may be satisfaction index, amount of sales, number of claims, number of failures, etc. Here, the "characteristic" is an index or the scales for measurements.
> ◆The desired level of the characteristic is the "vision to reach" and the current level shows the "current status" and current situation level.

### Implementation item ②   Decision on the Investigation Items

Decide on the approach of analysis (investigation items). The investigation items are to be grasped by stratifying the elements that constitute the theme. As the points for stratification, "4M" (Man, Machine, Materials, Methods) and "7M+E+T", "7S" are generally used (Refer to Table 3.3).

> **ONE POINT**
> 
> ◆Required items for the tasks required from outside, and focusing items for creative tasks should be selected as the investigation items.

### Implementation item ③   Grasping the Desired Level

For each investigation item, grasp the desired level (system, function, performance and level, etc. that are newly required.)

> **ONE POINT**
> 
> ◆Example of the desired levels: ①  Upper policy(directed value), ②  function/performance level that reflected as attractive,  ③  target level by benchmarking, ④  new regulation value or moves of competitors, ⑤  obstacles or losses that seem to occur in the near future, ⑥  required levels set intentionally.

Understand the Task Achieving Procedures

### Implementation item ④ Grasping the Current Level

Grasp the current level against the desired level. That is to grasp the current way of work or situation and level contrasted to the desired level. At this stage, it is not the purpose to find out the degree of poorness of current status, but to recognize the difference (gap) from the desired level and to grasp it as the necessary information to consider the attack points.

Here, the sequence of grasping the "desired level" and the "current level" in the implementation item ③ and ④ does not matter so much. Important thing is to grasp both of them.

#### ONE POINT

◆ If the object of examination is totally new and there is no current status, grasp based on the similar events or related situations.

### Implementation item ⑤ Grasping Gaps

Grasp the difference (gap) between the desired level and current level. The gap between the desired level and the current level should be grasped by quantitative data (numerical data). When, depending on the theme, there is no choice but to express by verbal information (language data), it is important to make it practical as much as possible grasping the facts and not by guesses.

### Implementation item ⑥ Consider the Candidates for the "Attack Points"

Consider the candidates for attack points as the "direction of the countermeasure ideas". An attack point is not the countermeasure themselves but it specifies the span, area and focus point of establishing the measures to eliminate the gap. That is, it is the attack point that shows where the measures should be focused considering the gap and capability of the shop floors. Therefore, if an attack point is set as a small area, many measures are not generated, and it is better to decide the attack point from higher perspective and broader ways of looking.

> **ONE POINT**
> ◆The attack points is to clarify the direction and points to consider the measures.

For each of the remaining investigation items, repeat the implementation items ③ to ⑥.

### Implementation item ⑦　Decide on the Attack Points

It is usual that there are many attack points and it is necessary to narrow them to effective and efficient ones, utilizing the "Attack Points Selection Sheet" (Tool 3-6), etc.

As examples of investigation items, there are such that "the possibility of eliminating the gaps (Is it possible to eliminate it considering the environment of the shop floor or capability?)", "capability of the shop to cope with (Is it possible to cope with ourselves?)", "wishes of customers (or previous and following processes) (the degree of demand by the customers)", etc.

If you proceed with some prospect with rough effects forecasting on whether you can achieve the targets with the narrowed down attack points, the failure to achieve the target will become difficult to occur.

## Implementation Step 2　Setting Targets

① Based on the clarification of the attack points, establish the 3 elements of target ("what", "how far" and "by when").

② Clarify the reason for the setting the target and get the prospect on the achieving the target.

③ Depending on the needs, make the "activity plan" concretely that comes after the step 3 "planning of the measures".

If there are plural attack points, for each attack point, set the target (secondary target) and make it possible to achieve the overall target (primary target) all together. The target should be aimed at challenging and enthusiastic level, But if the target is irrational, it will not be achieved.

Understand the Task Achieving Procedures

It is a rule to state the target quantitatively with the characteristic of the theme. When it is difficult to express by quantitative value, you need to devise some quantification by replacing it with alternative characteristic [Note], or by utilizing questionnaire or making evaluation criteria.

(Note) Alternative characteristic: Other quality characteristic used because it is difficult to directly measure the quality characteristic required (from JIS Quality Management terminology). For example, the alternative characteristics of customer satisfaction are such as percentage of satisfaction based on questionnaire or percentage of claims.

## Step 3　Planning Measures

This step is divided into 2 implementation steps and to generate many candidates of measures (ideas) based on the attack points and to select those that have large expected effects.

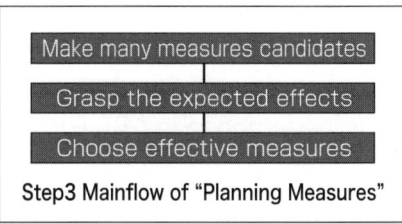

Step3 Mainflow of "Planning Measures"

### Implementation Step 1　Listing up Candidates of Measures

① Utilizing such as "Idea Conception method", and focusing on the attack points, generate many measures (ideas) which effects are expected large.

### Implementation Step 2　Narrowing down the Measures

① Forecast the effects for each of the measures candidates generated.
② For each attack point, select the measures candidates that have large expected effects, rank them from the largest to smallest and narrow down the measures candidates that you want to adopt.

*11*

# Chapter 1

## Step 4 — Pursuing the Success Scenarios

This step is made up of 4 implementation steps to examine realizable scenarios on the narrowed down measures candidates (ideas) and to forecast the estimated effects.

Evaluate totally among the scenarios, abolishing those with difficulty of removal of obstacles and side effects, and to decide the success scenarios.

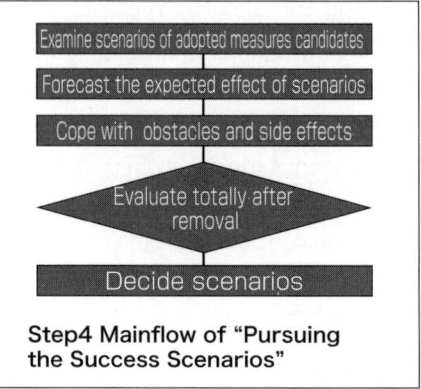

**Step4 Mainflow of "Pursuing the Success Scenarios"**

## Implementation Step 1 — Examination of the Scenarios

Among the measures candidates, examine those scenarios (implementation methods) that are realizable and concrete.

### ONE POINT

◆ Make scenario candidates combining some of the measures.
◆ Break down one measures into practical implementation methods.

## Implementation Step 2 — Forecasting the Estimated Effects

For each scenario that is made practical, forecast the estimated effects.

### ONE POINT

◆ For each scenario, forecast the estimated effects using simulation or trial (pre confirmation), etc. and summarize it as scenario candidates examining the details.

Understand the Task Achieving Procedures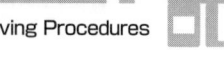

## Implementation Step 3 — Forecasting and Removals of Obstacles and Side Effects

① Forecast the obstacles that prevent each of the scenario implementation and bad effects to others (side effects) , and to think the ways to avoid them.

② Give up those scenarios that are difficult to remove the obstacles and side effects.

**ONE POINT**
- ◆ The bigger the estimated effects and/ or the higher the newness, the scenario is expected to have the bigger obstacles and/or side effects.
- ◆ Using various, methods the removal measures have to be examined, but if it is difficult to remove, give up the adoption after consulting to your boss.

## Implementation Step 4 — Selection of Success Scenarios

Decide the success scenarios judging the above process comprehensively.

**ONE POINT**
- ◆ Confirm that the total of forecasted effects of success scenarios is at the level to clear the target.

## Step 5 — Implementation of the Success Scenarios

This step is composed of 2 implementation steps, to make implementation plant of the selected success scenarios, and to implement then surely along with the planned procedures.

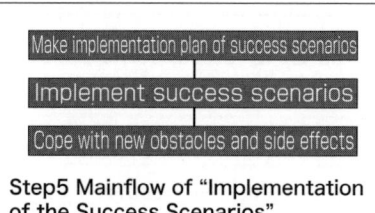

Step5 Mainflow of "Implementation of the Success Scenarios"

13

# Chapter 1

## Implementation Step 1　Making Implementation Plan

Make implementation plan to implement the Success Scenarios.

## Implementation Step 2　Implementation of the Success Scenarios

① Each person in charge implements the detailed implementation items following the implementation plan.

② For each scenario, grasp the effects and problems.

③ Take countermeasures when some problems like side effects other than the ones taken action of beforehand occur.

# Step 6　Confirmations of Effects

This step is divided into 2 implementation steps to judge the degree of achievement of the targets and to confirm the tangible and intangible effects. When growth targets of the group and/or individuals were set, confirm the degree of achievements of them.

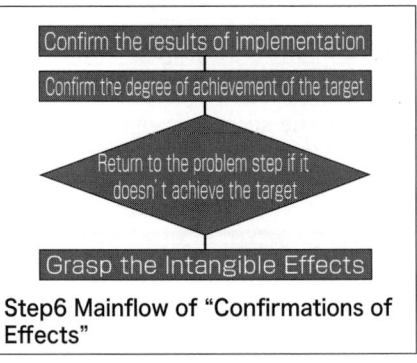

Step6 Mainflow of "Confirmations of Effects"

## Implementation Step 1　Grasping the Tangible Effects

① Confirm the results of implementation for each item of the success scenarios by actual performances.

② As to the characteristics set, confirm the degree of achievement of the target. If the target was not achieved, return to the step where the pro-blems had occurred and re-challenge perseveringly, aiming at the achievement of the target.

Understand the Task Achieving Procedures

③ Grasp the cost needed to implement the success scenarios and adverse effects.
④ Grasp the side effects and ripple effects other than the ones aimed at.

## Implementation Step 2　Grasping the Intangible Effects

① Confirm the degree of growth of the group and individuals.
② Grasp other intangible effects (environment, safety, morale, etc.).

## Step 7　Standardization and Fixing of the Control

This step is divided into 3 implementation steps to examine the methods for maintenance and to control so that the implementation effects are attained continuously and to institutionalize them.

> Standardize the success scenarios
> Make the new way of work known to all
> Confirm the degree of fixing the control

**Step7 Mainflow of "Standardization and Fixing of Control"**

## Implementation Step 1　Standardization

As to the success scenarios that were effective, decide on the methods and mechanism to maintain and control them and establish or revise "standards", "criteria", "manuals", etc.

## Implementation Step 2　Make them Known to All

① Decide the dates to implement the new way of work and make them known to all the relevant peoples along with the purpose of the revisions.
② Educate and train the relevant people so that they can surely implement the new way of works.

## Implementation Step 3　Fixing the Control

It should be confirmed by data that the new standards are surely observed, and the effect is continuing.

# Chapter 1

## 1-4
## Tools Useful for Task Achieving that are Explained in this Book

Table 1.1 summarized the outline of the implementation procedures of each step of Task Achieving Type and the tools effective for each step that are explained in this book.

Table 1.1 Outline of Implementation Procedures and Effective Tools of Task Achieving Type

| Step | Implementation Procedure Outline | Effective tools |
|---|---|---|
| 1. Theme selection | •Ferret out problems and tasks, and narrow down to what you want to select for theme<br>•Judge the procedure to tackle with the theme<br>•Clarify the necessity to tackle with the theme, and decide reasonable theme, make overall plan | Problems and tasks digging up checklist<br>Problems and tasks selection sheet<br>Problems and tasks narrowing down evaluation table<br>Improvement procedures selection method<br>Gantt chart |
| 2. Clarification of attack points and setting target | •Grasp the desired level and current level of the characteristic that reflect the theme as a whole, and clarify confirm the achievement level<br>•Decide on the approach of analysis (investigation items) by using 4M, and grasp these desired level and current level, clarify these gaps<br>•Consider and dig out the candidates for attack points to eliminate the gaps as the direction of the countermeasure ideas, and decide the attack points<br>•Decide the concrete target from overall characteristic and attack point | Stratification<br>Investigation items selection table<br>Benchmarking<br>Questionnaire survey<br>QC seven tools<br>New QC seven tools<br>Attack points selection sheet<br>SWOT analysis |
| 3. Planning of measures | •Focus on the attack points and utilize such as Idea Conception method, generate many effective measures candidates<br>•For the each attack points, select the measures candidates that have large forecasted effects and narrow them down | Brain storming method<br>Tree diagram<br>Brain writing method<br>Wish points listing method<br>Defects points listing method,<br>Focused object technique<br>Checklist method<br>Visual connection technique |
| 4. Pursuing success scenarios | •Examine realizable scenario and forecast the estimated effects<br>•Forecast obstacles and side effects that prevent the scenario implementation, and examine the measures<br>•Evaluate totally among the scenarios, and decide success scenarios | PDPC method<br>Obstacles/Side effects exclusion examination table<br>Merit/Demerit table<br>FMEA<br>Quality table<br>Worksheet for pursuit of success scenarios |
| 5. Implementation of success scenarios | •Make implementation plan of success scenarios, and implement them<br>•Grasp effects and problems for each scenario<br>•Take countermeasures when some new problems and side effects exist | Gantt chart<br>Arrow diagram method<br>PDPC method<br>5W1H matrix diagram |
| 6. Confirmations of Effects | •Confirm the results of implementation of each item of the success scenario by actual performances and degree of achievement of the target. If the target was not achieved, return to the necessary step. Grasp the side effects and ripple effects<br>•Grasp the Intangible Effects | QC seven tools |
| 7. Standardization and Fixing of control | •Standardize success scenarios to maintain and control<br>•Make the new way of work known to all the relevant peoples, and educate/train them<br>•Follow up status of observation of standards and continuing effects | 5W1H matrix<br>QC seven tools |

Understand the Task Achieving Procedures

## 1-5

# A Case Example to Learn the Procedures of Task Achieving Type

Before learning the tools effective for each step, a case example of Task Achieving utilization is introduced below. Get a perspective on what kind of tools are used at which step.

## This will do All right! Childcare Leave
## —How to Get Childcare Leave without Anxiety—

HAKUTSURU SAKE Brewing Co., Ltd. Personnel Department
"Yatto deta Circle (Finally Emerged Circle)"

**Excerpted from Presentation materials at 5064th QC Circle Conference held by Hyogo district of QC Circle Kinki Chapter.**

---

HAKUTSURU SAKE Brewing Co. Ltd. is located at "Nada Gogo" of Kobe City and is a company of 265 years from establishment that is producing and selling centered around the sake Hakutsuru, that is famous with "Maru", and sweet sake, shouchu, plum wine. The "Yatto deta Circle" belongs to the personnel department, which is in charge of broad area, from employment, personnel, education, labor, salary, social insurance and to other welfares.

This case example enhances the sense of security and satisfaction of the employees who are subject to get childcare leave, by making an easy to understand manual and establishing an information network to connect workplace and home so that they can take the leave with sense of security and to get back to the workplace without anxiety.

*17*

# Chapter 1

## Step 1  Theme Selection

### Implementation Step 1  Ferreting out (Examining) Problems and Tasks

After the reviews of the themes that we were considering as candidates and ferreting out newly annoying things and those that can be improved more, we found 11 candidates for the theme (Refer to Fig. 1.3).

◎ 3pt.  ○ 2pt.  △ 1pt.

| Problems and tasks \ Evaluation items | Necessity | | | | QC circle capability | | Overall evaluation | Priority to table |
|---|---|---|---|---|---|---|---|---|
| | Importance | Urgency | Easiness for tackling | Upper policy | Is the timing right? | Is the work possible to cope with ourselves? | | |
| Making manual for employees subject to childcare leave | ◎ | ◎ | ○ | ◎ | ◎ | ○ | 16 | 1 |
| Sorting file cabinet (Naming drawer) | ○ | △ | ◎ | △ | △ | ○ | 10 | 3 |
| Ensure to record personal information changes | ○ | ○ | ○ | △ | △ | ○ | 10 | 3 |
| Systematize the ledger health insurance | △ | △ | △ | △ | △ | △ | 6 | 6 |
| Review the way to print and crimping the pay slip | ○ | ○ | ○ | △ | △ | ○ | 10 | 3 |
| Put employee directory into data | ○ | ○ | △ | △ | △ | ○ | 9 | 4 |
| Utilize the ledger data | △ | △ | △ | △ | △ | △ | 6 | 6 |
| Organize company residence-related business | ○ | ○ | ○ | ○ | △ | ○ | 11 | 2 |
| Make a checklist for new employee | △ | △ | ○ | △ | △ | ○ | 8 | 5 |
| Make checklist of bank seals | △ | △ | ○ | △ | △ | ○ | 8 | 5 |
| Create a manual on procedures in a public employment security office | ○ | ○ | ○ | △ | ○ | ○ | 11 | 2 |

Fig.1.3  Ferret out and narrow down the problems and tasks

### Implementation Step 2  Narrowing down the Problems and Tasks

As the results of evaluation of the theme candidates with the items like importance, urgency, easiness for tackling, upper policy, we picked up the highest score theme, "Making Manual for Employees subject to Childcare Leave" (Refer to Fig. 1.3).

### Implementation Step 3  Selection of Improvement Procedures

We applied the "improvement procedure selection method", and because it is "a work which we didn't have any experience with", we decided to tackle it with task achieving type of QC Story.

## Implementation Step 4    Clarification of the Reason of Theme Selection

Due to the "Act on Advancement of Measures to Support Raising Next-Generation Children" promulgated in 2003, our company was obliged to submit "an action plan of employers regarding countermeasures to support the development of the next generation" to the jurisdiction of the department of labor, and the establishment of the manual that was to be included in the plan was the most prioritized task.

With these backgrounds, we decided the theme as "This will do All right! Childcare Leave —How to Get Childcare Leave without Anxiety—".

## Implementation Step 5    Making the Overall Activity Plan

We decided the person in charge of each step, and made the overall activity plan like Fig. 1.4.

Plan : ········▶    charge
Implementation : ━━━▶    Date Created: June 08, 2007

| Step | Person in charge | 2007 June | July | August | September | October | November |
|---|---|---|---|---|---|---|---|
| Theme selection | Kakiuchi | ···▶ | | | | | |
| Procedure selection | Kakiuchi | ···▶ | | | | | |
| Activity plan | Kakiuchi | ···▶ | | | | | |
| Setting attack points and targets | Tsuchida | ···▶ | | | | | |
| Planning of measures | Tsuchida | ···▶ | | | | | |
| Pursuing success scenarios | Tanaka | | ···············▶ | | | | |
| Implementation of success scenarios | Tanaka | | | ···············▶ | | | |
| Confirmations of effects | Kiyama | | | ···▶ | | | |
| Standardization and fixing of control | Kiyama | | | | ···········▶ | | |
| Reflection and future tasks | Kiyama | | | | | ···▶ | |
| Next theme selection | Kiyama | | | | | | ···▶ |

Fig.1.4   Activity plan

# Chapter 1

## ONE POINT

◆ The reason why they could list up theme candidates more than 10 including new problems and tasks is due to the various angles and perspectives. It is a good practice to include boss's policy as one of the evaluation item and to prioritize them in the order of the scores. It is also an appropriate decision to select the task achieving type with the reasoning that it was one which they didn' t have experience before.

## Step 2  Clarifications of Attack Points and Setting the Target

### Implementation Step 1  Clarification of Attack Points

**(1) Grasping the Vision to Reach and the Current Status**

The overall characteristics was made to "the feeling of security (the degree

---

Request to cooperate to the questionnaire                                  2007.06.10
                                                                Personnel Department
                                                                      Yatto deta Circle

Always thanking you for your help
This time, our QC circle is working "maternity, child care leave" and related subject
In order to improve the situation, we made a questionnaire as follows.
We ask your cooperation.

| 1. Did you sometimes feel anxious about returning to work during maternity and childcare leave? | | Number |
|---|---|---|
| 1—① | 1. Felt very easy    4. Sometimes felt anxious<br>2. Felt easy         5. Felt very anxious<br>3. Neither | |
| 1—② | ◆Fill in the reasons (concretely) | |

| 2. What do you think the supports of Presonnel department? | | Number |
|---|---|---|
| 2—① | 1. Very good         4. Bad | |

Fig.1.5  Questionnaire Paper

of security) of the employees who is subject to the Childcare Leave" and the investigation items are divided into 3 of "employee on childcare leave", "company" and "information" and for each of them the vision to reach was set. To grasp the current status against them, questionnaire survey was made to the employees on childcare leave and 10 employees who have returned to work after the leaves.

The questionnaire was made of 7 items, out of which 6 items on the question with 5 points scale evaluation with the reason for the evaluation, and 1 item of free answer as in Fig.1.5. Part of the results is shown on Fig. 1.6.

### Employee on the Childcare Leave

**1. Did you sometimes feel anxious about returning to work during maternity and childcare Leave?**

|   |       | Amount | Overall points |
|---|-------|--------|----------------|
| 1. Felt very easy | 5 pt. | 0 person | 0 pt. |
| 2. Felt easy | 4 pt. | 0 person | 0 pt. |
| 3. Neither | 3 pt. | 1 person | 3 pt. |
| 4. Sometimes felt anxious | 2 pt. | 7 person | 14 pt. |
| 5. Felt very anxious | 2 pt. | 2 person | 2 pt. |

☆ Desire to get back to the workplace
↓
Sense of security 38%

**2. What do you think the support of personnel department?**

| 1. Very good | 5 pt. | 0 person | 0 pt. |
|---|---|---|---|
| 2. Good | 4 pt. | 7 person | 28 pt. |
| 3. Neither | 3 pt. | 2 person | 6 pt. |
| 4. Bad | 2 pt. | 1 person | 2 pt. |
| 5. Very bad | 1 pt. | 0 person | 0 pt. |

☆ Support of personnel department
↓
Satisfaction of respondents 72%

**3. Was there the anythings you don't understand about the various procedures related to childcare leave?**

| 1. Knew well | 5 pt. | 0 person | 0 pt. |
|---|---|---|---|
| 2. Knew most | 4 pt. | 6 person | 24 pt. |
| 3. Neither | 3 pt. | 1 person | 3 pt. |
| 4. Knew a littles | 2 pt. | 3 person | 6 pt. |
| 5. Knew nothing | 1 pt. | 0 person | 0 pt. |

☆ Understanding for various procedures
↓
Degree of understanding 66%

**4. About Information from company**

| 1. Very satisfied | 5 pt. | 0 person | 0 pt. |
|---|---|---|---|
| 2. Satisfyied | 4 pt. | 4 person | 16 pt. |
| 3. Neither | 3 pt. | 5 person | 15 pt. |
| 4. Dissatisfied | 2 pt. | 1 person | 2 pt. |
| 5. Very dissatisfied | 1 pt. | 0 person | 0 pt. |

☆ Information from company
↓
Degree of satisfaction for information 66%

Fig.1.6  Questionnaire result

# Chapter 1

## (2) Clarification of Gaps and Attack Points

For each of the investigation item, vision to reach and current status was summarized on the "Attack Points Selection Sheet" and the gap for each of them was grasped and the candidates for attack points was considered.

We thought all of them are needed to resolve the task, and adopted them as attack points (Refer to Table 1.2).

Table 1.2  Clarification of attack points

Attack point selection sheet

| Overall characteristic | Vision to reach (ideal) | Current status (current situation) | Achieving level |
|---|---|---|---|
| The feeling of security of the employees who is subject to the Childcare Leave | The degree of security 100% | The degree of security 38% | The degree of security 100% |

| Classification | Item | Vision to reach (ideal) | Current status (current situation) | Gap | Attack point (candidates) | Possibility to remove gaps | Adoption or rejection |
|---|---|---|---|---|---|---|---|
| The employees who is subject to the Childcare Leave | The sense of security to return to the jobs | The degree of security 100% | The degree of security 38% | 62% | Increase the sense of security during the leave and vacation | ○ | Adoption |
| | Understanding for various procedures | Degree of understanding 100% | Degree of understanding 66% | 34% | | | |
| Company | Support of personnel department | Satisfaction 100% | Satisfaction 72% | 28% | Raise the degree of satisfaction of support in personnel department | ○ | Adoption |
| | Personal knowledge in personnel department | Grasped by all people | Not grasped | | Knowledge varued | | |
| | Management of works and employee's history | Grasped and managed by all | Individually managed | | Unclear management | Grasp and manage in all people | ○ | Adoption |
| Information | Company information | Degree of satisfaction for information 100% | Degree of satisfaction for information 66% | 34% | Increase the degree of satisfaction for company information | ○ | Adoption |

Targets: Raise the feeling of security of the employees who is subject to the childcare leave to 100% by Sep.2007

## Implementation Step 2  Setting the Targets

From overall characteristics, the target was decided as "To make feeling of security of Employee on the Childcare Leave to 100% by September 2007".

Understand the Task Achieving Procedures

## ONE POINT

◆ In JHS(Jimu, Hambai, Service: Clerical works, Sales and Services) sections, there are often cases where there is no numerical data as the management items. Here, a questionnaire was used to quantify the investigation items to clarify the vision to reach, the current status and the gap. It is recommended as a reference point. Although the attack points are also plausible, if the evaluation items were subdivided further, the judgments and priority can be made more clear.

## Step 3  Planning of Measures

### Implementation Step 1  Listing up Candidates of Measures

We generated the candidates of measures, all participating, for each of the attack points decided on the Attack Points Selection Sheet (Refer to Table 1.3).

Table 1.3  Planning of measures

Raise the feeling of security of the employees who is subject to the childcare leave     5 : High ～ 1 : Low

| Attack point | Measures candidates (ideas) | Expected effects | | | Adoption or rejection |
|---|---|---|---|---|---|
| | | Easiness to tackle | Continuity | Overall evaluation | |
| Increase the sense of security during the leave and vacation | Make manual to understand easily | 5 | 5 | 10 | OK |
| | Tabulate each procedure flow | 5 | 5 | 10 | OK |
| | Summarize and tabulate questionnaire | 5 | 5 | 10 | OK |
| | Summarize regulation and rules | 4 | 4 | 8 | OK |
| Increase degree of satisfaction of the supports of personnel department | Understand the level of personal knowledge in personnel department | 4 | 5 | 9 | OK |
| | Get information of other companies | 5 | 4 | 9 | OK |
| | Make everyone able to support the minimum | 4 | 3 | 7 | OK |
| | Fix the person in charge | 3 | 2 | 5 | NO |
| Increase the degree of satisfaction of company information | Make personnel department easy to contact | 5 | 5 | 10 | OK |
| | Communicate information | 5 | 5 | 10 | OK |
| | Listen to concerns and explain before the leave | 3 | 3 | 6 | OK |
| | Communicate information to others | 5 | 4 | 9 | OK |
| | Set chances to explain to the eligibles | 5 | 4 | 9 | OK |
| Grasp and manage by all people | Eliminate mistakes and omission | 5 | 5 | 10 | OK |
| | Fix the person in charge | 3 | 1 | 4 | NO |

# Chapter 1

## Implementation Step 2　Narrowing Down the Candidates of Measures

We decided to adopt items of total points of 6 or above after evaluation by 2 angles of easiness of tackling and continuity as the expected effects (Refer to Table 1.3).

### ONE POINT

◆ Although it is good that they could list up many candidates of measures, they could have made the narrowing down more concretely if the evaluation items have been set with the ones with more clean implementation effects.

## Step 4　Pursuing the Success Scenarios

Arranging the adopted candidates of measures and summarizing into 10 items, practical implementation methods were examined for each of them. As the results, all of them were decided to be effective, they were put together for each of the grouping of investigation items and the timing of implementation and summarized into 6 success scenarios (Refer to Table 1.4).

### ONE POINT

◆ The methodology could be a good reference to make the candidates of measures as practical and the summarizing the success scenarios by grouping by the grouping and implementation timing. It could have been better if they could judge the scenarios by the size of the expected effects by using evaluation of 5 points scale.

## Understand the Task Achieving Procedures

### Table 1.4 Pursuing success scenarios

Increase the feeling of security of the employees who is subject to the childcare leave

| | Measures candidates (idea) | Concrete measures | Possibility of implementation | Success scenarios |
|---|---|---|---|---|
| Manual | Make an easy to understand manual | Put the table of Contents | Yes | Scenario ① |
| | | Glossary | Yes | |
| | Make the list of the flow of procedures | Make a table of easy to understand flow of the leave | Yes | |
| | | Make a (photo) list of the persons in change personnel department | Yes | |
| | | Summarize the rules | Yes | |
| | | How to see pay slips | Yes | |
| | | Procedures and the flow of health insurance and employment insurance | Yes | |
| | | Explanation of distant learning and news delivery | Yes | |
| | Summarize and tabulate questionnaire | Frequently asked questions | Yes | |
| Personal knowledge in personnel department | Understand the level of personal knowledge in personnel department | Conduct understanding test | Yes | Scenario ② |
| | Get information of other companies | Distribution of newspaper clips | Yes | |
| Information | Increase the degree of satisfaction to supports of personnel department | Create an E-mail address for the persons on leave | Yes | Scenario ③ |
| | | Make a (photo) list of persons in change of personnel department | Yes | |
| | Communicate the information | Issue "Hakutsuru News" monthly | Yes | Scenario ④ |
| | Make the information known to others | Post manual and information of department page on intranet board | Yes | |
| | | Post information in personnel department page on intranet | Yes | |
| | Set chances to explain to the eligibles | Personnel department in head office, by phone in branch office | Yes | Scenario ⑤ |
| Control | Eliminate mistakes and omission | Manage employee's history by making check sheet specified to personnel department | Yes | Scenario ⑥ |

## Step 5  Implementation of Success Scenarios

### Implementation Step 1  Making Implementation Plan

To surely implement the 6 success scenarios, the schedule and role allocation were decided as in Table 1.5.

Table 1.5 Making implementation plan

| Success scenarios | What | When | Who(person in change) |
|---|---|---|---|
| ① Make a manual to distribute to the target group | Put the table of contents | By August 15, 2007 | By all people |
| | Make the table of easy to understand flow of the leave | | Kiyama |
| | Make a (photo) list of person in charge personnel department | | Kakiuchi |
| | Summarize the rules | | Kakiuchi |
| | How to see pay slips | | Tanaka |
| | Procedures and the flow of health insurance and employment insurance | | Andou |
| | Explanation of distant learning and news delivery | | Kiyama |
| | Frequently asked questions | | Kakiuchi |
| | Glossary | | Kiyama |
| ② Increase personal knowledge in personnel department | Conduct understanding test | In September | Kiyama |
| | Distribution of newspaper clips | As nesessary | Kakiuchi |
| ③ Information 1 : For target group ~ Increasing communication tools | Create an E-mail address for the person on leave | By August 31 | Kiyama |
| | Make 「Hakutsuru News」 once a month | Every month | Kakiuchi |
| ④ Information 2 : Inform for employees by Intranet information | Post manual and information of department page on intranet board | After completion | Kiyama・Kakiuchi |
| | Post information in personnel department page on intranet | After completion | Kiyama・Kakiuchi |
| ⑤ Information 3 : Explain in person | Personnel department in head office, by phone in branch office | As nesessary | By all people |
| ⑥ Checksheet of management employee's history | Manage employee's history by making check sheet specified personnel department | Till end of october | Andou |

## Implementation Step 2  Implementation of Success Scenarios

### (1) Making Manual

In addition to the contents, the flow of the procedure for the childcare leave and Q&A, the face picture of personnel department people and the jobs in charge are also included. We aimed that the people at the branch and local offices can make inquiries at ease by knowing the face of the person in charge (Refer to Fig. 1.7).

### (2) Enhancement of the Knowledge of the People in the Department

Current main person in charge made a comprehensive test on the Childcare Leave and made the member to answer without referring to the manual, etc. Also, to let the member know the related social situation and the other

Fig.1.7　Making manual for childcare leave

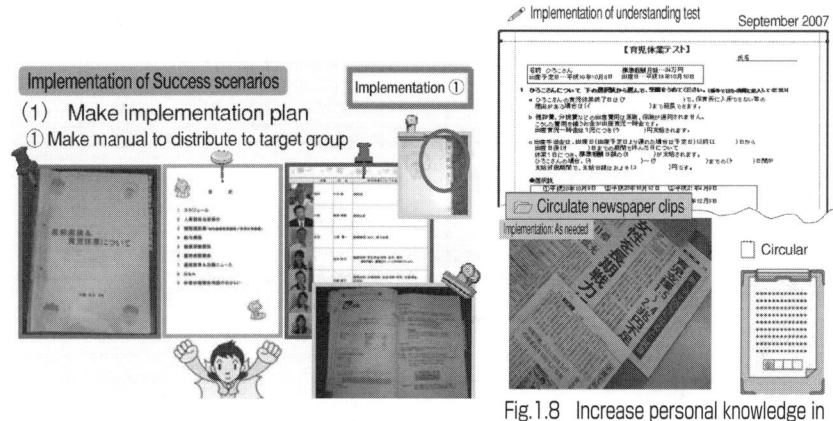

Fig.1.8　Increase personal knowledge in personnel department

companies practices, we circulated clips of newspaper articles to the members as necessary (Refer to Fig. 1.8).

## (3)　Information ①　To the employees who are subject to Childcare Leave

To let the people know the company situation even when they are on the leave, we send "Hakutsuru News" once a month, and to avoid it to become one direction, we made an e-mail address only for employees on the leave "Jinji Papa Mama (Personnel Dept. Papa Mama)" so that they can send e-mails whenever convenient if they have something unsecure and/or questions (Refer to Fig. 1.9).

## (4)　Information ②　Communication to Employees

Not only for those subject to the leave, to let the employees who are thinking to take the leave and the people in the department to know the procedures, we published the manual and rules on the website of personnel department on the in-house intranet. We also opened a page to introduce the anxiety and question the persons on the leave have in Q&A form. On the bulletins board, to let the information known, the link was made to the purpose and the place of publication (Refer to Fig. 1.10).

Fig.1.9 Communication to the employees who is subject to the Childcare Leave

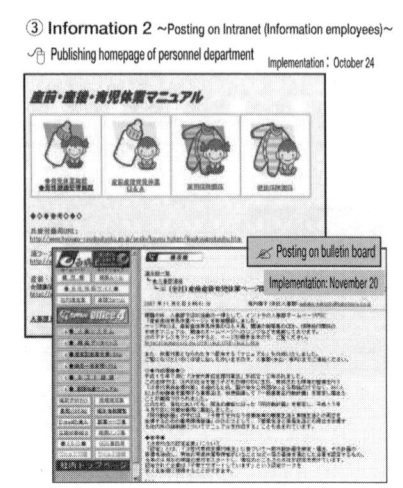

Fig.1.10 Provision of information to employee

## (5) Information ③ Prior Explanation

Revising the prior explanation by mail and telephone call done so far, the explanation is done face to face in the personnel department a couple of days before using the manual and flows and to answer questions. To those in branch offices, we started to send the manual and to explain along with the manual on the phone.

## (6) History Control Checksheet

We made a checksheet to make the prevention of mistake and omission and to make the history control complete. On the checksheet, we record the supplies from the mutual aid association, supplied dates and question and others for each of the persons on the leave.

### ONE POINT

◆They are effective implementations where there are women like fineness, considerations, and that will give sense of security here and there, such as the manuals and communication tools.

Understand the Task Achieving Procedures

## Step 6  Confirmations of Effects

### (1)  Overall Effects

We asked the 10 people who we answered questionnaire first to confirm the manual and success scenario, and questionnaire was answered again. Results was the big enhancement of the understanding of the peoples on the Childcare Leave, and the sense of security after the return to the jobs became 80% (Refer to Fig. 1.11).

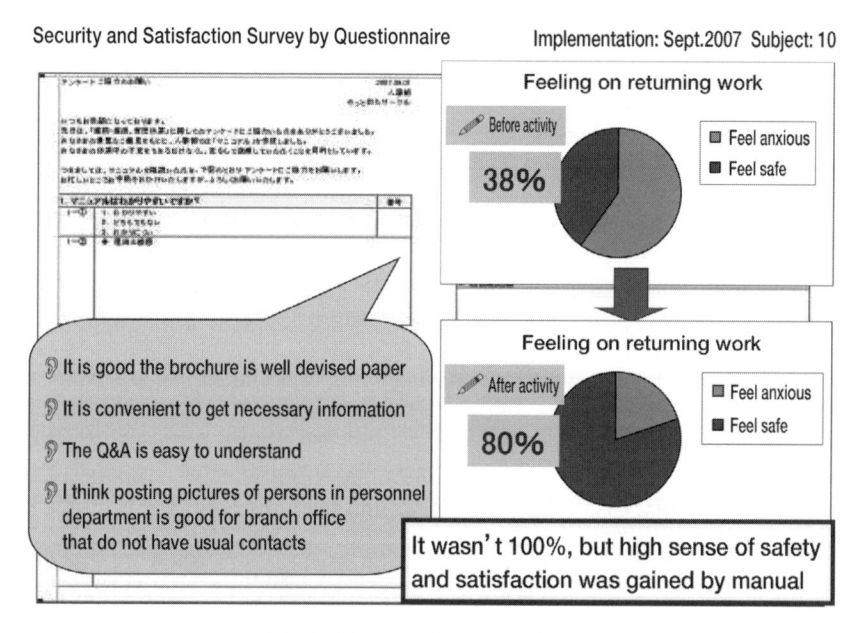

Security and Satisfaction Survey by Questionnaire        Implementation: Sept.2007  Subject: 10

Feeling on returning work
Before activity
38%
■ Feel anxious
■ Feel safe

⚡ It is good the brochure is well devised paper
⚡ It is convenient to get necessary information
⚡ The Q&A is easy to understand
⚡ I think posting pictures of persons in personnel department is good for branch office that do not have usual contacts

Feeling on returning work
After activity
80%
■ Feel anxious
■ Feel safe

It wasn't 100%, but high sense of safety and satisfaction was gained by manual

Fig.1.11   Confirming effects

### (2)  Effects of Each of the Success Scenarios

① Manual

Impressions like well devised, necessary information can be obtained, Q&A is easy to understand, etc. were received and favorably received.

② Enhancement of the members knowledge

We did the comprehensive test and the knowledge was improved 30% on average.

③ Information Related Activities

We could know that each of the information provision was well received, and it is read with interests, and e-mail address was utilized 5 times within 3 months after the setting up. History control is being done without any omissions.

**ONE POINT**

◆Although large effects were obtained but ended up with un-achievement of the target, therefore, it is needed to reflect on which step had problems, if the target was too high aiming at 100%, and if it should be challenged again. These should be made a consensus among the QC Circle members.

## Step 7  Standardization and Fixing of the Control

To maintain and fixing the effects, we tackled with making manual for distribution, checksheet preparation, holding study meeting and updating the website of the personnel department intranet, clarifying the 5W1H (Refer to Table 1.6).

Table 1.6  Standardization and fixing of control

|  | When | Who | What | Why | How |
|---|---|---|---|---|---|
| Make manual to distribute to target group | Upon receipt of the application | All | Part of the manual in charge | To hand out | Check Print |
| Making checksheet | when eligibles come | Nakagawa | Checksheet | To confirm | Make |
| Hold study session | When eligibles come | All | Contents | To confirm | Review |
| Website of personnel department on intranet | As necessary | Tanaka | Contents | To update information | Update |

# Chapter 2

## Tools Effective for "Theme Selection"

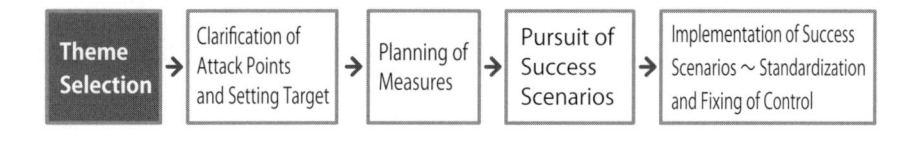

| Theme Selection | → | Clarification of Attack Points and Setting Target | → | Planning of Measures | → | Pursuit of Success Scenarios | → | Implementation of Success Scenarios ~ Standardization and Fixing of Control |

# Chapter 2

# Points and Tools of "Theme Selection"

"Theme Selection" is a common step to all the problem solving, First, select candidates of the theme with high priority from among the problems and tasks that were examined broadly from various angles, and them clarify which problem solving type is used for further steps, to decide on the theme, and make activity plan.

Implementation procedures is made up of 5 steps that is shown on Table 2.1 and we are going to introduce 5 tools effective for this step.

Table 2.1 Implementation procedures and the tools that are useful for "Theme Selection"

| [Implementation Procedures] | [Effective Tools] |
|---|---|
| 1. Ferreting out Problems and Tasks | Tool2-1 Problems and Tasks Digging up Checklist |
| 2. Narrowing down Problems and Tasks | Tool2-2 Problems and Tasks Selection Sheet |
| 3. Selection of Improvement Procedures | Tool2-3 Problems and Tasks Narrowing down Evaluation Table |
| 4. Clarification of the Reason for the Theme Selection | Tool2-4 Improvement Procedures Selection Method |
| 5. Establishing the overall Activity plan | Tool2-5 Gantt Chart |

These are only basic tools, and we also introduce case example of theme selection combining various points of view.

## (1) Points for "Ferreting out Problems and Tasks"

When conducting improvement activities, it is a very important point to decide on the theme. When people who are tackling a theme for the first time tackle a task far above their capabilities, there is a risk of failures on the way. On the other hand, we often hear that they are at a loss to find out good themes. Even when we observe various presentations, we cannot understand well how they have dug out the theme.

## Tools Effective for "Theme Selection"

Therefore, it is important to ferret out problems and tasks that could be the seeds of the theme utilizing "Problems and Tasks Digging up Checklist" and "Problems and Tasks Selection Sheet."

1) At this stage, do not classify problems and tasks, and ferret out those you have some concerns from various angles without any omission. As viewpoints, ferret out from the things around yourself to the company level, on the time scale, from past to the possible happenings in the future. Involve bosses and related peoples to ferret out problems and tasks, and it become possible to ferret out from broader viewpoints.

2) Problems and tasks should be sought out from following viewpoints.
   ① The tasks that emerged from reflection on previous activities and remained problems
   ② The problems that surround you like things that trouble you every day and those you are thinking it is inconvenient
   ③ Upper policy and problems and tasks in the work place
   ④ Desire or requirements and complaints from customers including previous and following processes and other departments
   ⑤ Things that should be solved beforehand when introducing new businesses
   ⑥ Things that should be addressed beforehand based on the risks in the future
   ⑦ Things that should be further strengthened or enhanced
   ⑧ Things that you want to achieve higher level than the current level

### (2) Points of "Narrowing down the Problems and Tasks"

1) It will be better to narrow down those as a theme utilizing "Problems and Tasks Narrowing down Evaluation Table" and so forth, to evaluate using evaluation items like following items, and to narrow down to those

that have high overall evaluation points.

① Degree of agreement with company policy and upper policy

② Degree of necessity to solve from urgency, expected effects and future perspectives

③ Own capability level, willingness to challenge, satisfaction, etc

2) It will become easier to proceed if you consult your boss about the narrowed down candidates for the theme and if you can confirm the limitations and coordination with other departments, after agreeing that it is the most prioritized items.

## (3) Points for "Selection of Improvement Procedures"

1) "Selection of Improvement Procedures" is to judge which Procedures among the Problem Solving type, Task Achieving type or Measures Implementing Type to apply to the narrowed down themes utilizing the flowchart for "Improvement Procedures Selection Method".

2) When issues are already happening and when the causes and measures are almost known, or in case a task was given to implement, choose the procedures for Measures Implementing type.

3) When issues are already happening and when the causes are not known, choose the procedures for Problem Solving type.

4) When the issues are not happening but when you want to cope with new works, when you are taking up tasks in the near future, when you want to make a radical breakthrough of the work already exists, or when it is a theme that belong to the tasks like creation of attractive quality, choose the procedures for Task Achieving type.

## (4) Points of "Clarification of the Reason for the Theme Selection"

1) "Clarification of the Reason for the Theme Selection" is to clarify the

necessity to tackle with the theme, and name the theme expressing the aim and functions to achieve, concretely, simply and understandably. When it is necessary, add sub-title.

2) It would be better to clarify the necessity like the following items concretely based on the facts data and information.

① Necessity from current situation or level

② Requirement or request from customers or related parties including following processes

③ Necessity judged from comparison with competitors or future perspective

④ Necessity judged from desirable conditions or levels, or undesirable conditions or loss

# Chapter 2

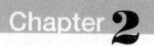

## Tool 2-1

# Problems and Tasks Digging up Checklist

## (1) What is Problems and Tasks Digging up Checklist

At the "Implementation step 1 Ferreting out Problems and Tasks" in the Theme Selection, the "Problems and Tasks Digging up Checklist" is useful for ferreting out problems and tasks from various angles.

It helps to digging up problems and tasks through checking the problems and tasks list that are accumulated every day, or to check if there is any omission in the problems and tasks found at the ferreting out meeting.

Table 2.2 "Problems and tasks digging out checklist" from the points of view of QCDPSME, the management items of workshop

| | Checkpoint | What concerns you |
|---|---|---|
| Q | What are the problems and tasks on quality | |
| C | What are the problems and tasks on cost | |
| D | What are the problems and tasks on delivery time | |
| P | What are the problems and tasks on productivity | |
| S | What are the problems and tasks on safety | |
| M | What are the problems and tasks on moral | |
| E | What are the problems and tasks on environment | |

Even looking at the case examples, it is not explained detail enough how they have dug up the theme, but in addition to the list above, if you use the following perspective as checklist, they are useful to ferret out problems and tasks from various angles.

1) At this stage, do not distinguish problems and tasks and ferret out what concerns you. When doing it, it will also be useful to prepare the scope of investigation in the form of checklist like Fig. 2.1.

Tools Effective for "Theme Selection"

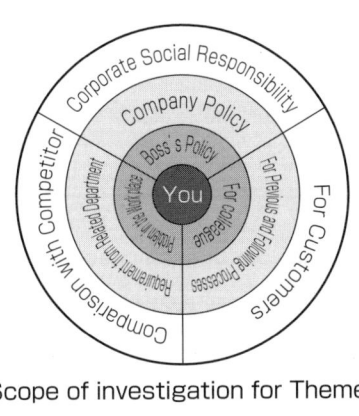

Fig.2.1  Scope of investigation for Theme Selection

(Source : Ayano, Katsutoshi, ed., *QC Circle Kanagawa District Task Achieving Study Group ed., Kadai Tassei Jissen Manual, 2nd revision* (*Task Achieving Practice Manual 2nd revision*), JUSE Press, Ltd., 2001.)

2) Also, if you examine on the time line of past, present and future like Fig. 2.2 to dig out problems and tasks, it is useful to get ideas on various problems or tasks.

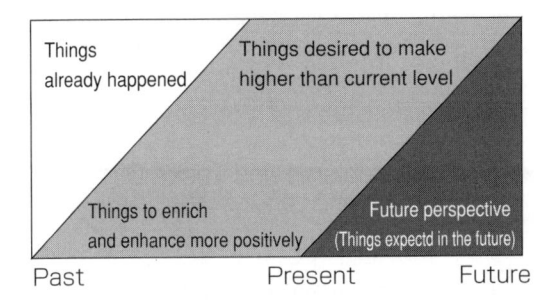

Fig.2.2  Examine Problems and Tasks on the Time Line

(Source : Ayano, Katsutoshi, ed., *QC Circle Kanagawa District Task Achieving Study Group ed., Kadai Tassei Jissen Manual, 2nd revision* (*Task Achieving Practice Manual 2nd revision*), JUSE Press, Ltd., 2001.)

## (2)  Procedures for Making "Problems and Tasks Digging out Checklist"

### Step 1. Clarify the checkpoints for ferreting Problems and Tasks

Clarify the checkpoints by listing up the checklist discussing the scope of ferreting out problems and tasks.

In case of new circles, many problems and tasks will be ferreted out just by clarifying problems and tasks from all the angles, taking up the QCDPSME, the management items of workshop like Table 2.2.

In case of veteran circles, not only these in your own workshop but, if you make a checklist with the view points of Fig 2.1 and Fig. 2.2, you can ferret out problems and tasks from wider perspectives.

**Step 2. Fill in what concerns you for each checkpoints of the checklist**

In the cases of QC circles that are continuing improvement activities, they may have a list of problems and tasks that have not been tackled yet, even they had been raised as themes so far. They can be filled in the appropriate column of the checklist, and as to the checkpoint that are not filled in, check whether there is anything that concern you and fill in.

If there is no past themes that has been carried over, or if it is the first improvement activity to tackle with, hold a meeting to ferret out problems and tasks and list up what concerns you or what is discussed usually with all the members participating on the each view point of the checklist, and fill in to the column of "what concerns you" of the Problems and Tasks Digging out Checklist.

## (3)　Case Example of "Problems and Tasks Digging up Checklist"

Fig. 2.3 is an example that uses upper policy, employee, future forecast and one which desired higher than current level as checkpoints and ferreting, out problems and tasks, and combined with the "Problems and Tasks Selection Sheet".

Tools Effective for "Theme Selection"

(Point allotment) ○ :3pt. △ :2pt. × :1pt. 05/06/02

| Checkpoint | What concerns you | What is known | What is unknown | Tentative theme | Importance | Urgency | Possibility | Cost | Boss's policy | Effects | Overall evaluation |
|---|---|---|---|---|---|---|---|---|---|---|---|
| What is upper policy? | Does the work place have safety most priority? | Awareness of safety is still low | Safety rules are not observed | How to let them observe the safety rule surely | ○ | △ | △ | △ | △ | ○ | 144 |
| | Self-development is low | Personal motivation for development is low | understanding on methods for self development | How to activate self-development | △ | × | × | ○ | ○ | × | 18 |
| | QC circle activity is not active | QC circle only for presentation. There is no time to join in QC circle activity | Understanding methods and technique | How to activate QC Circle activity | △ | △ | × | ○ | ○ | △ | 72 |
| | Work improvement suggestion activity isn't active | There is no time to revise idea to as suggestion | | How to activate work improvement suggestion activity | △ | △ | × | ○ | ○ | △ | 72 |
| What is empoyee's demand? | Employee service in director office insufficuat | There is some complaints in branch office | Each department satisfied | How to improve satisfaction for employee service | ○ | △ | △ | △ | ○ | △ | 144 |
| What are problems and tasks predicted to happen in the future? | Low resolution rate of charge payable on utility poles | It will worsen if left | Lack of information of land owner | How to raise resolution rate of charge on utility poles | ○ | ○ | △ | × | ○ | ○ | 162 |
| What are the things desired higher than current level ? | Complaint to some of delivery classes for next genelation | Demand for class is rising | What are wanted | How to improve quality of delivery class for next generation | ○ | △ | ○ | △ | ○ | △ | 216 |

Fig.2.3  Combining "Problems and tasks selection sheet" and "Problems and tasks Digging out checklist"

(Source : Kansai Electric Power Co. Ltd., "Hino kuruma (Wheel of Fire) Circle" Presentation Materials at the 4970th held by the QC Circle Headquarter.)

# Chapter 2

## Tool 2-2
# Problems and Tasks Selection Sheet

### (1) What is "Problems and Tasks Selection Sheet"?

Another useful tool that is effective for "Implementing step 1 Ferreting out Problems and Tasks" is "Problems and Tasks Selection Sheet." The "Problems and Tasks Selection Sheet" is useful to organize that concerns, what is known or what is unknown, and to decide on the tentative theme.

Many of the problems and tasks are recognized as rough images, but many of them are vague in that they have unclear scopes or they are not grasped quantitatively, etc. In those cases, it is important to clarify "what is known" or "what is unknown" for the contents of each problem or task and to decide "tentative theme" using the "Problems and Tasks Selection Sheet" with the format like Table 2.3.

Table 2.3  Form of "Problems and Tasks Selection Sheet"

| | What is concerned | What is known | What is unknown | Tentative theme (Candidates for the theme) |
|---|---|---|---|---|
| 1 | | | | |
| 2 | | | | |
| 3 | | | | |

(Source : Ayano, Katsutoshi, ed., *QC Circle Kanagawa District Task Achieving Study Group ed., Kadai Tassei Jissen Manual, 2nd revision* (Task Achieving Practice Manual 2nd revision), JUSE Press, Ltd., 2001.)

### (2) Procedure for Making "Problems and Tasks Selection Sheet"

#### Step 1. List up Problems and Tasks

Table the problems and tasks listed up on the "Problems and Tasks Selection Checksheet."

## Step 2. Fill in the current status of grasping

Clarify what is known at present or what is not known for each of what concerns you and fill them in the respective column of "what is known" or "what is unknown" of the "Problems and Tasks Selection Sheet."

## Step 3. Decide Tentative Theme

For each of Problems and Tasks, decide tentative theme.

## (3) Case Example of "Problems and Tasks Selection Sheet"

Fig. 2.4 is a case example that problems and tasks are listed up along with the upper policy of "big improvement of efficiency at workplace" and arranged on the "Problems and Tasks Selection Sheet." It is an efficient method to ferret out only that are within the limitation of policy and scope, etc.

| What concern you | What is known | What is unknown | Tentative theme |
|---|---|---|---|
| 1. Man-hour is increased because of adding measure points of trunk capacity | Tasks do not finish within allocated time because it is increasd 220 minutes per experiment | Measurement man- hour for each type of a car, Measure time and method and equipment of other office | Measurement of car trunk capacity takes too much time |
| 2. Preparing for quantity evaluation experiment exceeds standard time in RV | Passenger cars are within standard time  RV car exceed the limit by 42 minutes | Gaps among processes | Measurement preparation takes too much time |

Fig.2.4  Case Example of "Problems and Tasks Selection Sheet"

(Source : Nissan Motor Co., Ltd., "Performance Circle" Presentation Materials at the 3780th QC Circle Convention held by the QC Circle Kanto Branch, Kanagawa District.)

*41*

## Tool 2-3

# Problems and Tasks Narrowing down Evaluation Table

### (1) What is "Problems and Tasks Narrowing down Evaluation Table"?

A tool useful for the "Implementation Step 2 Narrowing down Problems and Tasks" in the step of Theme Selection is the "Problems and Tasks Narrowing down Evaluation Table." It is also called as "Theme Selection Matrix" from its shape.

Basically, like Table 2.4, rank them with plural evaluation items like upper policy, urgency, expected effects, improvement desire, etc. If necessary, weights are given to the evaluation items. It is used to get consensus among the concerned people using the data usable or facts, information at the maximum.

In actual utilization, you should review if the evaluation items are appropriate to yourselves, and to prioritize the evaluation.

Table 2.4 Form of "Problems and Tasks Narrowing down Evaluation Table"

| Tentative theme (Candidates for the theme) | Evaluation items | | | | Overall points | Judgment |
|---|---|---|---|---|---|---|
| | Boss's policy | Urgency | Expected effects | Willingness to challenge | | |
| Weight | 1 | 1 | 1 | 2 | | |
| | | | | | | |

(Source : Ayano, Katsutoshi, ed., *QC Circle Kanagawa District Task Achieving Study Group ed., Kadai Tassei Jissen Manual, 2nd revision* (*Task Achieving Practice Manual 2nd revision*), JUSE Press, Ltd., 2001.)

### (2) Procedure for Making "Problems and Tasks Narrowing down Evaluation Table"

**Step 1.** Decide on the evaluation items used for selection of problems and tasks

It is recommended to include following viewpoints in the evaluation items.

① Consistency with company policy or boss's policy
② Urgency, expected effects, needs for solution, difficulty of solution, etc.
③ Own capability, desire for solution, satisfaction, etc.

**Step 2.** Decide the weights for each evaluation item

**Step 3.** Evaluate on each evaluation item and calculate the overall weighted points and decide on the priority

## (3) Case example of "Problems and Tasks Narrowing down Evaluation Table"

Table 2.5 is an example where own indigenous evaluation items are added.

Table 2.6 is an example where 12 problems (A-L) were narrowed down to 5 from urgency view point, and evaluation is done from the degree of importance, and the Table 2.7 is the evaluation table for the second stage. It can be used to narrow down the themes that fit to your own evaluation method.

Table 2.8 is an example where indigenous methods are used to devise a theme selection table, from ferreting out to the evaluation.

For ferreting out the theme, ferreting out of problems of own workplace is done from "4 *naru* (become)" checkpoints of "*yokunaru* (become better)" "*Yasukunaru* (become cheaper)" "*Hayakunaru* (become faster)" and "*anzenninaru* (become safer)", and the problems taken up and evaluation are arranged in

Table 2.5  Example of theme selection matrix table

| | Effects | Emergency | Necessity | Hopes | Company Policy | Total |
|---|---|---|---|---|---|---|
| Reduce overwork time | 3 | 3 | 4 | 5 | 3 | 18 |
| Housekeeping | 2 | 3 | 4 | 3 | 3 | 15 |
| Sales promotion of nonmedicinel products | 4 | 3 | 5 | 4 | 5 | 21 |
| Decrease waiting time | 3 | 4 | 4 | 3 | 5 | 19 |

(It matches to company's policy — pointing to "Company Policy")
(Judge with unit price per Prescription (Sales of nonmedicinel products ÷ number of prescription))

(Source: Bohsei Pharmacy, "Ayaka 3 Months Circle", *QC Circle Magazine*, Aug. 2008, Case Example 1, JUSE.)

Table 2.6 Example for urgency evaluation table

Evaluation criteria : High urgency=3pt. Common urgency=2pt. Low urgency=1pt.

| Zone / Item | Documents | | Sales | | | | | Ticket examination | | Ticket vending machine | | Loner |
|---|---|---|---|---|---|---|---|---|---|---|---|---|
| Label | I | K | B | D | F | G | L | C | J | A | H | E |
| Score | 12 | 6 | 12 | 11 | 11 | 14 | 8 | 10 | 8 | 9 | 7 | 10 |

| | |
|---|---|
| I 12pt. From documents | : Document is not organized and have trouble finding. |
| G 14pt. From selling | : Air ticket selling is not known well and feel anxitous. |
| C 10pt. From ticket examination | : Too much time is spend to deliver lost property. |
| A 9pt. From ticket vending machine | : Ticket vending machine is too complex to understand its operation. |
| E 10pt. from loner | : It is difficult to work because narrow windows |

(Source : East Japan Railway Company, "Sweet Potato Circle" , *QC Circle Magazine,* April 2007, One Point Case Example, JUSE.)

Table 2.7 Example of evaluation table for importance

Important: 3pt. some important: 2pt. usual: 1pt.

| Label | Evaluation items / Problems | Feasibiliy to realize | Urgency | Commonalities | Possibility to end in period | Supporter's opinion | Possibility to obtain data | Overall points | Rank |
|---|---|---|---|---|---|---|---|---|---|
| I | Document is not organized and non trouble finding | 15 | 11 | 9 | 17 | 10 | 5 | 67 | 4 |
| G | Air ticket selling is not known well and feel anxious | 12 | 10 | 12 | 15 | 10 | 13 | 72 | 3 |
| C | Too much time spend to deliver lost property | 15 | 15 | 15 | 10 | 15 | 15 | 85 | 1 |
| A | Ticket vending machine is too complex to understand its operation | 12 | 9 | 13 | 14 | 12 | 13 | 73 | 2 |
| E | It is difficult to work because of narrow windows | 15 | 8 | 15 | 7 | 5 | 5 | 55 | 5 |

(Source : East Japan Railway Company, "Sweet Potato Circle", *QC Circle Magazine,* April 2007, One Point Case Example, JUSE.)

matrix diagram and evaluation is done. Evaluation criteria are also devised to change depending on the item, not giving equal weights to each item.

From the evaluation results, the theme candidates are narrowed down to one, the treatment of other candidates are made clear by setting them as the candidates for improvement suggestion and next activity theme.

Tools Effective for "Theme Selection"

Table 2.8  Example of combining "Problem and Tasks Digging up Checklist" with a "Theme Selection Matrix"

| 4 naru (become) checkpoint | | Problems in workplace | Evaluation | | | Boss's policy | | | | | | Overall evaluation | Theme | Theme leader | Activity period |
|---|---|---|---|---|---|---|---|---|---|---|---|---|---|---|---|
| | | | Importance | Possibility to do ourselves | Possibility to do in short period | Quality | | Cost | | | Delivery / Safety | | | | March — June |
| | | | | | | Improvement of process capability | Defect reduction | Man-hour reduction | Failure cost reduction | WIP reduction | Equipment reduction / Improvement of ability to predict risk | | | | |
| Yoku naru (Change better) | Existence of defects | Abnormality in F/C inside diameter control chart | ◎3 | ◎3 | ◎3 | ◎3 | | | | | | 81 | Changing shape of bytes | | (Improvement suggestion) |
| | Existence of abnormality | Occurrence of man-hour for rework | ◎5 | △1 | △1 | | ◎3 | ◎3 | | | | 45 | (Improve equipment) | | Request to boss or staff |
| | Existence of adjustment | Defect caused by lack of right packing | ◎5 | ◎3 | ◎3 | ◎3 | | | | | | 135 | Improve packing | | March ×××× |
| Yasuku naru (Change cheaper) | Existence of bad effect to following processes | | | | | | | | | | | | | | |
| | Existence of Pokamisu(careless miss) | | | | | | | | | | | | | | |
| | Existence of muda(waste) | A loss in multi tasks | ◎5 | ◎3 | ◎3 | | ◎3 | | | | ◎3 | 135 | Kaizen of v/p by reduction of loss and waste | | May ×××× |
| | Existence of muri(over burden) | | | | | | | | | | | | | | |
| | Existence of mura(variation) | | | | | | | | | | | | | | |
| | Existence of efficiency down | | | | | | | | | | | | | | |
| | Man-hour as planned | | | | | | | | | | | | | | |

Importance: ◎ 5pt.:high / ○ 3pt.:middle / △ 1pt.:low
Difficulty: ◎ 3pt.:easy / ○ 2pt.:normal / △ 1pt.:hard
Period: ◎ 3pt.:short / ○ 2pt.:middle / △ 1pt.:long
Level of unit: ◎ 3pt.:high / ○ 2pt.:middle / △ 1pt.:low

(Source : Komatsu Ltd., "TM Checker man Circle", *QC Circle Magazine*, April 2010 series, JUSE.)

Chapter 2

## Tool 2-4

# Improvement Procedures Selection Method

## (1) What is "Improvement Procedures Selection Method"?

The tool useful for "Implementation step 3. Selection of Improvement Procedures" in Theme Selection is the "Improvement Procedures Selection Method." When the Task Achieving type QC Story was first proposed, "QC Story Application Judging Table" and "Procedures Confirmation Chart" were used, but along with the proposal of Measures Implementing type, it became common to select one with the flowchart like Fig. 2.5.

```
                         ┌─────────┐
                         │  Theme  │
                         └────┬────┘
                              │
                    ┌─────────┴─────────┐
          What is the object which    The works that you have
          you tackle with?            never experienced before
                    │
          The works that you have been doing so far
                    │
         ┌──────────┴──────────┐
     Are the measures
     already known?
                    │
         ┌──────────┴──────────┐
The factors and measures          The factors and measures
are already known                 aren't already known at all
         │                                  │
         │              Can you analyze factors?
         │                                  │
         │                   ┌──────────────┴──────────────┐
         │              Factors can be analyzed    Analyzing the factors
         │                                          is difficult
         ▼                         ▼                         ▼
┌──────────────────────┐  ┌──────────────────────┐  ┌────────────────────┐
│ Measures Implementing│  │ Problem Solving type │  │ Task Achieving type│
│        type          │  │                      │  │                    │
└──────────────────────┘  └──────────────────────┘  └────────────────────┘
```

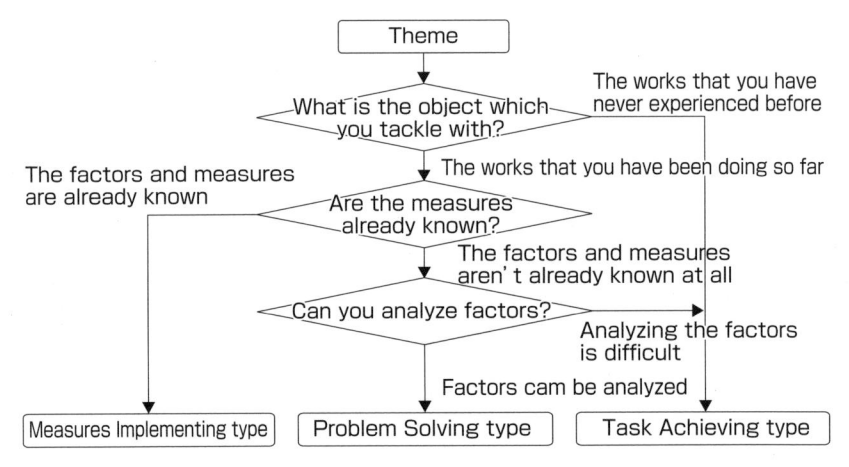

Fig.2.5 The flowchart for improvement procedures selection methods

(Source : Hosotani, Katsuya, ed., *Suguwakaru Mondai Kaiketsu ho* (*Quickly Understandable Problem Solving Method*), JUSE Press, Ltd., 2000.)

However, it doesn't mean that you have to apply one of the improvement procedures to a theme as a whole. Refer to the case example introduced later.

Tools Effective for "Theme Selection"

## (2) Procedures for Utilization of the "Improvement Procedures Selection Method"

1) First judgment is on whether it is a work that you have experienced so far. When it is a theme that is related to the works that you have never experienced before, select Task Achieving Type Procedures.
2) In case it is a work that you have been doing, and if the factors and measures are already known, select Measures Implementing Type Procedures.
3) In case you have no idea on the factors and countermeasures, basically select Problem Solving Type Procedures, but in case you cannot analyze factors, select Task Achieving Type Procedures.

## (3) Case Example of Utilization of "Improvement Procedures Selection Method"

Fig. 2.6 is an example where Problem Solving Procedures were selected according to the contents of the problems separating the badness that were made clear by current situation grasping into recurrence preventions and preventions.

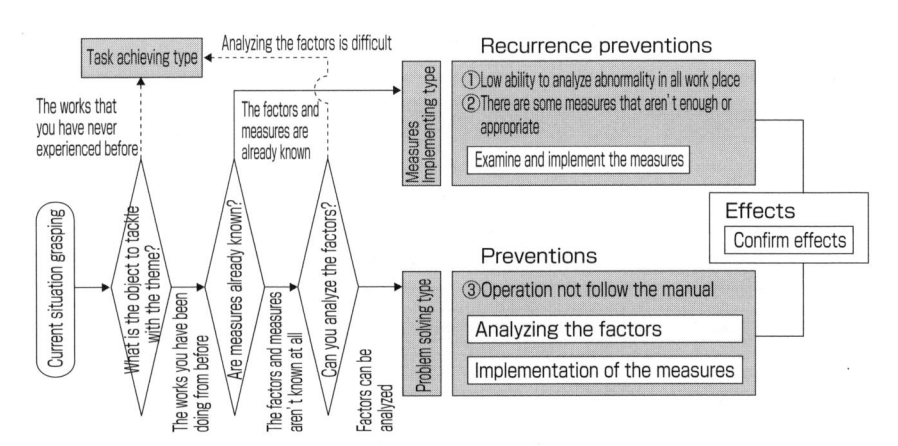

Fig.2.6 Selection of Procedure fit to the Problems

(Source : Konica Minolta Medical & Graphic, Inc., "Chienowa (Puzzle Ring) Circle", *QC Circle Magazine*, Dec. 2007, One Point Case Example, JUSE.)

# Chapter 2

## Tool 2-5

# Gantt Chart

## (1) What is "Gantt Chart"?

To implement the theme selected surely and without any omission, it is important to decompose each step into detailed implementation items and to make overall schedule plan and to put them into implementation.

Most frequently used for the scheduling plan and scheduling control of the operation and works that correspond to implementation items is the "Gantt Chart" and it is also called as Bar Chart, Yokosen Kotei Hyou (horizontal process table), or line table. On the Gantt Chart, arrange implementation items on the vertical axis and dates (month and day) on the horizontal axis. Basics are the plan is drawn with thin line or dotted line and the actual are drawn with thick line or solid lines (refer to Fig. 2.7). "Gantt Chart" is used in the cases of relatively simple and rough plan and when the number of operation items are not so many.

Scheduling is used in any problem solving procedures, and in the Task Achieving Type Procedures, it is also often used as the activity plan in the

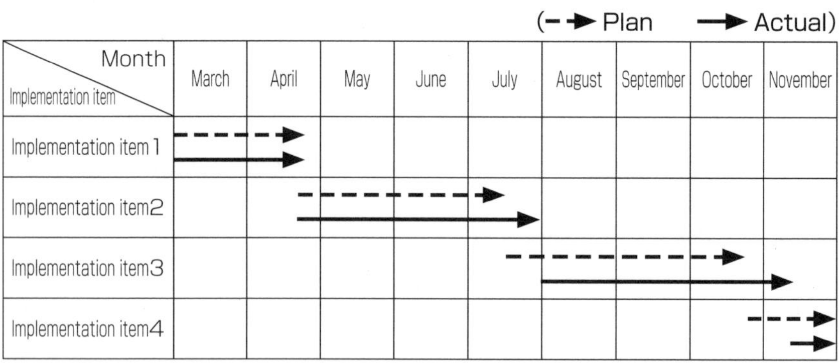

(-▶ Plan    ▶ Actual)

| Month \ Implementation item | March | April | May | June | July | August | September | October | November |
|---|---|---|---|---|---|---|---|---|---|
| Implementation item 1 | --- | -▶ | | | | | | | |
| Implementation item 2 | | | --- | --- -▶ | | | | | |
| Implementation item 3 | | | | | | --- | --- --- -▶ | | |
| Implementation item 4 | | | | | | | | | --- -▶ |

Fig.2.7  Basic Example of "Gantt Chart"

"Clarification of Attack Points and Setting Target" and "Implementation of Success Scenarios."

## (2) Procedures for making "Gantt Chart"

### Step 1. Decompose to implementation items

Decompose the project or theme into implementation items such as steps or implementation steps (operation or work tasks).

### Step 2. Estimate the necessary time

Estimate the time (days) needed to execute each item.

### Step 3. Enter vertical axis and horizontal axis

Write those implementation items on the vertical axis like Fig. 2.7 and set time like months, weeks, or days on the horizontal axis, and express the time needed for each items as plan line (bar or arrow). When writing, make the beginning point of the line to show the beginning of the operation and the end point to show the end of the operation.

The "Gantt Chart" shows the operation time at one glance, and it is easy to understand for the manager of the overall projects and for each operator in charge, and it is effective for progress control. In progress control, if you write actual time needed as a implementation line under the plan line, you can grasp the gaps (late or early) against the operation schedule.

## (3) Case Example of "Gantt Chart" Utilization

An example of overall schedule is shown on Table 2.9.

In this example, 5W1H is clarified for each step and a system of step leader/sub-leader is adopted, and what kind of techniques is used for each step is also examined, these are the features. To proceed the activities efficiently, it is important to decide as much as possible on how to tackles by clarifying the approaches from 5W1H viewpoints at the planning stage.

## Table 2.9 Implementation Example of Scheduling that uses to Gantt Chart

| Class | Why (Purpose) | What (Implementation) | Where (Place) | Who (Leader) | Who (Sub) | When March | April | May | June | July | August | September | October | How (Methods, QC methods) |
|---|---|---|---|---|---|---|---|---|---|---|---|---|---|---|
| P | Setting attack point and target | Clarification of attack point | Office/jobshop | Okabe | Fujimori | --→ | | | | | | | | Selection table of investigation items / Attack point digging out sheet |
| P | Setting attack point and target | Setting target | Office | Okabe | Fujimori | --→ | | | Plan ---→ Actual —→ | | | | | Bar graph |
| P | Planning Measures | Listing up candidates of measures | Office/jobshop | Fujimori | Jinno | | --→ | | | | | | | Tree diagram |
| P | Planning Measures | Narrowing down the measures | Office | Fujimori | Jinno | | --→ | | | | | | | Matrix diagram |
| P | Pursuit of Success scenarios | Examined success scenarios | Office/jobshop | Jinno | Atou | | --→ | | | | | | | Brain-storming |
| P | Pursuit of Success scenarios | Forecasting the estimated effects | Office/jobshop | Jinno | Atou | | --→ | →| | | | | | Brain-storming |
| P | Pursuit of Success scenarios | Forecasting and removals of obstacles | Office/jobshop | Atou | Tateno | | | --→ | → | | | | | In-process test / Table for removing obstacles |
| P | Pursuit of Success scenarios | Selection of success scenario | Office/jobshop | Atou | Tateno | | | | --→ → | | | | | |
| D | Implementation of success scenario | Making implementation plan | Office | Tateno | Sunayama | | | | --→ → | | | | | Graph |
| D | Implementation of success scenario | Implementation success scenario | jobshop | Tateno | Sunayama | | | | | -------→ | | | | In-process test |
| C | Confirm effects | Grasping tangible effects | Office/jobshop | Sunayama | Suzuki | | | | | | ------→ | | | Bar graph |
| C | Confirm effects | Grasping intangible effects | Office/jobshop | Sunayama | Suzuki | | | | | | ------→ | | | Research |
| A | Standardization of and fixing of control | Standardization | Office | Suzuki | Katou | | | | | | | --→ | | Operation procedure manual |
| A | Standardization of and fixing of control | Making them known to all | Office/jobshop | Suzuki | Katou | | | | | | | --→ | | Education for operator |
| A | Standardization of and fixing of control | Fixing of the control | Office/jobshop | Suzuki | Katou | | | | | | | --→ | | Daily inspection |
| A | Reflection and future addressing | Reflection on activity | bar | Katou | Okabe | | | | | | | | --→ → | Reflection meeting |
| A | Reflection and future addressing | Making next plan | Office | Katou | Okabe | | | | | | | | --→ → | Brainstorming |

(Source : Hitachi Global Storage Technologies, "25TEST Circle", *QC Circle Magazine,* March 2009, Case Example 1, JUSE.)

## ONE POINT

◆Gantt Chart is devised by an American Engineer, Henry L Gantt. Origin is the method to illustrate the sequence of production process devised at the beginning of 1900, and after his death, his subordinate Wallace Clark has disseminated the name of Gantt Chart and the technique, and it came to be used for many development and construction work scheduling. Main stream is the Task Gantt Chart that allocates tasks, but there are other charts derived like Milestone Chart and chart that shows the dependence relationship among the tasks.

# Chapter 3

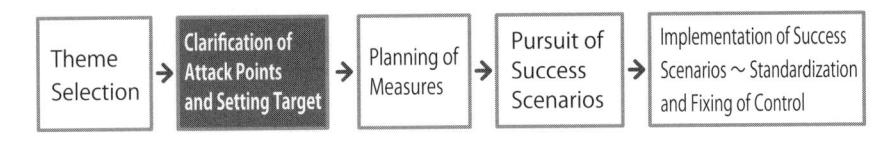

## Tools Effective for "Clarification of Attack Points and Setting Targets"

Theme Selection → **Clarification of Attack Points and Setting Target** → Planning of Measures → Pursuit of Success Scenarios → Implementation of Success Scenarios ~ Standardization and Fixing of Control

# Chapter 3

# Points and Tools for "Clarification of Attack Points and Setting Targets"

Step of "Clarification of Attack Points and Setting Targets" is composed of 2 implementation steps. The first is the "Clarification of Attack Points" where the task is broken down to clarify the attack points. The second is the "Setting Targets" to clarify the practical targets that corresponding to the "Clarification of the Attack Points."

The "Clarification of Attacking Points" is further decomposed to a couple of implementation items. Its outline, and the effective tools introduced in this book are shown in Table 3.1.

Table 3.1 Effective tools and implementation procedures/items for "Clarification of Attack Points and Setting Targets"

| 【Implementation steps】 | 【Effective tools】 | |
|---|---|---|
| 1. Clarification of Attack Points | Tool 3-1 | Stratification |
| · Grasping overall characteristics | Tool 3-2 | Investigation Items Selection Table |
| · Deciding investigation items | Tool 3-3 | Benchmarking |
| · Grasping desired level | Tool 3-4 | Questionnaire Survey |
| · Grasping current level | Tool 3-5 | QC Seven Tools and New QC Seven Tools |
| · Grasping difference (gap) between both of them | | |
| · Examination of candidate attack point | Tool 3-6 | Attack Points Selection Sheet |
| · Deciding attack points | | |
| 2. Setting Targets | Tool 3-7 | SWOT Analysis |

## (1) Points of "Clarification of Attack Points"

This step is the most important step in the task achieving type and it can be said that this is the step the feature of task achieving type appears. Although the detailed implementation steps are as explained in Chapter 1, it is reproduced in Fig. 3.1.

# Tools Effective for "Clarification of Attack Points and Setting Targets"

① To decide on the investigation items (approaches) to analyze the task taken up as the themes, it is recommended to utilize "Stratification" and "Investigation Items Selection Table."

For the classification of stratification, 4M, 7M+E+T, 7S, etc. are frequently used (Refer to Table 3.3).

② Desired level (where you want to be) is grasped for all the investigation items.

Desired level is clarified from the following items on the system, functions, performances, and levels newly required.

 ・From bosses policy (directed value)
 ・From the level of function and performance that looks attractive
 ・From target level through benchmark
 ・From new regulatory requirement and competitors trends
 ・Considering the expected obstacles and losses

③ Gap is the difference between the desired level (vision to reach) and present level (current status). If the level is numerical data, it is easy to grasp the gap. For example, if the investigated patient's shortest waiting time at an hospital was 20 min (desired level) and the average 60 min (present level) of own hospital, the gap is 40 min.

When the desired level and present level is in verbal data, make them as concrete expression as possible and take care that the attack points do not become vague.

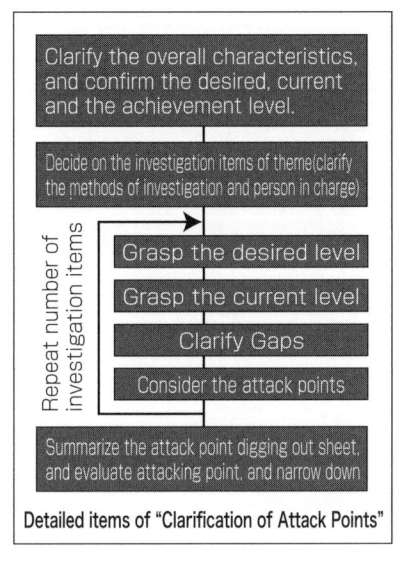

Fig.3.1 Detailed items of Clarification of Attack Points

To grasp and organize these desired level and present level, tools such as benchmarking and questionnaire survey and QC Seven Tools are utilized.

(Note) At ②③ above, it does not matter which of the desired level and present level is grasped first.

④ To eliminate the gaps, the measures candidates are ferreted out considering the capability of the workplace, but it is important first to examine where to focus to attack without thinking blindly.

This focus and the points of view is the "attack points" and therefore, it is desirable to consider bigger view points and from higher purposes. For each of the gaps, consider the attack points from various angles.

⑤ The attack points candidates that seem to eliminate large gap can be expected to bring large improvement effects, the attack points are decided narrowing down the attack points candidates to a few items using the evaluation items.

⑥ To effectively proceed with "Implementation step 1. Clarification of the attack points" and to summarize efficiently, "Attacking Points Selection Sheet" is appropriate to use.

## (2) Points of "Setting Targets"

① The final target is generally accord with the achievement level of characteristics that represents the theme (task) as a whole, but it is also realistic to decide separately consulting with supervisors depending on the situation.

② Because it is common that there are plural attack points in Task Achieving Type, it is important to decide the target for each of the attack points, and to confirm that the total of them satisfies the total target. If they do not satisfy, you have to add other attack points.

Tools Effective for "Clarification of Attack Points and Setting Targets"

## Tool 3-1

# Stratification

## (1) What is Stratification?

Stratification is to separate into some groups that has some common points or tendency, focusing on the features of the data. For example, dividing them into days of the week, or models, it becomes possible to see the difference in the occurrence situations of defectives.

There are two purposes in stratification.

The first purpose is, by dividing them into strata, to examine if the variance of the total data can be explained by the "difference in the averages of each stratum".

The second purpose is to examine, by looking at the distribution of the data for each data, if there are any kind of commonalities between the strata.

The stratification can largely divided into two. The first is the "stratification" by the characteristic of the data. And the other is the "stratification" by the phenomenon that the data represent.

### 1) "Stratification" by the characteristics of the obtained data

Examples of the items for "stratification" that is generally used are shown in Table 3.2.

### 2) "Stratification" by the phenomena that the data represent

① Good products or defectives
② Kinds of the defectives
   Example) Case of Voucher billing: entry omission, entry error, format error, count error, etc.

At the step of "Current Status Grasping" in problem solving type, "Strati-

*55*

Table 3.2 Example of items for "Stratification"

| Classification | Example of items for stratification |
|---|---|
| By time series | Month, Day, Hour, Day of the week, Daytime, Night, Season, etc. |
| By Worker | Individual, Group, Workplace, Age, Experience, Gender, etc. |
| By machine and equipment | Machine type, Model, Efficiency, Machine number, Tools, etc. |
| By material, raw material, component | Maker, Retailer, Time of purchase, Lot, Storage method, etc. |
| By working method, condition | Temperature, Humidity, Pressure, rpm, Line Speed, etc. |
| By measurement, Inspection | Measuring equipment, Measuror, Measuring place, Measuring method, Inspector, etc. |
| By environment, weather | Sound, Lighting, Temperature, Weather, Season, etc. |
| By client | Type of occupation, Gender, Age, Annual income, Hobby, etc. |
| By distribute channel | Channel, Market, salling Typed, Transportation method, etc. |

fication" is used to examine if there are any featured points in the badness of the control characteristics. Similarly, the "Stratification" can be utilized to examine the investigation items at the "Clarification of Attack Points" of Task Achieving Type.

After "Grasping Overall Characteristics" using such as graphs, Pareto diagram, what should be done is to decide the approaches (investigation items) for analyzing the theme. The investigation items, here, are those that are grasped by "stratifying" the elements that construct the theme. When deciding on the approaches (investigation items), it is effective to utilize 4M, 7M+E+T, 7S as the viewpoints for the "stratification" (Refer to Table 3.3).

Among them, 4M is famous and well known. 7M+E+T has been added based on the 4M. 7S is recommended to utilize as the viewpoints for thinking or investigating from the management or planning perspectives.

## (2) Procedures for "Stratification"

### Step 1. Clarify the purpose of the stratification

Clarify the purpose of the stratification: for what you are doing stratification.

Tools Effective for "Clarification of Attack Points and Setting Targets"

Table 3.3  Point of view in "Stratification"

| 4M | 7M + E + T | | 7S |
|---|---|---|---|
| Man | Man | Environment | System |
| Machine | Machine | Time | Skill |
| Material | Material | | Strategy |
| Method | Method | | Structure |
| | Measurement | | Style |
| | Management | | Staff |
| | Morale | | Shared value |

**Step 2. Decide on the characteristics (data)**

Decide on what the characteristics (data) to take: the object of stratification.

**Step 3. Think whether it can be stratified**

From standpoint of various angles of viewpoints, think whether it can be devided.

**Step 4. Decide on the items for stratification**

Decide on the items for stratification: how it can be divided (stratified).

It is recommended to utilize the viewpoints of "stratification" (4M, 7M+E+T), 7S, etc. to decide stratification items.

**Step 5. Gather data, or arrange existing data**

When new data is collected, gather stratified data. At this point, it is convenient to devise a checksheet, etc, so that the data on the characteristics decided at step 2 can be collected classified for each stratification item.

When you are re-arranging the existing data with the stratification thinking in mind, it is recommended to arrange them in a checksheet format.

**Step 6. Analyze data**

Using the collected data, analyze the differences among the stratification items. For this analysis, using QC Seven Tools like graph/ Pareto diagram/ scatter diagram/ histogram/ control chart, conduct the comparison among the stratification items on the characteristics considerd.

## (3) Case Example of "Stratification"

Fig. 3.2 is an example of utilizing "stratification" on the sales promotion of quasi drugs (non medical products) at a pharmacy. Not only by the trend

**Total sales trend of non-medicinal product**

— : Unit price
▩ : Sales

● Amount of sales : ¥120,419　● A unit price of prescription : ¥39/presciption

**Amount of sales by the price range**

■ : April
▨ : May
■ : June
□ : July

More than ¥1,000 — About 58% of all

**Number of sales by the price range**

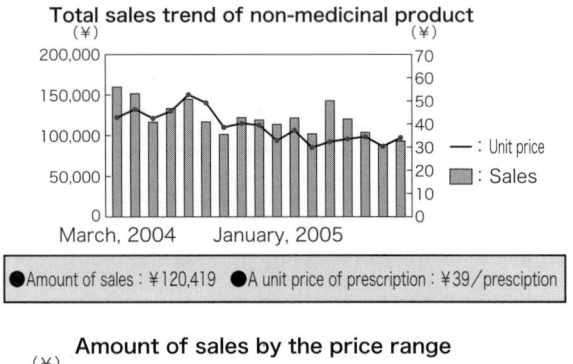

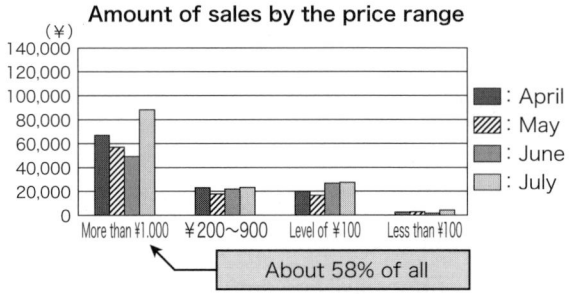

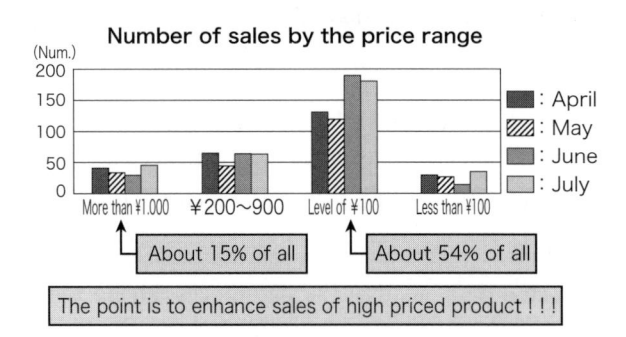

■ : April
▨ : May
■ : June
□ : July

¥200~900 — About 15% of all
Level of ¥100 — About 54% of all

The point is to enhance sales of high priced product ! ! !

Fig.3.2　Example of Stratification

(Source : Bohsei Pharmacy, "Ayaka 3 Months Circle", *QC Circle Magazine*, Aug. 2008, Case Example 1, JUSE.)

## Tools Effective for "Clarification of Attack Points and Setting Targets"

graphs of sales and the unit price of prescription, but also by "stratifying" sales amount separated by price range and number of sales stratified by price range, the tasks in the future are clarified.

Table 3.4 is an example that examined the investigation items with "4M" to clarify the attack points.

Table 3.4  Examination of investigation items utilizing 4M

| Classification | What | How | Who | When |
|---|---|---|---|---|
| Man | On/Off Timing | Behavior survey | Kitamura | Jan.8 |
| Material | Variation of air flow rate | Load factor by an hour | Fujitani | Jan.12 |
| Material | Air leak in equipment | Diagnosis by hearing in machine stopping day | Mizushima | Jan.10 |
| Material | Air leak in equipment | Grasping leak-rate | Mizushima | Jan.31 |
| Machine | Maximum load pressure | Setting for each equipment Pressure survey | Ikeda | Jan.17 |
| Method | Possibility of whole day stopping | Grasping actual situation in work place | Katagiri | Jan.9 |

(Source : Kobe Steel Co, Ltd., "Active Power Circle", *QC Circle Magazine*, July 2004, Case Example 3, JUSE.)

---

### ONE POINT

◆If the machine in the "4M" is limited to machines, facilities and equipments, a voice may be heard from the people at clerical works saying that there is no such thing. Do not limit to machines. It is necessary to understand them as the tools in a broader sense, like copy machine, equipment, (like PCs, projectors), office supplies.

In Table 3.3, "4M" has been listed, but depending on the type of jobs, "M" like Maintenance (maintaining), Market (market), Medium (Media), Mode (Style), Matter (materials), Merchandise (sales items) are utilized. It is convenient if you arrange necessary "M" needed to yourselves and to communalize them.

# Tool 3-2

# Investigation Items Selection Table

## (1) What is "Investigation Items Selection Table"?

After ferreting out the investigation items utilizing "Stratification" introduced at Tool 3-1, it is recommended to judge (evaluate) utilizing the "Investigation Items Selection Table." to select the investigation items.

A table to materialize step by step the voices like information/ desires/ requirements from customers and following processes, and to ferreting out and to extract the investigation items necessary for each item of the voices is the "Investigation Items Selection Table."

## (2) Procedures for making "Investigation Items Selection Table"

**Step 1. Ferret out investigation items utilizing "stratification"**

Ferret out as many investigation items as thinkable.

**Step 2. Ferret out detailed contents to be investigated**

Ferret out detailed contents to be investigated for investigation items.

**Step 3. Judge (evaluate) and select investigation items**

Make matrix diagram, judge (evaluate) and select investigation items.

## (3) Case example of "Investigation Items Selection Table"

An example of the Combination of investigation items selection and investigation plan is the Table 3.5 "Investigation Items Selection Table ①". As an alternative method for investigation items selection, there is a method to utilize the "Quality Table" of Quality Function Deployment (QFD). It is a method to materialize the requirements and desires from customers and following processes step by step (deployment of required quality), to ferreting out the investigation items (quality characteristics) needed, and to extract

Tools Effective for "Clarification of Attack Points and Setting Targets"

investigation Items. An example that has utilized "Quality Table" is the Table 3.6 "Investigation Items Selection Table ②". Let's utilize it even in the improvement activity of QC Circles. Please refer to Tool 5-5 for the detailed explanation of "Quality Table".

Table 3.5 Example of "Investigation Items Selection Table ①"

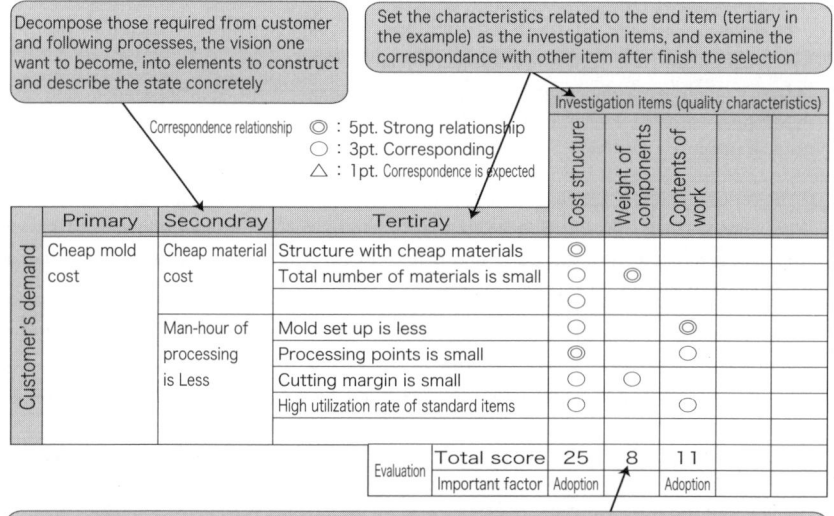

Examination of investigation items · Selection · survey plan table

Evaluation point ◎ : 5pt.
　　　　　　　　○ : 3pt.
　　　　　　　　△ : 1pt.

| Classification | Survey items | Contents | Influence | Extendability | Evaluation points | Rank | Allot survey · survey schedule | |
|---|---|---|---|---|---|---|---|---|
| | | | | | | | Who | When |
| Man | Designer | Man-hour for slide design | △ | △ | 2 | 3 | | |
| Material | Products | Shape of products | ◎ | ◎ | 10 | 1 | Kobayashi | Nov.10 |
| | Mold | Number of slide parts | ◎ | ◎ | 10 | 1 | Katou | Nov.10 |
| Method | Process | Design procedure | ○ | △ | 4 | 2 | | |
| | | Processing procedure | ◎ | ◎ | 10 | 1 | Izawa | Nov.15 |
| | Man-hour | Man-hour of processing | ◎ | ◎ | 10 | 1 | Komatsu | Nov.15 |

(Source : Ichiko Industries, Ltd., "Aun Circle" Presentation Materials at the 4100th QC Circle Convention held by the QC Circle Kanto Branch, Kanagawa District.)

Table 3.6 Example of "Investigation Items Selection Table ②"

[Decompose those required from customer and following processes, the vision one want to become, into elements to construct and describe the state concretely]

[Set the characteristics related to the end item (tertiary in the example) as the investigation items, and examine the correspondance with other item after finish the selection]

Correspondence relationship ◎ : 5pt. Strong relationship
　　　　　　　　　　　　　○ : 3pt. Corresponding
　　　　　　　　　　　　　△ : 1pt. Correspondence is expected

| | | | | Investigation items (quality characteristics) | | | |
|---|---|---|---|---|---|---|---|
| | Primary | Secondary | Tertiary | Cost structure | Weight of components | Contents of work | |
| Customer's demand | Cheap mold cost | Cheap material cost | Structure with cheap materials | ◎ | | | |
| | | | Total number of materials is small | ○ | ◎ | | |
| | | | | ○ | | | |
| | | Man-hour of processing is Less | Mold set up is less | ○ | | ◎ | |
| | | | Processing points is small | ◎ | | ○ | |
| | | | Cutting margin is small | ○ | ○ | | |
| | | | High utilization rate of standard items | ○ | | ○ | |
| | | | Evaluation | Total score | 25 | 8 | 11 |
| | | | | Important factor | Adoption | Adoption | Adoption |

When it is necessary to narrow down the scope of investigation due to activity period and information source, narrow down the investigation items by these score (However, wider the scope of investigation the more it is linked to quantitative grasping)

(Source : Ichiko Industries, Ltd., "Aun Circle" Presentation Materials at the 4100th QC Circle Convention held by the QC Circle Kanto Branch, Kanagawa District.)

# Chapter 3

## Tool 3-3

# Benchmarking

## (1) What is "Benchmarking"?

To grasp the desired level, it is effective to utilize "Benchmarking". "Benchmarking" is an management technique for finding out and improving the weak points of the management and work processes of own company/ own department, to conduct comparison analysis with the excellent cases (best practice) of other companies/ other departments, and to promote improvements and innovations setting a high innovative target (benchmark).

### Coffee break

#### Episode of Benchmarking

Fuji Xerox has won the Deming Prize (1980) through finding out the top in the world to utilize them to the management. The technique was utilized by American Xerox in their work improvement movement and named it as "Benchmarking" and "Benchmarking" gathered wide attention by they awarding of Malcolm Baldridge Award in 1989.

Selection of best practice is the key point of benchmarking. For example, American Xerox has learned from L.L. Beans Ltd. that is famous for the outdoor equipment for the best practice in storage work, and British Royal Mail (England Postal Service) benchmarked Yamato Transport Co., Ltd.

On the other hand, Southwest Airline (SWA) has benchmarked the fueling and maintenance processes of cock pit crew of car racing. SWA was a small local airline at their start, and against the average flight time of about one hour, fueling and maintenance was taking 45 min. When they investigated the fueling and maintenance time of other airline, it was found the average was about 50 min and was not helpful. Then they benchmarked the pit crew of Indie 500 mile racing where the fueling and maintenance time affects the results. As results, they have shortened the fueling and maintenance time to 15 min and they succeeded to enhance the operation rate of the aircrafts.

# Tools Effective for "Clarification of Attack Points and Setting Targets"

Clarifying the work processes that is the source of the strength of other companies/ other departments, by comparison with the work processes of own company/own department, examine what can be learned from there and link them to improvement and innovation.

When doing it, it is not necessary to limit the object of the benchmark to the other companies in the same industry.

## (2) Processes for Conducting "Benchmarking"

**Step 1. Assess the benchmark items**

Assess what is the issues of the own work place or circles.

**Step 2. Decide on the counterpart of benchmarking**

Among the leading company, work, workplace, decide the counterpart to benchmark.

**Step 3. Collect information**

Combining the techniques according to the investigation purpose, collect information. In the benchmarking, it is said that the investigating the best practice and to summarize the best practice is rather important than drawing out the target quantitatively in evaluation indexes.

**Step 4. Grasp the current status of the capability difference**

Carefully investigate the current situation of own workplace/ circle and the practices of objective of benchmarking.

**Step 5. Estimate the future capability level**

In addition to the current practice, it is necessary to know how the capability will change in the future.

**Step 6. Disseminate the findings**

Findings mean the best practice (excellent example) found by investigating the counterpart where information should be collected.

Explain them based on definite real data that will prove the correctness the findings to anyone to understand.

### Step 7. Set the target

Set the innovation target of the work.

### Step 8. Establish the action plan

Establish the action plan to implement the basic policy made based on the findings.

### Step 9. Implement the action plan

Introduce the best practice actually, and measure and evaluate the progresses periodically.

### Step 10. Re-benchmarking

Because the practice in the world is always changing, any plan should have some appropriate end point and findings themselves should be updated. For that purpose, re-benchmarking should be prepared.

Even in QC Circle activities, this thinking can be applied and there is a possibility of getting big results.

## (3) Case example of "Benchmarking"

Fig. 3.3 is a case example of benchmarking other circles to generate high quality improvement suggestions. Take the point that the sure comparison analysis was conducted.

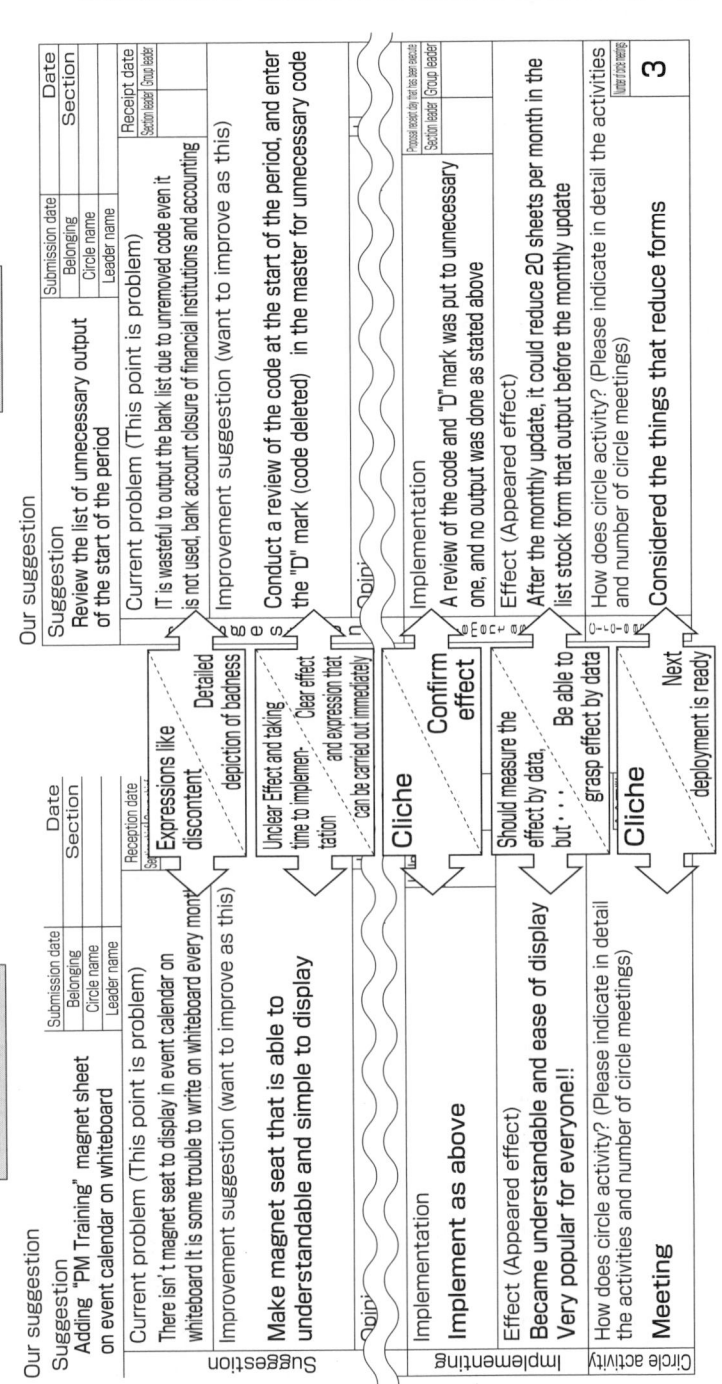

Tools Effective for "Clarification of Attack Points and Setting Targets"

| Ohizamoto circle | | Other circle | |
|---|---|---|---|

**Our suggestion**

| | | | | | | | |
|---|---|---|---|---|---|---|---|
| | Submission date | | Date | | Submission date | | Date |
| | Belonging | | Section | | Belonging | | Section |
| | Circle name | | | | Circle name | | |
| | Leader name | | | | Leader name | | |

Suggestion: Adding "PM Training" magnet sheet on event calendar on whiteboard

Suggestion: Review the list of unnecessary output of the start of the period

| Suggestion | | Reception date | | | | Receipt date |
|---|---|---|---|---|---|---|

Current problem (This point is problem): There isn't magnet seat to display in event calendar on whiteboard.It is some trouble to write on whiteboard every month

Current problem (This point is problem): IT is wasteful to output the bank list due to unremoved code even it is not used, bank account closure of financial institutions and accounting

→ Expressions like discontent / Detailed depiction of badness

Improvement suggestion (want to improve as this)

Improvement suggestion (want to improve as this)

Make magnet seat that is able to understandable and simple to display

Conduct a review of the code at the start of the period, and enter the "D" mark (code deleted) in the master for unnecessary code

→ Unclear Effect and taking time to implementation / Clear effect and expression that can be carried out immediately

**Implementation**

Implement as above

→ Cliche / Confirm effect

A review of the code and "D" mark was put to unnecessary one, and no output was done as stated above

Effect (Appeared effect): Became understandable and ease of display Very popular for everyone!!

→ Should measure the effect by data, but … / Be able to grasp effect by data

Effect (Appeared effect): After the monthly update, it could reduce 20 sheets per month in the list stock form that output before the monthly update

How does circle activity? (Please indicate in detail the activities and number of circle meetings)

→ Cliche / Next deployment is ready

How does circle activity? (Please indicate in detail the activities and number of circle meetings)

Meeting

Considered the things that reduce forms

| | | Proposal support line that has been executed | |
|---|---|---|---|
| | | Section leader | Group leader |
| Number of circle meetings | | | |
| 3 | | | |

Fig.3.3 Example of "Benchmarking"

(Source: Nagano Electronics Industrial Co., Ltd. "Ohizamoto (Home turf) Circle". QC Circle Magazine, May 2007, Case Example 3, JUSE.)

# Tool 3-4

# Questionnaire Survey

## (1) What is "Questionnaire Survey"?

When grasping the raw voice and desire level of the target peoples, "Questionnaire Survey" is effective. And it can be used for grasping current level.

"Questionnaire Survey" is a technique to grasp the recognition and desires of the customers, following processes, and people concerned quantitatively. Although it is effective to grasp the needs like desired items, it is necessary to examine the choice of the target persons, setting the questions, etc. deeply.

## (2) Procedures for conducting "Questionnaire Survey"

### Step 1. Decision on the survey theme

Clarify the purpose of the questionnaire survey and decide the survey theme.

### Step 2. Selection of the target people

Select the persons to ask for the cooperation to the survey.

### Step 3. Preliminary survey

Conduct a preliminary survey with cooperation of familiar persons.

### Step 4. Decision of the schedule

Decide overall schedule.

### Step 5. Examination of questionnaire items

Examine the questionnaire items based on the results of the preliminary survey.

### Step 6. Examination of answer items and methods

Examine the answer items and methods for questionnaire items.

### Step 7. Examination of analysis method

Examine the analysis methods of the survey results before doing the survey.

Tools Effective for "Clarification of Attack Points and Setting Targets"

### Step 8. Conducting Questionnaire Survey

Conduct the questionnaire survey to the selected persons.

### Step 9. Collection/ Counting/ Analysis of the survey results

Collect the results of the questionnaire survey and count/analyze.

### Step 10. Use them for the original purpose

Use them for the purpose of the questionnaire survey.

## (3) Case Example of Utilizing "Questionnaire Survey"

Fig. 3.4 is a case example where a circle, that belong to a company that has a system to present "cake coupon" on employee's birthday, conducted a "questionnaire survey" and summarized the opinions using "Affinity Diagram" for enhancement of satisfaction of use. Like this case example, "Affinity Diagram" is effective to summarize the opinions in free answer form.

---

**ONE POINT**

◆Quality of results in "questionnaire survey" depends on the question contents. When preparing questions, it is a good methodology to examine what kind of question contents should be given utilizing "affinity diagram". Also, it is necessary to examine beforehand the analysis method after the questionnaire collection.

Here, "SD techniques" is explained as the survey analysis method. "SD technique (Semantic Differential method)" is a technique to analyze characteristics (impression/ image) comprehensively, and it is a technique that uses object terms that reflect the characteristics, quantify and evaluate with 5 to 9 levels. Points are to make the levels of answer to odd number and to set the center to zero (Refer to Fig.3.5)
A case example of utilizing "SD technique" to enhance the customer satisfaction at a nuclear power plant tour is shown on Fig.3.6.

## Chapter 3

**Questionnaire about cake ticket**

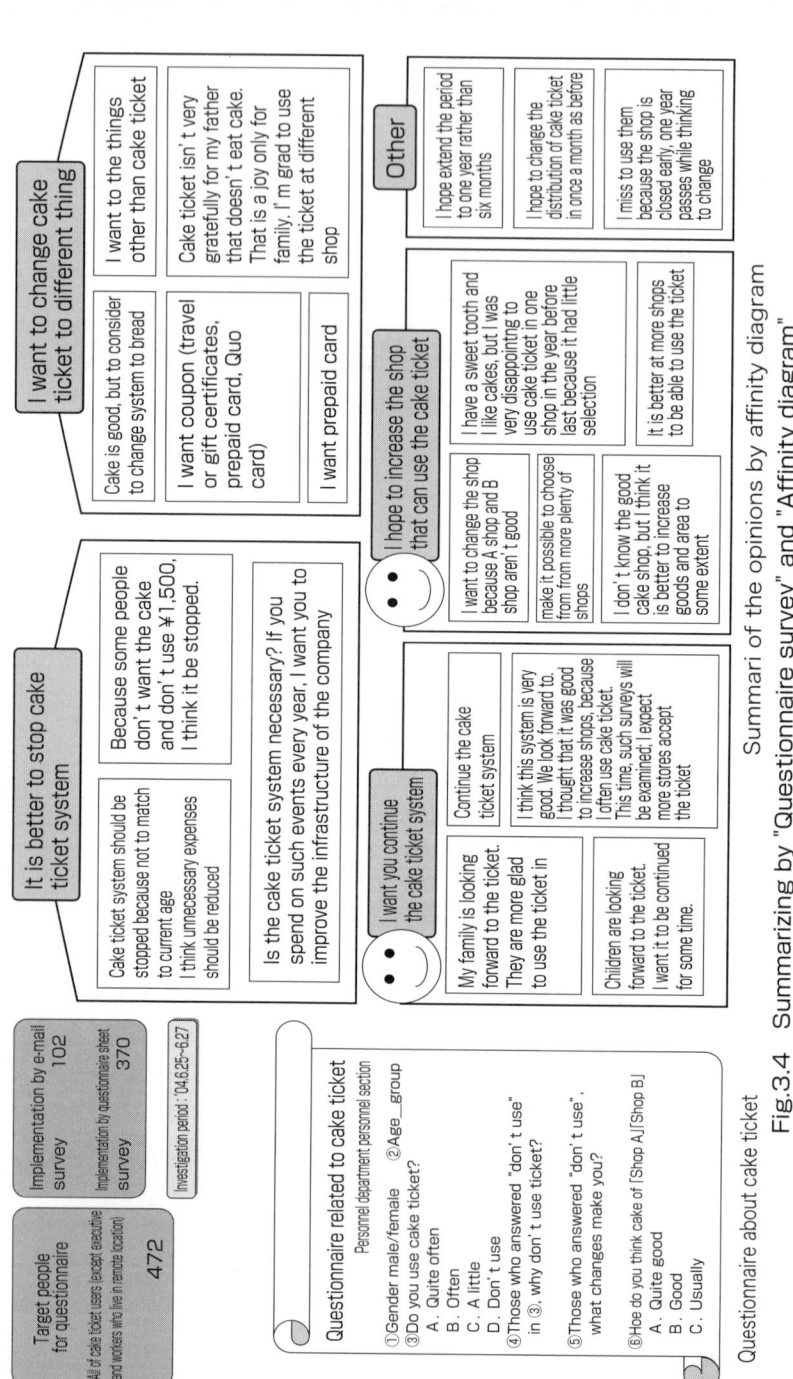

| Target people for questionnaire | Implementation by e-mail survey | 102 |
|---|---|---|
| All of cake ticket users (except executive and workers who live in remote location) | Implementation by questionnaire sheet survey | 370 |
| 472 | Investigation period : '04.6.25~6.27 | |

**Questionnaire related to cake ticket**
Personnel department personnel section

①Gender male/female  ②Age＿group
③Do you use cake ticket?
　A．Quite often
　B．Often
　C．A little
　D．Don't use
④Those who answered "don't use" in ③, why don't use ticket?
⑤Those who answered "don't use", what changes make you?
⑥How do you think cake of [Shop A]/[Shop B]
　A．Quite good
　B．Good
　C．Usually

### It is better to stop cake ticket system

- Cake ticket system should be stopped because not to match to current age
- I think unnecessary expenses should be reduced
- Because some people don't want the cake and don't use ¥1,500.
- I think it be stopped.
- Is the cake ticket system necessary? If you spend on such events every year, I want you to improve the infrastructure of the company

### I want to change cake ticket to different thing

- I want to the things other than cake ticket
- Cake ticket isn't very gratefully for my father that doesn't eat cake. That is a joy only for family. I'm grad to use the ticket at different shop
- Cake is good, but to consider to change system to bread
- I want coupon (travel or gift certificates, prepaid card, Quo card)
- I want prepaid card

### Other

- I hope extend the period to one year rather than six months
- I hope to change the distribution of cake ticket in once a month as before
- I miss to use them because the shop is closed early, one year passes while thinking to change

### I want you continue the cake ticket system ☺

- My family is looking forward to the ticket. They are more glad to use the ticket in
- Continue the cake ticket system
- I think this system is very good. We look forward to. I thought that it was good to increase shops, because I often use cake ticket.
- Children are looking forward to the ticket. I want it to be continued for some time.
- This time, such surveys will be examined; I expect more stores accept the ticket

### I hope to increase the shop that can use the cake ticket ☺

- I want to change the shop because A shop and B shop aren't good
- make it possible to choose from from more plenty of shops
- I don't know the good cake shop, but I think it is better to increase goods and area to some extent
- I have a sweet tooth and I like cakes, but I was very disappointing to use cake ticket in one shop in the year before last because it had little selection
- It is better at more shops to be able to use the ticket

Fig.3.4　Summarizing by "Questionnaire survey" and "Affinity diagram"
Summari of the opinions by affinity diagram

(Source : Takano Co. Ltd., "Hitohito (man-man) Circle", QC Circle Magazine, March 2006, Case Example 3, JUSE.)

# Tools Effective for "Clarification of Attack Points and Setting Targets"

### Questionnaire after attending training

Please put ○ mark to appropriate number in the following four topics.

1. Did you understand the contents?

+2   +1   0   -1   -2

I understood very much      I couldn't understand at all

Reason (What is the reason······item)
((Why······Teaching style, Textbook, Environment, etc.)

2. How was the contents of textbook?

+2   +1   0   -1   -2

Very easy to understand      Very difficult to understand

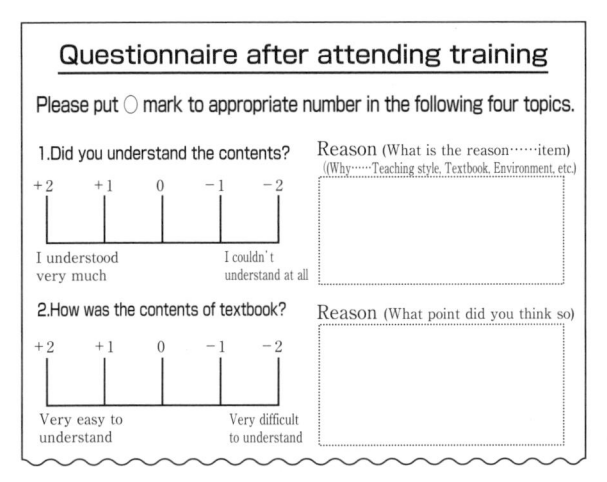

Reason (What point did you think so)

Fig.3.5  Example of SD(Semantic Differential) scale by questionnaire
(Source: "Rensai: Ikita Data no Torikata, Tsukaikata (Series: How to Take and Use Lively Data)", QC Circle Magazine, June, 2000, JUSE.)

Period: Apr.2000~Jan.2001  N=485

| Evaluation from customer | Very good | Good | Neither | Bad | Very bad |
|---|---|---|---|---|---|
| Number of people | 125 | 167 | 148 | 28 | 17 |
| Evaluation score | +2pt. | +1pt. | Opt. | -1pt. | -2pt. |
| Relationship for SD score | The positive effect 60.2% | | No effect 30.5% | Negative effect 9.3% | |

SD scale by customer questionnaire: 0.73

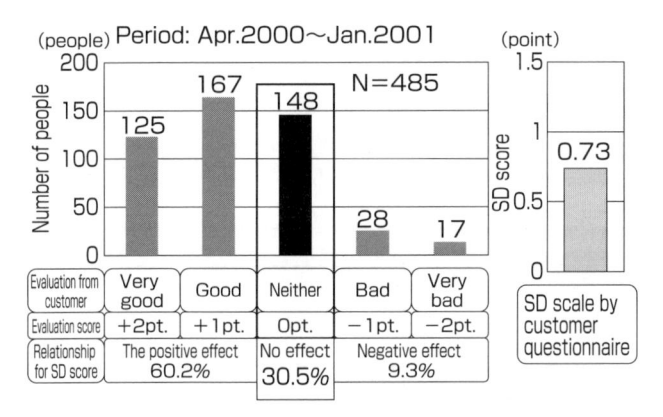

Fig.3.6  Questionnaire analysis by SD scale
(Source: Kansai Electric Power Co. Ltd., "Challenge Up Circle", QC Circle Magazine, Feb., 2003, Case Example 1, JUSE.)

# Chapter 3

## Coffee Break

### Separating is to understand.

It is explained in Tool 3-1 that "stratification" means focusing on the features of the data and to divide them into some groups that have some common points and trend.

We are using the term "wakaru（わかる：to understand)" in daily life. In fact, the etymology of this term is "wakatsu（わかつ：to separate)" and "wakatsu（わかつ：to separate)"="wakerukoto（わけること： to distinguish) is said to be connected to "wakaru（わかる：to understand). actually, " wakerukoto（わけること：distinguishing)" leads to "wakarukoto（わかること：understanding)", isn't it? Surely, we are doing seiri (sorting) and understanding by separating. This is the meaning of "understanding".

By the way, when we convert "wakaru（わかる)" into Chinese character, we get "解る (decipher)", "判る (discriminate)", and "分かる (understand)". How could we have a good command of them? I am consciously using "わかる" in hirakana without applying Chinese character forcibly. When I want to use Chinese character by all means, please refer to the following table.

I was once told to describe "わかったこと：what was understood" nearby when I utilized technique and made a chart and tables. At that time also, it was not in Chinese character, but "わかったこと" in hiragana.

| Chinese character | Meaning | Examples |
|---|---|---|
| Tokar (decipher) | Grasping<br>Academic "wakaru" of knowledge, theory, and reason etc. | English is understood<br>The meaning is understood<br>The answer is understood |
| Know (discriminate) | Prove<br>To determine<br>Seen by comparing the difference to distinguish | The differenceis is understood<br>Good and evil is understood |
| Understand | Share<br>Used in a general sense all "knowing" | |

Tools Effective for "Clarification of Attack Points and Setting Targets"

## Tool 3-5
# QC 7 Tools and New QC 7 Tools

### (1) What are "QC 7 Tools" "New QC 7 Tools"

When the "desired level" was grasped, then it is time to grasp the "current level" that corresponds to the "desired level". To grasp the current level, "QC Seven Tools" are useful. To investigate the current level is the same with the grasping status quo in problem solving type, it is important to conduct it well using the tools like QC Seven Tools (noted as Q7 hereafter) and New QC Seven Tools (noted as N7 hereafter).

Summary of Q7 and N7 is shown in Fig. 3.7 and Fig. 3.8.

### (2) Introduction of how to use them with a case example

Here, the procedure from the current level investigation that leads to the "Attack Points Selection Sheet" is explained using a concrete case example. (Source: Partly extracted from the presentation material of Powerful/Adventure Circle of Nissan Motor Co., Ltd. at the 5090th QC Circle National Convention held by the QC Circle Headquarter).

The case example used for the explanation is the one in which they tackled "Lead time reduction of piping assembly of cylinder head mold", and aimed at the large reduction of imposition time (5 days to 2 days) of the plumbing for cooling laid pipes in casting molds (Refer to Fig. 3.9).

This piping for water cooling is equipped to the upper and lower molds as cooling equipment. The cooling equipment is complicatedly penetrated as in the Fig.3.9, and as the structure is composed of piping and fittings, etc. , and it will cool the high temperature of aluminum by draining water into the pluming in the backside of the mold. The purpose of this equipment is the reduction of the cycle time and quality improvement of casting.

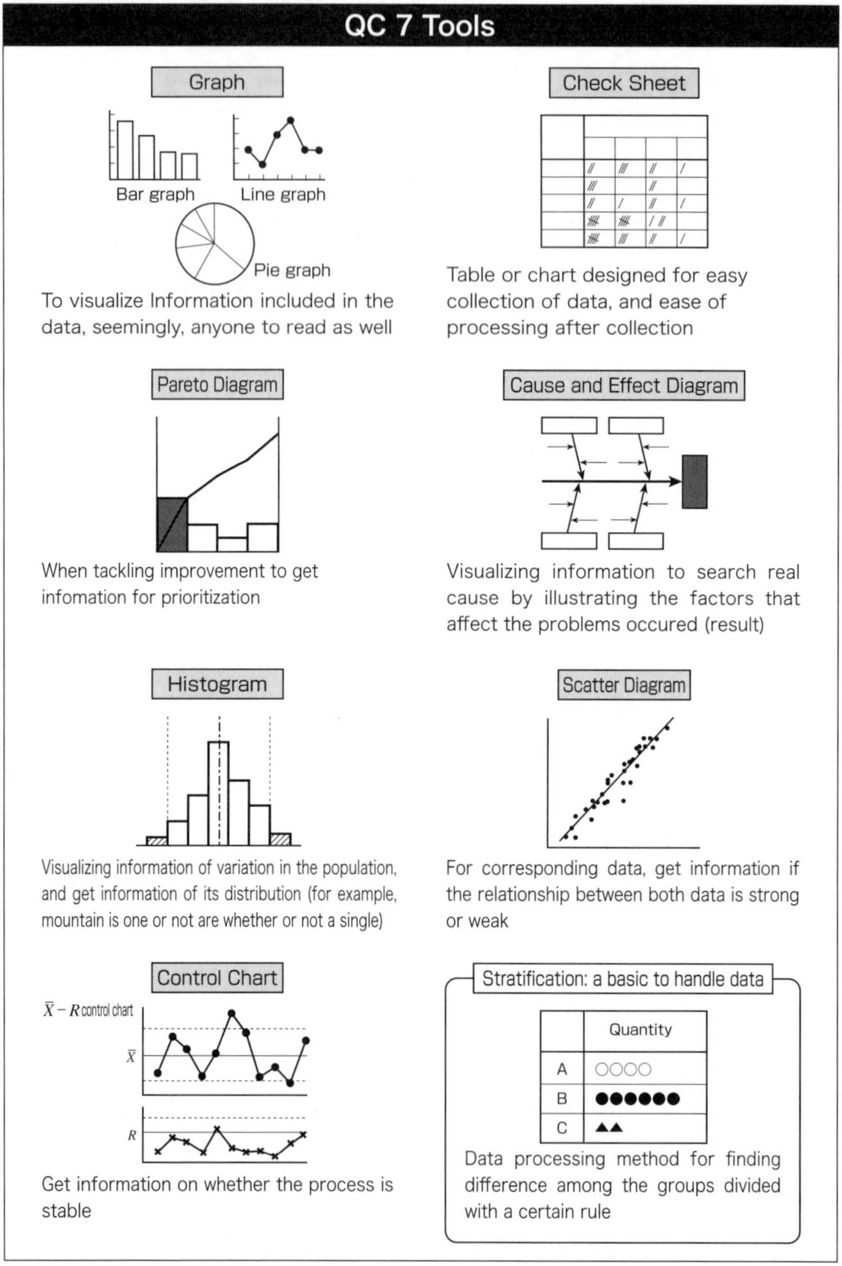

# Chapter 3

## QC 7 Tools

### Graph
Bar graph, Line graph, Pie graph
To visualize Information included in the data, seemingly, anyone to read as well

### Check Sheet
Table or chart designed for easy collection of data, and ease of processing after collection

### Pareto Diagram
When tackling improvement to get infomation for prioritization

### Cause and Effect Diagram
Visualizing information to search real cause by illustrating the factors that affect the problems occured (result)

### Histogram
Visualizing information of variation in the population, and get information of its distribution (for example, mountain is one or not are whether or not a single)

### Scatter Diagram
For corresponding data, get information if the relationship between both data is strong or weak

### Control Chart
$\bar{X} - R$ control chart
Get information on whether the process is stable

### Stratification: a basic to handle data

|   | Quantity |
|---|---|
| A | ○○○○ |
| B | ●●●●●● |
| C | ▲▲ |

Data processing method for finding difference among the groups divided with a certain rule

Fig.3.7 QC 7 Tools

(Source : Yamada, Yoshiaki, author and editor QC syuho no kihon to katsuyo, JUSE Press, Ltd. 2010)

# Tools Effective for "Clarification of Attack Points and Setting Targets"

## New QC 7 Tools

### Affinity Diagram

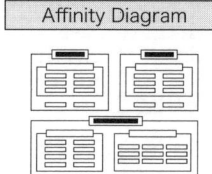

For uncertain situation to clarify the whereabout of problems grouping according to mutual affinity grasping them by language data like facts, opinions ideas.

### Relation Diagram

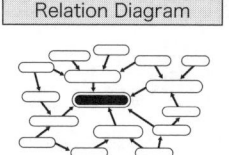

If problems are intertwined with various issues and causes complexly, to capture the causes and important phenomenon, and to find the clues by linking the causation and relationship with arrows

### Tree Diagram

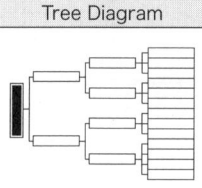

To deploy measures systematically(in a chain of targets and measures) to reach to a target purpose(goal), and to pursue the optimum means or methods to attain the purpose

### Matrix Diagram

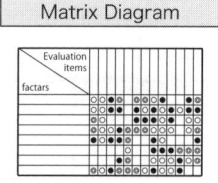

To grasp the ideas for problem solving by arranging the elements in a pair in to rows and colamns of the focused events and like cause and effect, target and measures to show the degree. relationships.

### PDPC Method

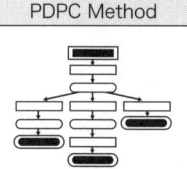

Abbreviation for Process Decision Program Chart. to decide the process to a desirable results avoiding expected risks of the implementation plan to achieve a target.

### Arrow Diagram Method

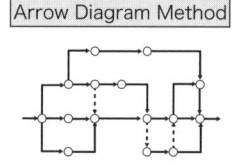

When forwarding a work, to clarify the segments of the jobs needed, to establish an optimum schedule and to control the progress efficiency.

### Matrix Data Analysis

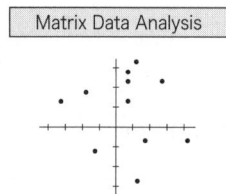

Only to technique that handle numerical data among the new QC Seven tool. Also known as prlnciple componet analysis. The relationship among the elements in a matrix are quantified, arrange them by computation to get good outlook.

### Language data and New QC 7 Tools

The data, not only numerical data, but verbal data "language" is also available. they are grasped utilizing New QC 7 Tools and used for problem solving like the QC 7 Tools.

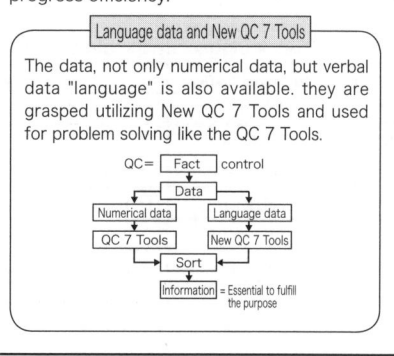

QC = Fact control
Data
Numerical data | Language data
QC 7 Tools | New QC 7 Tools
Sort
Information = Essential to fulfill the purpose

Fig.3.8 New QC 7 Tools

(Source : yamada, yoshiaki, author and editor QC syuho no kihon to katsuyo, JUSE Press, Ltd. 2010)

# Chapter 3

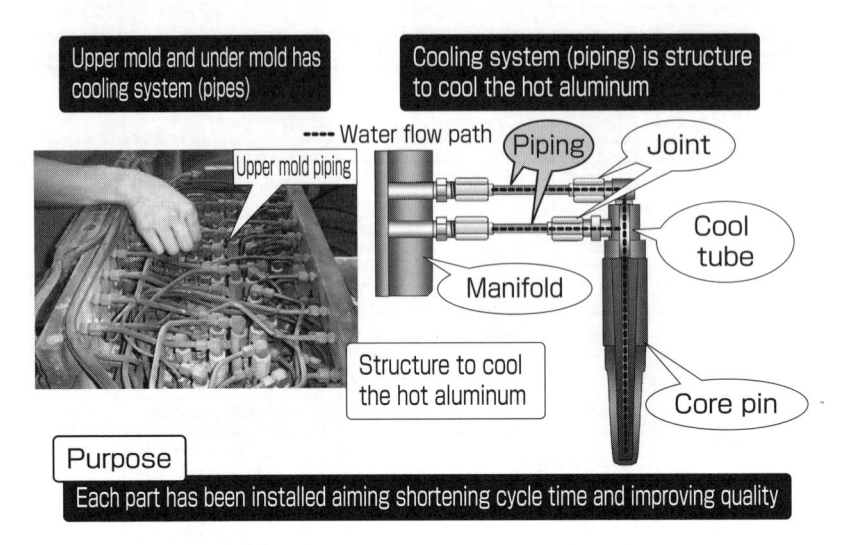

[Figure: Casting mold of water cooling pipes with labels: "Upper mold and under mold has cooling system (pipes)", "Cooling system (piping) is structure to cool the hot aluminum", "Water flow path", "Upper mold piping", "Piping", "Joint", "Cool tube", "Manifold", "Structure to cool the hot aluminum", "Core pin", "Purpose: Each part has been installed aiming shortening cycle time and improving quality"]

Fig.3.9 Casting mold of water cooling pipes

(Source: Nissan Motor Co. Ltd., "Powerful/ Adventure Circle" Presentation Materials, at the 5090th QC Circle Convention held by the QC Circle Headquarter.)

### Step 1. Decide investigation items

Decide investigation items utilizing 4M that is often used to ferret out factors in Cause and Effect Diagram. In the case example, Persons (Man), Materials/ parts (Material), Tools (Machine), methodology (Method) are used to decide the concrete investigation items together. Next, after clarifying who is to investigate by when using matrix diagram and each took responsibility and investigated them.

| Classifying | Investigation items | Role | When |
| --- | --- | --- | --- |
| Characteristic | Assembly time | Kikuchi | 9/10 |
| Man | Assembly man-hour | Kikuchi | 9/10 |
| Material | Amount of pipe | Nishihara | 9/15 |
| Material | Storage situation of piping | Nishihara | 9/15 |
| Method | The way of CAD assembly | Shibatani | 9/12 |
| Method | The way of assembly | Shibatani | 9/12 |
| Machine | CAD | Sasaki | 9/20 |
| Machine | Pipe bending machine | Sasaki | 9/20 |

### Step 2. Summarize the investigation results

The results of investigation should be summarized in a way easy to under-

Tools Effective for "Clarification of Attack Points and Setting Targets"

stand using table and list or Q7, N7. In this case example, only the investigation results on the 3 items that had gaps (man: assembly man hours, materials: number of plumbing, method: assembly method) are shown below.

### Step 3. Confirm the theme characteristics

It is important to properly "visualize" the overall theme characteristics that are to be tackled. In this case example, current level (5 days) and desired level (2 days) is compared concerning the lead time reduction of plumbing assembly.

When the current level (actual) and desired level was compared, it will become 60% reduction and we can see how challenging target it is. It can be said to be a theme to breakthrough using Task Achieving Type QC Story.

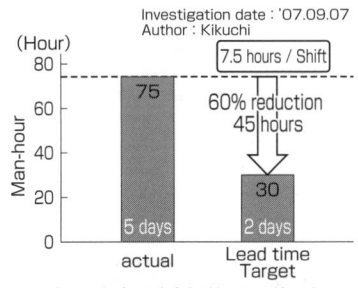

Fig.3.10 Confirmation of theme characteristics

### Step 4. Investigation on man (assembly man hours)

First, they investigated on man. Investigate if there is variation in assemble man hours depending on individuals. This time, group units (A-D groups) were investigated rather than individuals. The investigation results are shown on Fig. 3.11.

Each groups man-hours were summarized on a "bar graph". With this, one can see the variation of the man-hours of each group at a glance. The fastest group is 69 hours, and the slowest group is 80 hours and the gap was 11 hours.

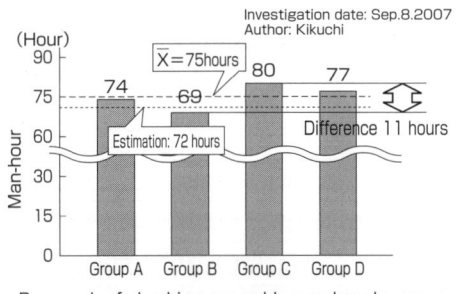

Fig.3.11 Investigation of plumbing assembly man-hour

## Step 5. Investigation on the materials (number of plumbing)

Next is the material (number of plumbing). They investigated where and how many plumbing were used. The results are shown on Fig.3.12. It proved that 266 of them were used in total. Here, it is not investigated, but to investigate by stratification on the plumbing materials or length will also become the grasping of status.

| Pattern | Pert of cooling | Number of Plumbing |
|---|---|---|
| Under mold | Chamber | 19 |
| | Core pin | ... |
| | Other | ... |
| Upper mold | Injection | ... |
| | Bulb lifter | ... |
| | Head bolt | ... |
| | Other | ... |
| Total number of necessary plumbing | | 266 |

Plumbing is being used for an average 266 in a mold set

Fig.3.12 Investigation of Number of plumbing

## Step 6. Investigation on method (assembly methodology)

Next is the method. Because the theme is the reduction of lead time of plumbing assembly, method is the plumbing methodology itself. Investigation was made, dividing them into processes, on the time spent on each process. The result is Fig.3.13. It was understood that the big part is "plumbing detach" "position confirmation" "assembly" and the order of assembly is not set, and that there is variation among the workers because it was left to the workers.

1. Checking the location of the plumbing is assembled in the drawing
2. Taking out the plumbing from the box
}  Detaching the plumbing 4 hours

3. Confirmation of plumbing direction
4. Confirmation of position
}  Confirmation of position 19 hours

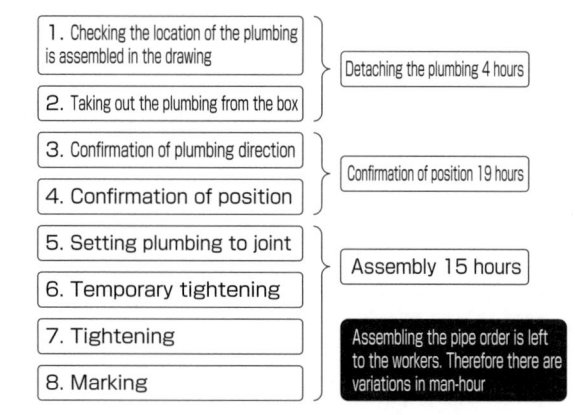

5. Setting plumbing to joint
6. Temporary tightening
7. Tightening
8. Marking
}  Assembly 15 hours

Assembling the pipe order is left to the workers. Therefore there are variations in man-hour

Fig.3.13 Investigation of assembly man-hour

Furthermore, actually, there was the matual interference among the plumbings during assembly and "re-assembly" was made every time it happens (Refer to Fig. 3.14).

# Tools Effective for "Clarification of Attack Points and Setting Targets"

As a result, it was "plumbing detach": 4 hours, "position confirmation": 19 hours, "assembly": 15 hours and "assembly rectification": 28 hours.

Above results is summarized in "Pareto Diagram" on the left of Fig. 3.15. From this Pareto diagram, reassembly and position confirmation occupies 62.6% of the total assembly man hours. Thinking that if these were improved, the target of 45 hours reduction can be achieved, attack points are marked using "ECRS Principle", one of the approaches of work improvement.

The assembly operation is actually needed work and value adding (primary) work. In contrast to this, reassembly is so to speak rework, and non value adding wasteful work. If it is a wasteful work, then it is important to seek to remove (Eliminate). Also, the position confirmation is an accompanied work to the primary work, assembly operation that has added value. However, think whether you cannot make it more simple (Simplify), or whether you

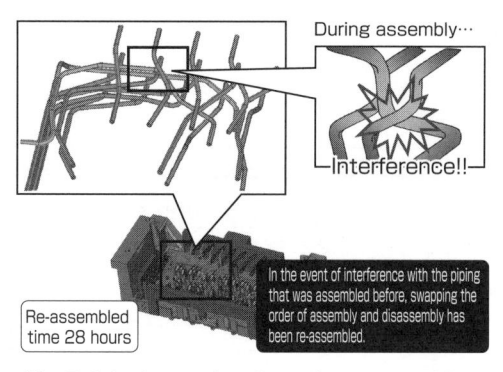

Fig.3.14  Investigation of re-assembing

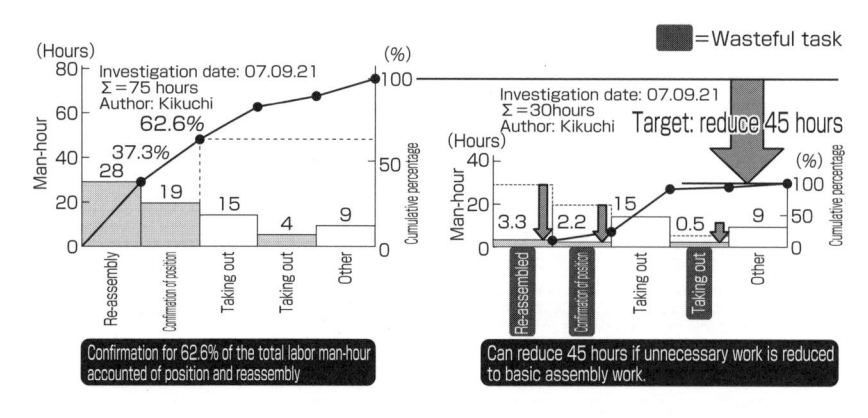

Fig.3.15  Summary of investigation into assembly man-hour

## Chapter 3

can assemble without(Eliminate) position confirmation. This is called ECRS principle.

> \* Principle of ECRS
> · <u>E</u>liminate   : Stop the worthless work
> · <u>C</u>ombine    : Consider to do it simultaneously
> · <u>R</u>earrange  : Change sequence
> · <u>S</u>implify   : Consider simplifying

In this case example, graph and Pareto diagram among QC Seven Tools are used many times. When graphs and Pareto diagrams were prepared, one can grasp the size and the differences in quantity or the time progresses, one can understand the current situation well, i.e. one can grasp the current status well. You will also get the shape of current situation if you draw graphs from various viewpoints. Only by using graphs that you have been familiar from elementary school age, information is organized like this case example, therefore you are recommended to use Q7, especially graph and Pareto diagram to investigate current levels.

Tools Effective for "Clarification of Attack Points and Setting Targets"

## Tool 3-6

# Attack Points Selection Sheet

### (1) What is "Attack Points Selection Sheet"?

To devise attack points, the "Attack Points Selection Sheet" like Fig. 3.16 is effective. This sheet is for organizing a series of procedures from evaluation of the desired/ current levels and the direction of measures (candidates of attack points) to resolve the gap using several items, through to narrowing down them effectively/ efficiently.

| Theme characteristic | Desired level | Current level | Achieve level |
|---|---|---|---|
| | | | |

| Investigation item | Desired level | Current level | Gap | Attack point (candidate) | Evaluation item | | | Adoption or rejection |
|---|---|---|---|---|---|---|---|---|
| | | | | | Capability of gap elimination | Degree of customer's desire | Total evaluation | |
| | | | | | | | | |
| | | | | | | | | |
| | | | | | | | | |

Fig.3.16 "Attack Points Selection Sheet"

### (2) Procedures for making "Attack Points Selection Sheet"

**Step 1. Decide the theme characteristics**

Clarify the characteristics of overall theme and grasp the desired (required) level, current level and the achievement level that is linked to target setting.

In the case example of the "Plumbing Assembly Time Reduction" that was introduced in Tool 3-5, it will becomes like below.

"Theme characteristics": Plumbing Assembly Man hours

"Desired Level": 30 hours

79

"Current Level": 75 hours

"Achievement level": 30 hours (The gap is 75 hours − 30 hours = 45 hours)

## Step 2. Decide investigation items

The investigation items are to grasp the elements that construct the theme by stratification. Pick up the elements that seem to influence the theme characteristics (characteristics that you want to improve), and decide the investigation items evaluating the degree of influence of each item.

In this case example, investigation items has been decided during investigation of current levels, those items are put into the investigation item column.

## Step 3. Decide the desired (required) level

To achieve the desired level of the theme characteristics, show the desired (required) level of each investigation item with numerical value with reasons, like work place required value or benchmarked level depending on each of investigation items. At that time, it is important to clarify the functions, performance and level, etc.

In this case example, drawing the "desired shape" of each investigation item, and the "desired shape" is made directly as the desired (required) level of each investigation item.

## Step 4. Grasping current levels

Grasp the current level in contrast to the desired level. However, there is a case where current level is not grasped such as new works.

In this case example, grasping the current status is done using Q7 taking data for each of the investigation item.

## Step 5. Ferreting out the gaps

Compare the desired (required) level and current level, the difference is the gap.

In this case example, for example, in case of the "Detaching out man hour", because the desired (required) level is "0.5 hours" and the current level is "4 hours", the gap will become "3.5 hours (4 − 0.5)" (Refer to Fig. 3.15). When the level was expressed by language data, it is difficult to generate the gap simply, and such cases are explained in the points for making in the following pages.

### Step 6. Decide candidate of attack points

From the gap, decide the candidates of attack points that show where to focus to think of the measures. The attack points is not the measures themselves, but is the one that indicates the scope or the area to plan the measures for the task achieving.

If the attack points are set small, it become difficult to think of many measures in the following steps, it is recommended to think from broader points of view. Taking the tree diagram as an example, it is an image to express the attack points not with the deployed expression of the detailed level of 2nd and 3rd, but with the first level expressions that include them. In other word, do not take it narrow and small but think the purpose from one step higher view point.

The cases are often seen where the reverse expression of gaps are made as the attack points, but that will limit the band of idea generation, it is important to think the expression carefully.

### Step 7. Evaluate the attack points candidates

To narrow down the attack points candidates, decide to adopt attack points evaluating the possibility of eliminating the gap (expected effects) and degree of desire of the customers.

Above is the explanation as procedures, but when it comes to actually making the "Attack Points Selection Sheet" and to decide the attack points candidates, measures line up or the richness of idea generation was narrowed from outset with the narrow scope.

This decision on the attack points is the most difficult and we will explain the points next.

## (3) Points of Making "Attack Points Selection Sheet"

The case examples that utilized "Attack Points Selection Sheet" are introduced in various books, but it is really difficult when it is actually made.

Especially, in case the gap can be expressed with quantitative values, the gap (difference) can be grasped immediately, but in case of language data, it is necessary to make it precise when grasping the gaps and expressing the attacking points candidates.

In the explanation of step 6, it was written that, "taking tree diagram, it is an image to express the attacking points with the first level expressions that include them", but when it comes to actually doing it, it is actually very difficult because expression becomes that of concrete measures.

In addition, when the desired (required) level and current level cannot express but only by language data, one will be at a loss to express the gap (difference). Taking much attention to these points, practical points of making the "Attack Points Selection Sheet" will be explained continuing the case example of "plumbing assembly time reduction".

## 1) On the Attack Points Candidates (when the level is numerical data)

First, clarify the theme characteristics. In the case example, the desired level is 30 hours against the current level of 75 hours and the gap becomes 45 hours and, the target achievement level becomes plumbing assembly man hours of 30 hours.

Next, grasp the investigated results based on the investigation items in terms of current levels against the desired levels, and the gaps. In the case example, current level of 11 hours of the maximum of the variation of assembly man hours among the groups was made to the desired level of 0 (none), and the gap becomes 11 hours. Likewise, in the similar way, current levels, desired levels and the gaps are summarized like the Fig. 3.17 "Attack Points Selection Sheet". If one could summarize the current levels, desired levels and the gaps on a "Attack Points Selection Sheet", next is to decide the candidates for the attack points. The point at that time is to make "the attack points candidates should be expressed in a way that may lead to the points of view

## Tools Effective for "Clarification of Attack Points and Setting Targets"

| Theme characteristic | Current level | Desired level | Targeted level |
|---|---|---|---|
| Plumbing assembly man-hour | 75hours | 30hours | 30hours |

| Classification | Investigation item | Current level | Desired level | Gap | Candidate of attack point |
|---|---|---|---|---|---|
| Man | Variation of assembly man-hour | 11 hour | 0 hour | 11 hour | Standardization |
| | Detaching man-hour | 4 hour | 0.5 hour | 3.5 hour | Review plumbing assembly method |
| Material | Number of pluming | 266 | 266 | None | — |
| Method | Confirmation of position | 19 hour | 2.2 hour | 16.8 hour | Confirmation of setting position |
| | Re-assembly | Occurring | Nothing | Occurring | Review plumbing assembly method |
| | Assembly procedure | Left to the workers | 1 pattern | Left to the workers | Standardization works |

Reduce 45 hours by reducing unnecessary work. ⇒ "Clarify procedure and methods"

Fig.3.17 Example of "Attack Point Selection Seet"

that is linked to the next step of "establishing measures".

Also, to make the generation of many ideas for measures candidates possible, the attack points candidates should be stated with the expression that widely covers the points of views without including concrete measures and means. Actually, the "expression that widely covers" is very difficult. In the case example, also, one can see the hardship they encountered in selection of attack points selection.

① **Case of investigation item "variation of assembly man hours"**

| Investigation item | Gap | Candidate of attack point |
|---|---|---|
| Variation of assembly man-hour | 11 hours | Standardization of works |

In the case example, because they simply thought standardization is necessary if it vary, the attack points became rather like measures. Here, among the variation of the assembly man hours, because B group was the most shortest, if the attacking point is expressed, for example, such as:,

Investigation of assembly method in B group ⇒ "Review assembly method" ⇒ Unify assembly method

Then, standardization will become one of the measures for unification and the band of measures in the next step would have been broadened.

② **Case of investigation item "method"**

| Investigation item | Gap | Candidate of attack point |
|---|---|---|
| Confirmation of position | 16.8 hours | Clarification of setting position |

In the case of position confirmation, the attack point candidate is set to "Clarification of setting position", the band of viewpoint is a little bit narrowed. In this case, how about if it is stated like as follows.

| Review of position confirmation method | ⇒ | Make the positional confirmation work to zero as much as possible |
|---|---|---|

When the attack point candidate is made to "Make the position confirmation work to zero limitlessly", then in the next step of "Establishing Measures", not only standardization but also many concrete measures ideas will be generated by the members of the circle based on "ECRS principle".

## 2) Case of Attack Points Candidate (in the case of the level is a language data)

How to express the gap when the desired level and current level are in language data, let's think taking the same case example again.

① **Case of investigation item "Sequence of assembly"**

| Investigation item | Current level | Desired level | Gap | Candidate of attack point |
|---|---|---|---|---|
| Assemble procedure | Left to the workers | 1 pattern | Left to the workers | Standardization of works |

In the case the level is in language data, what is not achieved or the current level is itself can be said to be the gap, and in this case example also expressed the current level as the gap. However, it would be better to devise the expression to lead to attack point candidates. In this example, how about thinking like below?

| Left to the workers ⇒ There is difference in work process by workers ⇒ Work process is not unified among workers |
|---|

## Tools Effective for "Clarification of Attack Points and Setting Targets"

Then the attack points can be thought like below.

| Gap | Candidate of attack point |
|---|---|
| Work process is not unified among workers | Unify the assembly method |

And the scope of investigation of measures will be broadened because improvement ideas of actual operation will be included as measures in addition to standardization.

Like this, if the level is in language data, the current level is apt to become the gap itself, but it is important to express from the view point of what is the fact concretely rather than writing them as the gaps.

② **In the case of investigation item "Reassembly"**

| Investigation item | Current level | Desired level | Gap | Candidate of attack point |
|---|---|---|---|---|
| Re-assembly | Occurring | None | Occurring | Review plumbing assembly method |

Here again the current level is made to the gap itself. If this fact is concretely expressed, the gap becomes "reassembly is conducted".

As to the attack points, it will become as below.

| Re-assembly ⇒ To make re-assembly to zero as possible ⇒ Assembly method |
|---|

And it becomes to possible to express the attack points well so that the plumbing method itself to become the point of view as the attack point. Then, just like the former case, isn't it possible to generate many ideas utilizing the "ECRS principles" and "5S", etc.? Also, by considering the plumbing method, not only the change of current plumbing method but also it become possible to generate novel ideas such that the cooling methodology itself to be changed to a different system. Task achieving type is not focused the possibility to realize, but the point is on generating many ideas to make breakthrough, and so it is important to make attack points that make it easy to generate many ideas.

# Chapter 3

## 3) Evaluation of Attack Points Candidates

After listing up the attack points candidates, next is the evaluation of the attack points to decide.

In this case example, listing up the attack points candidates, "Clarification of the sequence and methodology of assembly" as the attack points selected from all the candidates. As a usual method, as it has been explained in the step 7 of the procedures of making "Attack Points Selection Sheet", attack points (candidates) are narrowed down by evaluation of each item. In Fig. 3.18, for each attack points candidate, evaluation items (in this case, "expected effects" and "possibility of elimination") were decided, and the attacking points are narrowed down based on the results of evaluation.

| Characteristic · item | | Desired level | Current level | Gap | Candidate of attack point | Evaluation item | | Adoption or reduction |
|---|---|---|---|---|---|---|---|---|
| | | | | | | Expected effect | Possibility of elimination | |
| Characteristic | Total score of scored grade | Current situation, 20pt., up to 30pt. (50% up) | 20pt. | 10pt. | – | – | – | – |
| Item | (Man) Experience | Wealth of experience | Not much experience | Shape of experience | Gain experience | ○ | × | Rejection |
| | (Material) Manual | Practical manual are equipped | Only online manual | Manual is insufficient | Sufficient manual | ○ | ○ | Adoption |
| | (Machine) C A D | V2.1 | V2.0 | No big gap | – | – | – | – |
| | (Method) Learning | There is opportunity to learn | There isn't opportunity for learn | There is less opportunity for learn | Provide opportunities for learning | ◎ | ○ | Adoption |

Past learning method of three-dimensional scanning technology

- Experience in the introductory book → Learning is done during work, so progress and understanding differed.
- Gain experience on the job → Always do the only way that one knows. There are no time to examine or learn. Other persons are difficult to ask question because they look so busy
- Past learning session → Only some people participate, it is also fragmented content. Too diffcult to understand.

- Set chances of Learning
- Enhance Manuals

Decided as attack points

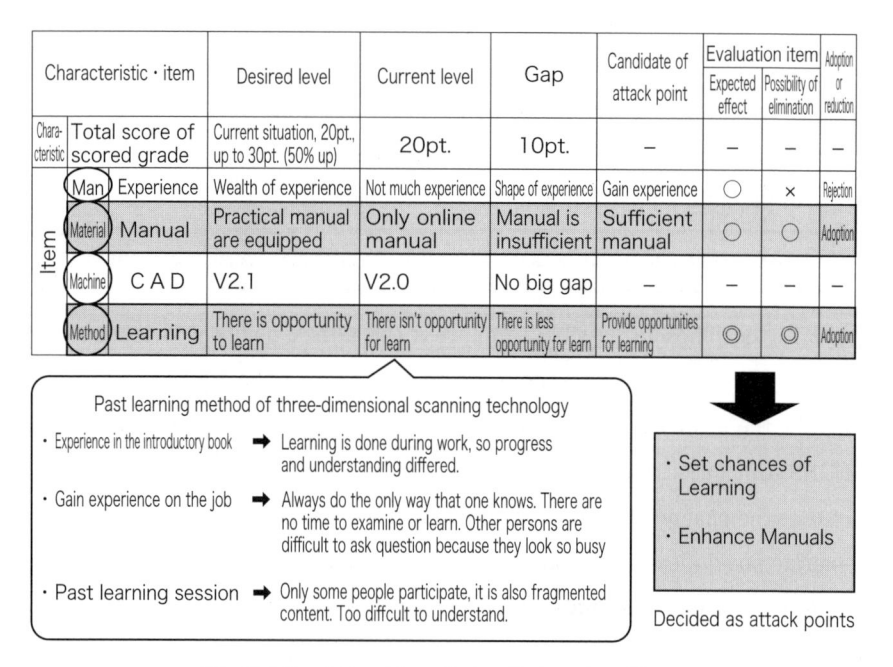

Fig.3.18 Attacking Point Selection Sheet

(Source：ONDA TECHNO Intl. Patent Attys., "3D Squadron CAD Ranger Circle", *QC Circle Magazine*, Dec. 2007, JUSE.)

Tools Effective for "Clarification of Attack Points and Setting Targets"

## Tool 3-7

# SWOT Analysis

In using the "Attack Points Selection Sheet", the "attack points" are decided, evaluating the attack point candidates and narrowing them down. Here, changing the viewpoint a little bit, a method is introduced. to derive attack points and to narrow them down using the "SWOT analysis".

## (1) What is "SWOT Analysis"?

The "SWOT analysis" is one of the tools and the name comes from the acronym taking following factors, and a tool to evaluate/ analyze dividing into these 4 items.

    [Internal factors]   S : Strengths     W : Weaknesses

    [External factors]  O : Opportunities  T : Threats

The "SWOT Analysis" was developed by Albert Humphrey of Stanford University in 1960's and it is a tool to conduct analysis of "own company" and "environment that surrounds the own company" and to use them for establishing management strategies.

It is a tool that can be used even by QC Circles, if "own company" is replaced with "own organization".

## (2) Procedures for Conducting "SWOT Analysis"

Concrete procedures for making it will be introduced taking activation of QC Circle activity.

**Step 1. List up the external factors, "Opportunities" and "Threats"**

As to the external environment where the QC Circle is positioned (for example, political/economical situations, performance of the company, existence of the rivals, etc.), arrange them dividing them if it is "an opportunity" or "a threat". For example, like the figure below,

# Chapter 3

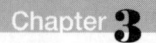

| We can't go to outside competition because of budget reduction due to performance downturn | ⇒ Threat |
|---|---|
| There is a chance to exchange with in house circles and the partner companies circles | ⇒ Opportunity |

Divide those external factors that you cannot control yourselves, like the changes in the external environment that surround QC Circles.

## Step 2. List up the "strengths"/"weaknesses" of own organization

List up the "Strengths"/"Weaknesses" of the QC Circles, referring to the "opportunities"/"threats", too. For example,

Strengths of the Circle
- Plural veterans who have rich experiences exist
- Have experience of winning silver award in company convention
- The number of suggestions is among the top class in the department.

Weaknesses of the Circle
- Member composition is divided to senior and young and the QC knowledge of young is poor
- There are those who dislike QC Circle activities
- Meeting participation rate is low due to shift work

List up internal factors that you can control dividing them into two like above.

## Step 3. Arrange them into a Matrix

Put in the items listed up by step 1 and 2 like Fig. 3.19 with external factors on the vertical axis and internal factors on the horizontal axis, and think about the strategies for each quadrant (intersection). For example, for the quadrant of "strengths" and "opportunities", think about active offensive strategies to defeat competitors with active offensive attacks. For the quadrant of "Strengths" and "Threats", think differentiation strategies like if threats can be evaded with strengths, or if differentiation from others can be made.

In the quadrant of "weaknesses" and "opportunities", since you may miss the precious chance with the weaknesses, think concrete step by step strate-

Tools Effective for "Clarification of Attack Points and Setting Targets"

|  |  | Intenal factors | |
|---|---|---|---|
|  |  | Strength | Weakness |
|  |  | · Plural veterans who have rich experiences exist<br>· Have experience of winning silver award in company convention<br>· The number of suggestions is among the top-class in the department | · Members composition is divided to senior and young and the QC knowledge of young is poor<br>· There are those who dislike QC circle activities<br>· Meeting participation rate is low due to shift work |
| External factor | Opportunity | Strategy of positive offence | Strategy of gradual measure |
| | · Supporters include many motivated bosses.<br>· Plant secretariat are lead to help us at any time<br>· Have the opportunity to interact with company circles and associate company circles | Utilize strong point of circle, what kind of opportunities grabbed. | Opportunities cannot be grabbed due to the weak point of the circle (what to do to prevent it) |
| | Threat | Strategy of differentiation | Exclusive defense strategy or withdrawal strategy |
| | · We can't go to outside competition because of budget reduction by performance downturn<br>· Circle in the next section has grown rapidly | Threats can be avoided by the strong point of the circle(Even they are threat to other companies. cant it made a differentiation factors?). | What does the threat affect to the weakness of the circle (what to do to prevent it). |

Fig.3.19   Matrix of "SWOT Analysis"

gies to prevent them. At the last quadrant of "weaknesses" and "threats", assuming the worst case and to think defensive security strategies, if it cannot be prevented, take retreat strategies.

From these points, SWOT analysis can be effectively used for current status grasping and to think attack point candidates. For example, there is practical use of it to analyze the current level (current figure) dividing them to 4 items of external factors and internal factors, and to think out desired level (desired shape) and attack point candidates at strategies level for each quadrant.

Next, it is recommended to evaluate those attack point candidates with appropriate evaluation items and to narrow down the attack points.

## (3) Case example of making "SWOT Analysis"

Fig. 3.20 is made utilizing the "opportunities", "threats", "strengths" and "weaknesses" introduced in the steps of "SWOT analysis".

If the strategies obtained by the analysis were made as the attack point candidates, this circle will grow steadily and is expected to become a top circle.

|  |  | Internal factors | |
|---|---|---|---|
|  |  | Strength | Weakness |
|  |  | · Plural veterans who have rich experiences exist<br>· Have experience of winning silver award in company convention<br>· The number of suggestions is among the top-class in the department | · Members composition is divided to senior and young and the QC knowledge of young is poor<br>· There are those who dislike QC circle activities<br>· Meeting participation rate is low due to shift work |
| External factors | Opportunity | Strategy of positive offence | Strategy of step by step |
| | · Supporters include many motivated bosses.<br>· Plant secretariat are lead to help us at any time<br>· Have the opportunity to interact with company circles and associate company circles | · Aim to get gold prize of all company competition and to participate in QC circle national conference with support of secretary and boss<br>· Incorporate a variety of expertise from prized circle in the company | · Increasing event and activity to enhance teamwork in the circle<br>· Plan to improve level by devising training and role allocation |
| | Threat | Strategy of differentiation | Exclusive defense strategy or withdrawal strategy |
| | · We can't go to outside competition because of budget reduction by performance downturn<br>· Circle in the next section has grown rapidly | · Including self participation, increasing the chance to study outside company<br>· Plan to be characteristic circle with creativity | · Make mid-term plan, advance keeping cool and steadily, and achieve target. |

Fig.3.20 Result of "SWOT Analysis"

# Chapter 4

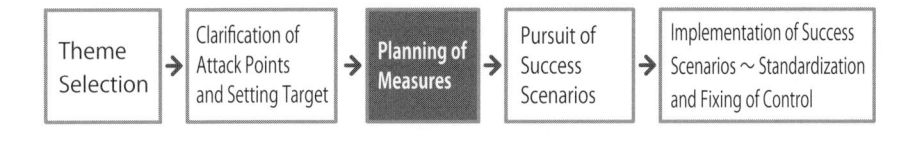

## Tools Effective for "Planning of Measures"

Theme Selection → Clarification of Attack Points and Setting Target → **Planning of Measures** → Pursuit of Success Scenarios → Implementation of Success Scenarios ~ Standardization and Fixing of Control

# Chapter 4

# Points and Tools for "Planning of Measures"

The "Planning of Measures" is a step to generate as many measures plan (ideas) that seem to have possibility of achieving the targets on the attack points (points of views) clarified at the step of "Clarification of Attack Points and Setting Targets", and to select effective measures among them evaluating them by the expected effects (degree of conformance to the target achievement).

The implementation procedures and the tools for this step introduced in this chapter are shown in Table 4.1. In actual idea generation, refer to the implementation procedures in the Table 4.2.

## (1) Points of "Listing up of measures plans (ideas)"

1) Measures plan (ideas) assume that all the adopted attack points are basically to be implemented. However, some of attack points may have close relationship and one of the attack points may have effects on other measures, and in that case it is recommended to list up the measures plans (ideas) by the following method.

Table 4.1  Implementation Procedures and Tools Effective for "Planning of Measures"

| 【Implementation procedures】 | 【Effective tools】 |
|---|---|
| 1. Listing up of measures plans<br>2. Narrowing down the measures plans | Tool 4-1 Brainstorming Method<br>Tool 4-2 Tree Diagram<br>Tool 4-3 Brain Writing Method<br>Tool 4-4 Wish-Points Listing Method<br>Tool 4-5 Defects Listing Method<br>Tool 4-6 Checklist Method<br>Tool 4-7 Focused Object Technique<br>Tool 4-8 Visual Connection Technique |

Tools Effective for "Planning of Measures"

Table 4.2  Procedures of Idea Creation in "Planning of Measures"

| Step | Implementation procedures | Contents for implementation |
|---|---|---|
| Preparation | 1. Understanding attack points | Review contents and background of the attack points (point of view) with all members |
| Idea creation | 2. Drawing ideas (Idea extraction) | Based on the attack points, draw out inspiration and ideas that seen to lead to goals. Own inherent technology is important to extract key ideas. |
| | 3. Develop ideas | Combine inspiration and ideas drawn out and polish and develop ideas by correcthing and adding |
| Summary | 4. Summarizing idea (planning of measures) | Polish futher to make the idea embodied, organize, and narrow them as measures plans |

① Narrowing down the focus to those attack points with large expected effect, examine them first.

② Thinking the attack points that seem to have interrelations together and list up the measures plans (ideas).

2) Gathering all the members' knowledge/ information, utilize effective tools to generate measures plan (ideas).

3) Do not be caught in the own way of doing work done so far, and customs and possibility of realization, and change the thinking and generate many measures plans (ideas) freely utilizing the procedures for idea generation and idea generating tools.

4) Investigate not only other workplaces within the company and other circles, but also information (the way of thinking, methodology, and case examples) of other companies and other industries, and refer them as hints.

## (2) Points of "Narrowing down the measures plan (ideas)"

1) Evaluation at the step of "Planning of Measures" should be conducted only on "size of expected effects" and do not evaluate the "feasibility of realization".

   It is because, if the possibility of realization is evaluated from the outset, there is a danger of extracting only those implementable, superficial, and ordinary measures plans, and there is a possibility of overlooking really effective measures. The meaning of the generation of various ideas with free thinking will be lost. And it is apt to become ordinary, mediocre measures.

2) Evaluation is conducted for each measures considering the scales of the theme characteristics calculating the expected effects.

3) It is the best to express the expected effects quantitatively as much as possible, but there are many cases where expressing quantitatively is difficult. In such cases, using the 5 points scale evaluation method, make it possible to rank them with relative evaluation of the predictable size of effects.

4) When the evaluation of the measures have been done, it is basic to conduct ranking for each group / range of attack points. In the cases where the attacking points are related each other, measures (ideas) generated for the range of related plural attacking points are compared and ranking is conducted.

5) When each measures has effects but the expected effects do not appear as predicted by themselves, it is important to confirm the effects totally in combination with other measures and to conduct ranking and to judge their adoption or rejection.

Tools Effective for "Planning of Measures"

| Divergent thinking methods | Free association methods | Brainstorming methods, Brainwriting methods |
| | Forced association methods | Check list methods, Characteristic listing methods, Morphological analysis methods, Wish-points listing method, Defects listing methods |
| | Analogy association methods | Virtual situation setting methods, Reverse thinking method, Input output method, Focused object technique |

| Convergent thinking methods | Space mapping methods | Inductive methods | Affinity diagram |
| | | Cause and effect methods | Relation diagram, cause and effects diagram |
| | Sequence mapping method | Tree methods | Tree diagram |
| | | Time series methods | PDPC methods, Arrow diagram |

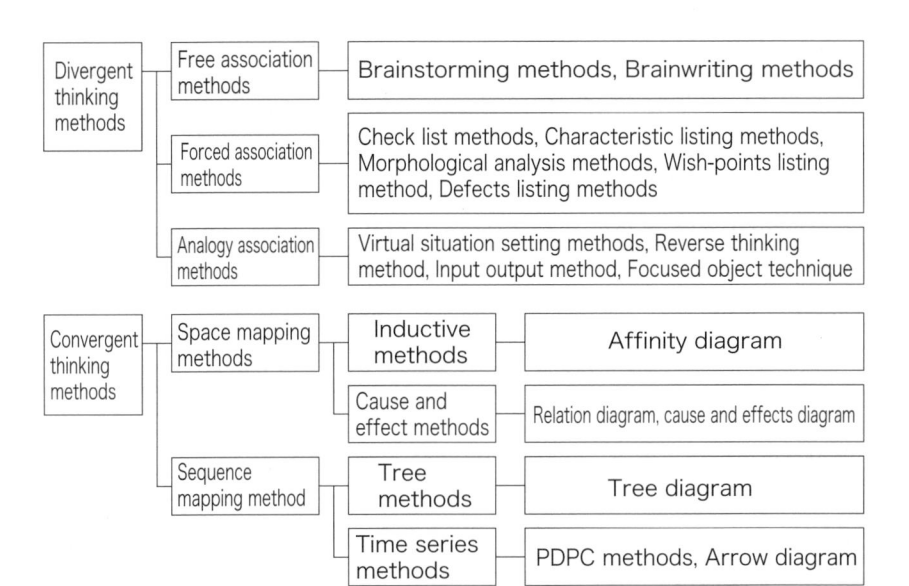

Fig.4.1 Classification of "Idea Creating Methods" and idea tools related
(source : Makoto Takahashi, ed. *Shinpen Souzoryoku Jiten* (*New Edition Creativity Dictionary*) , JUSE Press, Ltd., 2002.)

## (3) Points for using "Idea Creation Methods"

Various idea creation methods are introduced, but they are basically largely classified as is shown in Fig. 4.1 into the "divergent thinking methods" where the ideas are generated and ideas are widened freely without concerns to ranges and rules, and "convergent thinking methods" where the generated many ideas are narrowed down to match the purposes.

The divergent thinking methods are the general name given to various tools (creative methods) that are used in the process of generating many ideas, it widens ideas freely without concern to ranges and rules. "quantity rather than quality", "freely and boldly", "without judgment", and "combination" are important.

On the other hand, the convergent thinking method has a merit of

95

# Chapter 4

systematically summarizing the many ideas generated by divergent thinking method and to allow generation of additional idea creation at the stage of arranging them, and it is recommended to utilize them considering "analysis/synthesis", "refining through garbage out", "practically" and "with purpose". Do not forget to avoid wrong judgment and vague expression and to make them easy to understand.

It is important to utilize divergent thinking methods to expand own perspective and points of views, and how well to narrow down the ideas generated with widened viewpoints with convergent thinking method and how well to connect them to the ideas with effective and higher results. Do not forget to use them in combination utilizing the features of divergent thinking methods and convergent thinking methods.

The idea creation methods introduced below are tools and only tools. They will shine brilliantly when they are used repeatedly, and they get rust when not used. You have the keys who use the tools.

## Tool 4-1

# Brainstorming Method

## (1) What is "Brainstorming Method" (BS Method)?

Widely known as a basic tool of idea creation, and many people are using, is the "Brainstorming method". It is often thought that creativity and creativeness are the inborn ability of special people, but it is known that anyone can easily generate ideas if they use "brainstorming method", and it is used in various scenes in many companies.

A. F. Osborn who developed the tool stated as follows, and from there four basic rules are decided.

- Ideas are generated when there is no criticism.
- The more ideas and the better things are born.
- It is more productive when conducted as a group rather than individuals.

From these, four cardinal rules have been decided.

It becomes important to follow these basic four rules that follow.

| Withhold criticism | Don't discuss and criticize any idea |
|---|---|
| Welcome unusual ideas | Unusual and mdical ideas are welcome. These is no taboo to creative ideas |
| Focus on quantity | Quantity is the key. Quantity breeds quality |
| Combine and improve ideas | Piggypack on other people's ideas and for the develop combine |

As the things that have to be prepared before brainstorming and cautions, it is recommended to select quiet place where the meeting will not be interrupted by telephone or noises, and the arrangement of the seats should be in a circle so that everyone can hear and look all the members' faces. Also, prepare vellum and tag label to records ideas and blackboard, and start after deciding the leader and secretariat beforehand for smooth meeting.

## (2) How to proceed with "Brainstorming Method"

### Step 1. Clarify the purpose

① The purpose of the idea creation should be understood by all the members participating.

② To examine the purpose by the group will help the communalization of the purpose.

③ If there are limiting conditions, you should decide them.

### Step 2. Decide the theme concretely

Any kind of problem cannot necessarily be solved with "brainstorming method" A problems that has a possibility of generating many solutions is suitable.

① The more concrete the theme, the easier is the idea generation.

② A concrete theme do not invite difference in interpretation, and the direction of thinking will be unified.

### Step 3. Generate ideas

① The matter which is reminded at once should be submitted as an idea.

② Anyway, generate ideas steadily following the four rules.
- Modify partly of the ideas experienced in the past, similar ideas, or already generated ideas.
- Think changing those that exist now to new way of use, and cheaper in price without changing the functions.

③ Record all the ideas generated, but take care not to exclude those words that provoke ideas.

④ The number of ideas should be targeted to at least 10 items per person.

### Step 4. Summarize ideas

After finishing generation of ideas, take about an hour of break and then restart.

① Group the generated ideas into the areas and categories of easy to summarize (in affinity). Make classifications (categories) of 5-6 ideas and duplicated ideas should be removed.

② Group to broader categories with the affinity of categories and arrange them.
③ If new ideas come out during the arranging, add them.

**Step 5. Evaluate the ideas and narrow them down**
① Reconfirm the purpose and target of idea generation with the members.
② Select the category items that match the purpose and target (ideas of lone wolf should be handled equal with the category items) and choose good ideas from among the extracted category items.
③ Inherent technologies owned should be the evaluation criteria, but evaluate with "effectiveness" and "feasibility" [Note], etc. However, when new ideas are sought, add "indigenousness/ originality" and "newness".

(Note) In task achieving type, the evaluation with "feasibility" should be after entering the step of "Pursuit of Success Scenarios".

## (3) Case example of "Brainstorming Method" using cards

● ● ● ● ● ● ● ● ● ● ● ● ● ● ● ● ● ● ● ● ● ● ● ● ● ● ● ● ● ● ● ● ● ● ● ● ● ● ● ● ● ● ● ● ●
Theme: Utilize Task Achieving Type QC Story Effectively
● ● ● ● ● ● ● ● ● ● ● ● ● ● ● ● ● ● ● ● ● ● ● ● ● ● ● ● ● ● ● ● ● ● ● ● ● ● ● ● ● ● ● ● ●

① Record ideas generated by all the members on the theme on cards (Refer to Fig. 4.2).
② Arrange card in each of the categories.
In the case example, all member have confirmed the recorded cards and grouped them into 4 categories arranging them to similar contents and in affinity (Refer to Fig.4.3).
・Grouped categories: "Education/ study method", "Consciousness/ motivation", "Theme/ activity", "Benchmarks", etc.
③ Evaluate the ideas and narrow them down.
In the case example, all the members confirmed the arranged cards into categories, and evaluated them with Matrix diagram from 2

# Chapter 4

| Understand the effect of QC story | Understand the meaning of task achieving | Understand the company's policy | Everyone Speaks |
|---|---|---|---|
| Try to use anyhow | Join the outside seminar | Understand the task in workplace | Realize the task achieving and win the victory in company conference |
| Hold group study meeting | Join QC circle conference | Learning idea creation methods | Join the inhouse study meeting actively |
| Read "QC circle magazine" | Study QC tools | Motivate onselves | Study by cases in and out of company |
| Buy books and study | Teaching by promoter | Think theme that we can feel fulfillment | Exchange with other QC circles |
| Gain experience of activity | Gather members | Share role by everyone | Conduct activity with senior circles |
| Activity involving boss | Work on themes that have no sense of obligation | Experience joy of using | Benchmark the excellent case |
| Ask help of promoter | Planning the theme that fit to task achieving type | Implementing data collecting effectively | Study at the supporting tools |
| Utilize for problems and tasks linked to actual work | Reasonable planning by all members | Have a challenge spirit | Challenge to familiar things |
| Gain experience of success | Don't spend the time to gather data and information | Observe the activities of other companies | Have flexible mind |

Fig. 4.2  Recording the idea to cards

**Education · Meeting to study**

| Teaching by promoter |
| Hold group study meeting | Buy books and study |
| Study at the supporting tools | Learning idea creation methods |
| Join the outside seminar | Study QC tools |

**Awareness · Motivation**

| Have flexible mind |
| Share role by everyone | Gather members |
| Experience joy of using | Have a challenge spirit |
| Join the inhouse study meeting actively | Gain experience of success |
| Challenge to familiar things | Try to use anyhow |

**Benchmarking**

| Benchmark the excellent case |
| Study by cases in and out of company | Observe the activities of other companies |
| Exchange with other QC circles | Join QC circle conference |

**Theme · Activity**

| Think theme that we can feel fulfillment |
| Work on themes that have no sense of obligation | Utilize for problems and tasks linked to actual work |
| Planning the theme that fit to task achieving type | Activity involving boss |
| Understand the task in workplace | Understand the meaning of task achieving |
| Understand the company's policy | Understand the effect of QC story |
| Conduct activity with senior circles | Realize the task achieving and win the victory in company conference |

Fig.4.3  Card arrangement to each category

Tools Effective for "Planning of Measures"

aspects of "Effects" and "Involvement of all members" toward the realization of the theme.

④ As to the ideas adopted, the practical implementation methods/ implementation plans and the role allocation of the members have been examined and decided to tackle toward implementation.

Evaluation score: ○ (3pt.) ／△ (2pt.) ／× (0pt.)

| | Planned ideas | Effect | All members participation | Total score | Adoption/Rejection |
|---|---|---|---|---|---|
| Education・Study meeting | Teaching by promoter | △ | △ | 4 | |
| | Buy books and study | ○ | △ | 5 | |
| | Hold group study meeting | ○ | ○ | 6 | Adoption |
| | Study supporting tools | ○ | × | 3 | |
| | Learning idea creation methods | ○ | ○ | 6 | Adoption |
| | Join the outside seminar | ○ | × | 3 | |
| | Study QC tools | △ | △ | 4 | |
| Awareness・Motivation | Have flexible mind | ○ | ○ | 6 | Adoption |
| | Share role by everyone | △ | ○ | 5 | |
| | Gather members | × | △ | 2 | |
| | Experience joy of using | △ | △ | 4 | |
| | Have a challenge spirit | △ | △ | 4 | |
| | Join the meeting to study actively in company | ○ | ○ | 6 | Adoption |
| | Gain experience of success | △ | × | 2 | |
| | Challenge to familiar things | ○ | ○ | 6 | Adoption |
| | Try to use anyhow | × | △ | 2 | |

Fig.4.4   Evaluation and narrowing down by matrix diagram

## ONE POINT

### One point of Brainstorming Method

◆ Every one of the members participate to think and speak and stimulate each other.
◆ Proceed surely following the "4 rules" of the basics of brainstorming
◆ At the scene of generating ideas, never evaluate good or bad of the generated ideas.
◆ Spend more time for idea evaluation than idea generation and refine and brush up the ideas.

## Tool 4-2

# Tree Diagram

## (1) What is Tree Diagram?

The "Tree Diagram" is one of the New QC Seven Tools, and as a tool to find countermeasures from factors, it is widely used by from managers/ specialist engineers to QC Circles.

The features of the "Tree diagram", are: when the goals like purpose, target, and results are established, to think first the measures to achieve the purpose, and then further to think measures to achieve the measures regarding the measures as the next level of proposes.

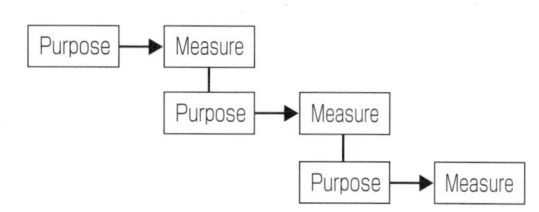

There are basically two types of "Tree Diagram"

① Measures Deployment Type: Used in cases to get the methods (measures) of solving (achieving) problems (tasks).

② Component Deployment Type: Used in cases to clarify the "contents" of objects of improvement.

Here, the measures deployment type of "Tree Diagram" that are generally often used in QC Circle is explained.

## (2) How to make "Tree Diagram"

Since it is important to arrange the generated ideas and to visualize for the members to share, it is important to make them visible to all the members. Also, although the "tree diagram" is classified to convergent thinking method, at the same time it is divergent thinking method and the ideas hit during making a tree diagram are steadily added.

Tools Effective for "Planning of Measures"

Step 1. Set the purpose/ target

① Confirm the purpose (target) with all the members and write it on a card and post it on a vellum.

Problem (task) to solve be expressed in a form of "to make ○○ to do △△" and set it as the purpose or target to achieve. Purpose should be made clear and simple, in an expression that can be understood by everyone, and short sentence is acceptable if necessary.

② If there is any limiting conditions, add them.

Step 2. Consider the primary means

① Consider the primary means that is the direct means to achieve the purpose.

② Write the primary means on cards and arrange them vertically on the right of the purpose card.

・The primary means usually do not become implementable level immediately.

・Not one means but at least 3 to 4 means should be written out.

・If the card is written with the form of "to make ○○ to do △△", then it will become easier to deploy the next means.

Step 3. Deploy means of the secondary and further

① Regarding the primary means as the purposes, and the means to achieve the purposes should be written on cards and place them right side of the primary cards.

② Similarly, deploy third, fourth levels till they become implementable means.

The means below the secondary level should be made more than two items and avoid the means to become in a series.

Step 4. Confirm the relationship of purpose and means (Refer to Fig. 4.5)

① To verify the relationship of purpose and means, ask "To achieve this purpose, is this means effective?" (starting from the left to the right).

② Next, from the lower level means to the higher levels, confirm

*103*

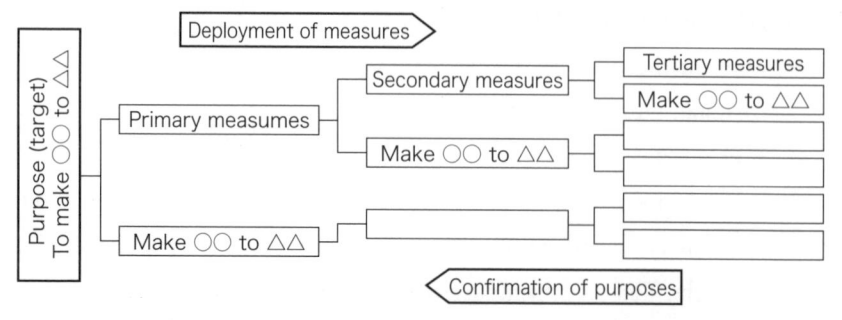

Fig.4.5 Confirmation of relations between purposes and measures

reversely, asking "By implementing this means, the purpose can be attained?" (starting from the right to the left).

③ In the process of confirmation, if necessary means are newly discovered, add them and eliminate those unnecessary, and modify those of wrong expressions.

This step is the most important part of tree diagram. Do not be robbed of heart to the deployment of means to the tree and arranging, and do not be hasty in making.

④ Connect the relationship of purpose and means by lines, and put in the necessary items like the theme, dates of making and the members.

## Step 5. Evaluation of means of implementable level

① Evaluate each, one by one, if the deployed means are appropriate.
② Methods of evaluation vary, but it is recommended to evaluate items like the followings.

Innovativeness/ importance/ effects/ economy/ time, period/ difficulty/ feasibility [Note], etc.

(Note) At the step of "Planning of measures" of task achieving, feasibility is not used for evaluation.

③ For the evaluation, you may set 5 point scale method or 3 point scale method of your own, but it is important to clearly decide the evaluation criteria before the evaluation.

Tools Effective for "Planning of Measures"

### Step 6. Making implementation plan

Means and ideas are further materialized and refined to feasible level and make implementation plan.

---
**ONE POINT**

### One point of making tree diagram

◆ At the stage of mutually generating means and ideas, never consider the preconditions, limiting conditions, and feasibility and so forth, and generate steadily.

◆ It is usual that there are several means to achieve a certain purpose. It is a principle that as we proceed to the lower level it branches off and will widen toward the end. When it narrows toward the end as we proceed to lower level, it is not called deployment. It is often observed when abstraction occured and you should take care.

◆ When the language expression is poor or the thinking is not organized, the means deployment tends to become one to one.

# Chapter 4

## (3) Case example of Using "Tree Diagram"

① Tree diagram which is conducted to 3rd level deployment (Refer to Fig. 4.6).

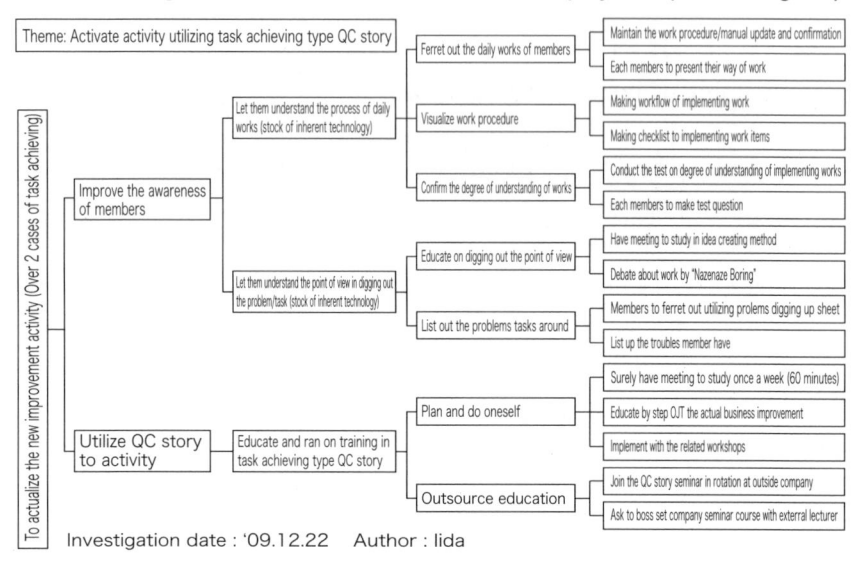

Theme: Activate activity utilizing task achieving type QC story

- To actualize the new improvement activity (Over 2 cases of task achieving)
  - Improve the awareness of members
    - Let them understand the process of daily works (stock of inherent technology)
      - Ferret out the daily works of members
        - Maintain the work procedure/manual update and confirmation
        - Each members to present their way of work
      - Visualize work procedure
        - Making workflow of implementing work
        - Making checklist to implementing work items
      - Confirm the degree of understanding of works
        - Conduct the test on degree of understanding of implementing works
        - Each members to make test question
    - Let them understand the point of view in digging out the problem/task (stock of inherent technology)
      - Educate on digging out the point of view
        - Have meeting to study in idea creating method
        - Debate about work by "Nazenaze Boring"
      - List out the problems tasks around
        - Members to ferret out utilizing prolems digging up sheet
        - List up the troubles member have
  - Utilize QC story to activity
    - Educate and ran on training in task achieving type QC story
      - Plan and do oneself
        - Surely have meeting to study once a week (60 minutes)
        - Educate by step OJT the actual business improvement
      - Implement with the related workshops
      - Outsource education
        - Join the QC story seminar in rotation at outside company
        - Ask to boss set company seminar course with exterral lecturer

Investigation date : '09.12.22    Author : Iida

Fig.4.6    Tree diagram of deployment to 3rd level

② Example of listing up means and narrowing down with tree diagram + matrix diagram (Refer to Fig. 4.7).

Date: 07.08.15
Author: Powerful Adventure Circle

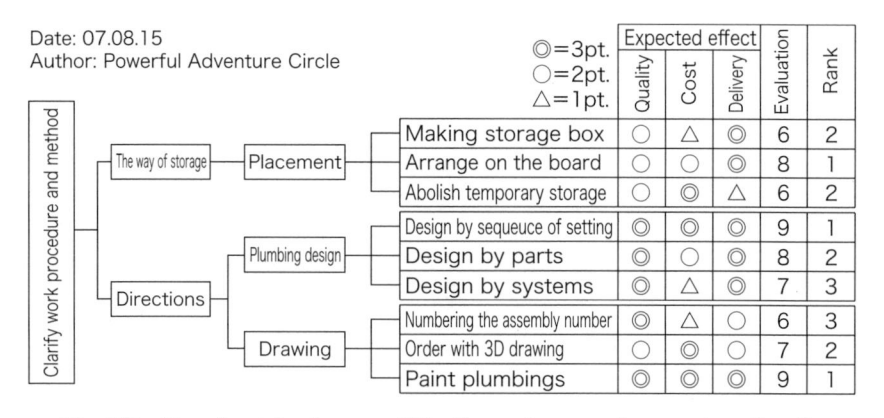

◎=3pt.
○=2pt.
△=1pt.

| Clarify work procedure and method | | | | Expected effect | | | Evaluation | Rank |
|---|---|---|---|---|---|---|---|---|
| | | | | Quality | Cost | Delivery | | |
| The way of storage | Placement | Making storage box | ○ | △ | ◎ | 6 | 2 |
| | | Arrange on the board | ○ | ○ | ◎ | 8 | 1 |
| | | Abolish temporary storage | ○ | ◎ | △ | 6 | 2 |
| Directions | Plumbing design | Design by sequeuce of setting | ◎ | ◎ | ◎ | 9 | 1 |
| | | Design by parts | ◎ | ○ | ◎ | 8 | 2 |
| | | Design by systems | ◎ | △ | ◎ | 7 | 3 |
| | Drawing | Numbering the assembly number | ◎ | △ | ○ | 6 | 3 |
| | | Order with 3D drawing | ○ | ◎ | ◎ | 7 | 2 |
| | | Paint plumbings | ◎ | ◎ | ◎ | 9 | 1 |

Fig.4.7    Tree/matrix diagram "Clarify work procedure and method"
(Source : Nissan Motor Co,. Ltd., "Powerful/ Adventure Circle" Presentation Materials, at the 5090th QC Circle Convention held by the QC Circle Headquarter.)

Tools Effective for "Planning of Measures"

## Tool 4-3

# Brain Writing Method

## (1) What is "Brain Writing Method" (BM method)?

It is also called "Silent Brainstorming" and the ideas, different from "Brainstorming method", is written on a paper (Brain Writing Sheet) rather than "mouth".

## (2) How to Proceed with "Brain Writing Method"

Just like "Brainstorming method", select quiet place where the meeting will not be interrupted by telephone or noises, and the arrangement of the seats should be in a circle so that everyone can hear and look all the members' faces.

Also, prepare "Brain Writing Sheet (BW form: Fig. 4.8)" to record ideas, and start after deciding the leader and secretariat beforehand for smooth meeting.

### Step 1. Clarify the purpose

① Understand the purpose of idea generation with all the participating members.

② It helps to communalization of the purpose to examine the purpose as a group.

③ If there is any limiting conditions, you should decide them.

### Step 2. Decide the theme concretely

① The more concrete the theme, the easier for the idea to come out.

② Concrete theme does not bring difference in interpretation, the

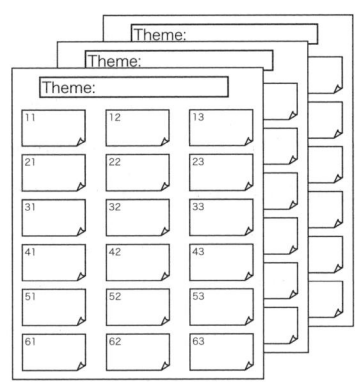

Fig.4.8 Brain Writing Sheet

*107*

direction of thinking can be unified.

**Step 3. Each member sit in a circle having brain writing sheet**

Take seats so that members can look around each other.

**Step 4. Generate 3 ideas in 5 minutes**

① With the signal of start by the leader, write 3 of one's own ideas in the top column (11,12,13) of the sheet.

② Write the idea contents concretely without abstraction.

③ At first, avoid blanks and fill it out surely.

**Step 5. After 5 minutes has passed of all members writing, hand the paper to the right side person (Decide the rotation direction)**

Read the ideas on the sheet turned around well.

**Step 6. Write additional 3 ideas within 5 minutes**

Write additional 3 ideas of own in the columns (21, 22, 23) below (11,12,13) where the ideas are already written.

**Step 7. In the similar manner, turn around the sheet in sequence adding ideas till the signal of finish by the leader**

① Write 3 ideas within 5 minutes and hand it to next until all the member to have a turn.

② When the former idea is utilized, write ↓ (arrow) at the boundary of the frame.

③ When new ideas are not generated and move to ideas of differant idea category, pull a bold line at the border of the frame.

④ Above ② and ③ do not need to be written.

**Step 8. Evaluate ideas and narrow them down**

① Reconfirm the purpose and objective of idea generation with members.

② Select category items (treat lone wolf idea equal to category items) that fit to the purpose/ objective, and choose good ideas from the selected category items.

③ Inherent technologies owned should be the evaluation criteria, but evaluate with "effectiveness" and "feasibility" [Note], etc. However,

## Tools Effective for "Planning of Measures"

when new ideas are sought, add "indigenousness/ originality" and "newness".

(Note) In task achieving type, the evaluation with "feasibility" should be after entering the step of "Pursuing Success Scenario".

## ONE POINT

### One point of "Brain Writing Method"

◆ When filling in the "Brain Writing Sheet", write it simple and clearly. Also never hand it to next person with blank.

◆ Try to think from broader viewpoint like "Brainstorming Method".

◆ Write in the brain writing sheet without speaking. Never do private talk.

◆ Young and veteran, boss and subordinate, without regard to the position, write in ideas freely.

◆ "Brain Writing Method" can generate many ideas within a short time.

## (3) Example of a Brain Writing Sheet
(Refer to Fig.4.9)

| Theme: How to make better communication at workplace? | | |
|---|---|---|
| 11<br>Go drinking together | 12<br>Have a common hobby | 13<br>Take lunch together |
| 21<br>Call each other by nicknames | 22<br>Work accompanied by family | 23<br>Change lunchboxes |
| 31<br>Go to toilet together | 32<br>Make a break time | 33<br>Commute by group |
| 41<br>Play games at lunch break | 42<br>Allow them to bring pets | 43<br>Release a pheromone |
| 51<br>Share the memory in shameful event | 52<br>More time to break during 1-3 pm | 53<br>Bring the album and look together |
| 61<br>Mimic the fellow by all members | 62<br>Rotate to do all the odd job by the all members | 63<br>Hold a Christmas party |

Fig.4.9  Example of Brain Writing Sheet

Tools Effective for "Planning of Measures"

## Tool 4-4

# Wish-Points Listing Method

We can usually generate many ideas if we have some cues.

"Brainstorming Method" and "Brain Writing Method" are tools to generate ideas making opinions of members so forth as the cues. Here, we will introduce wish-points listing method to generate ideas making own (member) dreams and desires as the cues.

### (1) What is Wish-Points Listing Method?

"Wish-points Listing Method" is a tool to generate ideas making own dreams and wishes as cues/ hints. It is said that forward looking dreams and wishes are born out of own self-advancement mind and the pursuit of the dreams and that is connected to free point of view/ imagination and creative idea. Wish points span from small wishes (reverse of weak points/ shortcomings) to forward looking big wishes (ideals and desires).

### (2) How to proceed with "Wish-Points Listing Method"

Basic way of proceeding is to follow the 4 rules of "Brainstorming" and to follow the same procedures.

**Step 1. Clarify the purpose**

① The purpose of the idea creation should be understood by all the members participating.

② To examine the purpose by the group will help the communalization of the purpose.

③ If there are limiting conditions, you should decide them.

**Step 2. Decide the theme concretely**

① The more concrete the theme, the easier is the idea generation.

② A concrete theme do not invite difference in interpretation, and the direction of thinking will be unified.

③ Take care so that the theme scope do not become too large (There is a worry that the dreams and wishes escalate and become out of control).
- On the contrary, take care not to limit it too much and it becomes only about the reverse of weak points and shortcomings.

## Step 3. Record any dreams/ wishes that hit relating to the theme

① Following the 4 rules of brainstorming, generate wish-points that hit with all the members (aim at 10 items per person at the least).
- Generate steadily without making judgment (whatever is OK like a flash/ a whim).
- Generate many, making the dreams and wishes of all the members as cues (absurdity is welcome).

② Record all the wish-points generated (on memo pad, vellum, tag, etc.). Try to utilize brain writing sheet.

## Step 4. Group the wish-points generated

① After fishing generating wish-points, have a break for relaxation (more than 30 minutes).

② After finishing generating wish-points, have a break for relaxation (more than 30 minutes).

③ Eliminate those duplicated wish-points, and leave those wish-points that are difficult to group.

④ During the grouping, if new wish-point appears, add it and take record of it.

## Step 5. Evaluate the wish-points grouped and narrow them down

① Reconfirm the purpose and target of idea generation against the theme with all the members.

② When selecting the wish-points, make own dream/ target of workplace or company as an important criteria (if there is a problem provider, respect the independence/ desire/ intention of the person).

Tools Effective for "Planning of Measures"

Step 6. Consider the idea to realize or materialize the wish-point that are adopted

① About the wish-points evaluated/selected, generate ideas that realize and materialize them (Analyse and unify the ideas, remove any garbage and refine and polish, and think concretely).

② Finish up the ideas that were made concrete by further evaluating/ selecting as much as possible.

## ONE POINT

### One point of "Wish-Points Listing Method"

◆ To dig up forward looking ideas utilizing the words that lead to dreams and wishes well, try to make such words as hints.

Great/ ingenious/ tomorrow/ in the future/ whacked/ Stirring/ 120 full point/ ultimate/ supreme/ breast inflatable/ unusual/ impressive/ elegant/ gorgeous/ new/ incredible/ deceptively/ beautiful/ lovely/ cute/ outstanding top/ fashionable/ big/ dreamy/ remarkable/ nice/ awesome, etc.

## (3) Case Example of "Wish-points Listing Method"

∙∙∙∙∙∙∙∙∙∙∙∙∙∙∙∙∙∙∙∙∙∙∙∙∙∙∙∙∙∙∙∙∙∙∙∙∙∙∙∙∙∙∙∙∙∙∙∙∙∙∙∙∙∙
### Theme: Refrigerator of Our Dream
∙∙∙∙∙∙∙∙∙∙∙∙∙∙∙∙∙∙∙∙∙∙∙∙∙∙∙∙∙∙∙∙∙∙∙∙∙∙∙∙∙∙∙∙∙∙∙∙∙∙∙∙∙∙

· thin · big capacity · with sensor for consumption expiration · no need for electric power · no need of cleaning · hanging on wall · no chlorofluorocarbon used · hand can enter without door opening · glow in the night · embedded on wall · calorie calculation function · cooking · dry proof · wanted can be taken out instantly · rust free · transparent to look inside · remind of day of trash · can freely move · keep household accounts · store tableware · flexible · change old milk to yogurt · morphed into heating box · with range and TV · quiet · cold water served · help cooking menu · quiet · low price · rotate · no need to wrap raw materials · buzzer sounds when kept open · can enter whole pot · can become talking companion

⬇

Evaluation wish-points grouping them into "shape" "materials" "ease of handling (function)", etc.

Shape: · Folding   · Transparent   · Light
      · Rotatable   · Free color, etc.
Material : · Rust free   · Small motor sound
      · Durability   · Shock proof, etc.
Function : · Dry proof
      · Remind consumption date
      · With Range &TV , Cooking
      · Storable without wrap
      · Cold water supply, etc
→ Finished with the refrigerator of dream like the picture on the right.

Tools Effective for "Planning of Measures"

## Tool 4-5

# Defects Listing Method

## (1) What is "Defects Listing Method"?

We are apt to become critical for everything in everyday life and work in many cases. The "defects listing method" is a tool that is going to utilize this critical power (finding fault and nitpicking, etc.) as an underhand with our characteristics/ tendency. It is also called "Reverse Brainstorming" and is used frequently especially as a tool for problem finding at workplace and also for convergence and evaluation of the ideas. We recommend the use for "problems finding of work and workplace" in the QC Circle activities, etc. While the "Wish-points Listing Method" is to generate ideas making dreams and wishes as cue, the "Defects Listing Method" is to generate ideas making defects of things and dissatisfaction.

To use this tool, it is important not only to list up the defects that hit, but to list up many defects, while proceeding with "Brainstorming Method", to look at the defects of the theme from various viewpoints/ perspective, without judging the fitness and good or bad. It become important to generate ideas by finding out the missed points and latent problems and defects, making the defects as cues.

## (2) How to proceed with "Defects Listing Method"

### Step 1. Clarify the purpose

① The purpose of the idea creation should be understood by all the members participating.

② To examine the purpose by the group will help the communalization of the purpose.

③ If there are limiting conditions, you should decide them.

## Step 2. Decide the theme concretely

① The more concrete the theme, the easier is the idea generation.

② A concrete theme do not invite difference in interpretation, and the direction of thinking will be unified.

## Step 3. Record any defects and dissafisfation that hit relating to the theme

① Following the 4 rules of brainstorming, generate defects that hit with all the members (aim at 10 items per person at the least).
  - Generate steadily without making judgment (list up even it cannot be said defects).
  - It is important to think defects only from own position or environment.

② Record all the defects/ dissatisfactions generated (on memo pad, vellum, tag, etc.). Try to utilize brain writing sheet.

## Step 4. Group the defects generated and decide the direction of improvement

① After finishing generating defects, have a break for relaxation (more than 30 minutes).

② Group them into domain or categories that are easy to group (with affinity).

③ Eliminate those duplicated defects.

④ If new defect appears, during the grouping, add it and take record of it.

⑤ Examine and select those groups, and examine the direction of improvement.

⑥ With all the members, confirm the concrete direction of improvement.

## Step 5. Consider the idea to realize or materialize along with the direction of improvement

① Generate ideas that realize and materialize the improvement (Analyze and unify the ideas, remove any garbage and refine and polish, and think concretely).

② Finish up the ideas that were made concrete by further evaluating/

## Tools Effective for "Planning of Measures"

selecting as much as possible.

③ Against the ideas evaluated/ selected, further criticize and make them live ideas.

---

### ONE POINT

**One point of "Defects Listing Method"**

◆ It is up to the boss and seniors and members to smash or foster ideas. Make environment where, without picking up young buds, to let the flower bloom and to finish fruits. Do not use the kind of words like followings that pick up the bud of ideas.

· Impossible. We have already done such a thing!
· Do not think such bizarre and foolish things!
· Not a significant idea, and strange!
· Because it is going well and there is nothing to do particularly, isn't it!.
· Cost too much time and money, let's think next time. Can you make it later!
· The thought has been decided and such a opinion will not be accepted.

# Chapter 4

## (3) Case Example of "Defects Listing Method"

### Theme: Vending Machine which is cute and convenient

·Many sold out of what we want to drink  ·Hard to take  ·Hard to put in  ·No choice of quantity  ·Cigarette and beverages are separated  ·Location is difficult to see  ·Only Japanese Yen  ·Stocks cannot be seen  ·Higher bills cannot be used  ·Hands become wet on rainy days  ·Number of products carried are small  ·No trash equipped  ·No use during blackout  ·Unfriendly  ·No undo function  ·Changes are difficult to pick when dropped  ·Easily press wrong button  ·Makers are limited  ·Button need to be pushed  ·Heavy in weight  ·No use if there is no change  ·Bag is not provided  ·Do not win roulette  ·Different from the sample  ·No receipt/ voucher issued  ·Often out of stock  ·Beyond the reach of children  ·Space- consuming  ·Cannot buy the amount of drink  ·Sell only soft drinks  ·Often out of changes, etc.

⬇

Evaluation was made grouping the defects into "Products", "Functions", "Machine" and so forth.

Product : ·Variety is small
　　　　　·Only limited makers' drinks
　　　　　·Do not win the roulette
Machine : ·Space Consuming
　　　　　·Always installed at the same place
　　　　　·Design is nerdy
　　　　　·Easily press wrong button
Function : ·Tasting is not possible
　　　　　·Returning goods not allowed
　　　　　·No voucher (receipt) issued
　　　　　·Unfriendly  ·Insects gather
　　　　　·No bags provided, etc.

➡ The opinion was expressed, and it became such a vending machine with the charm

Tools Effective for "Planning of Measures"

## Tool 4-6

# Checklist Method

## (1) What is Checklist Method?

The "Checklist Method" is a tool to generate ideas of the things hit and things thought along with the items set beforehand. There are those checklists like the versatile "Osborn's Checklist", and those with original set of purposes/ usages.

The "5W1H Checklist" that is for reviewing the status and to generate ideas converging the ideas by the combination of the reasons or causes, and their improvement and the standards to realize them, the "GE Checklist" that is used for improvement and planning of product, and the "GM Checklist" that is said to be effective for idea generation to aim at cost reduction of manufacturing process are well known (Refer to Table 4.3).

Table 4.3 Kind of Checklist

| Classify | Name of checklist | Inventor | Use · Characteristic |
|---|---|---|---|
| General Checksheet | Osborn checklist | Alex·F Osborn | Easy to use/High generality |
| Matrix checklist | 5W1H checklist | — | Easy to use |
| Checklist for advertisement | Idea creating checklist | ABW association | For copywriter |
| Checklist made by own company | Checklist of GE<br>Checklist of GM<br>Checklist of MIT | GE company<br>GM company<br>MIT | For value analysis |
| Checklist of play on words | DA SA KU NI TA O CHI (Note) | — | Check by play on words |

(Source : Sugiura, Tadashi, ed. *Konnani Yasashii Aidea Hasso ho* (*Such a Easy Idea Generating Method*), JUSE Press, Ltd., 1999.)

(Note) One of the checklists used in Japan taking the first symbole of following Japanese phrases.
· Daiyo shite mitara (How about substitute it?)
· Sakasama ni site mitara (How about reverse it?)
· Kumiawase te mitara (How about combine it?)
· Nitamono wa naika (Is there anything similar?)
· Tano youto wa naika (Is there any other usage?)
· Ookiku shitara (How about making it larger?)
· Chiisaku shitara (How about making it smaller?)

*119*

## (2) How to Proceed with "Checklist Method"

Here, we will introduce the most famous Osborn's Checklist which is easy to use and with high versatility.

### Step 1. Clarify the purpose
① The purpose of the idea creation should be understood by all the members participating.
② To examine the purpose by the group will help the communalization of the purpose.
③ If there are limiting conditions, you should decide them.

### Step 2. Decide the theme concretely
① The more concrete the theme, the easier is the idea generation.
② A concrete theme do not invite difference in interpretation, and the direction of thinking will be unified.

### Step 3. Prepare checklist
① To get accustomed to the "Checklist Method", we will use the Osborn's checklist, but when accustomed, depending on the objective, it is recommended to make a checklist with members and to use it.
② Decide the leader and the secretary, so that idea generation should be conducted smoothly.

### Step 4. Generate ideas and polish the ideas further
① Basics of procedure is to follow the 4 rules of the "Brainstorming Method".
② About the ideas with large effects, further create ideas toward the realization and polish and foster the ideas.

### Step 5. Summarize ideas
① Summarize several ideas as a concept. Do not discuss if it can be realized actually, and try to make good use of ideas generated.

## ONE POINT

### One point of the "Checklist Method"

◆ The "Checklist Method" is a tool which is easy to use. Generally, the easier the tool, the results that is aimed do not come out easily. However, the effect of the tool begins to appear slowly when repeatedly used without giving up on the way. Please pay attention to the following points when it is conducted in a group.

① All the members discuss with forward looking will.
② Generated ideas should be shared by all the members.
③ Repeat it until members are satisfied and conduct about three times with the same theme.

- 1st round : Generate ideas along with the items on the checklist
- 2nd round : Review the existence of deficiency of the listed items from the ideas generated and complete the list.
- 3rd round : Draw ideas along with the items on the checklist again.

## (3) Case example of Osborn's Checklist Utilization
(Refer to Fig. 4.10)

| | Theme: Product development of new generation type ballpoint pen | |
|---|---|---|
| No. | Checklist | Created idea |
| 1 | Other uses?<br>(New ways to use as is? / Other uses if modified) | Magnetic type ballpoint Ballpoint for both bold and fine |
| 2 | Adapt?<br>What else is link this? What other idea does this suggest?/Does past offer parallel?/What could I copy?/Whom could I emulate? | Ballpoint with light |
| 3 | Modify?<br>(New Twist?/Change meaning? colour, motion, odour, taste, form, shape? other change?) | Ballpoint changes ink color by temperature and humidity |
| 4 | Magnify?<br>What to add?/More time?/Greater frequency?/Stronger?/Higher?/Larger?/Longer?/Thicker?/Heavier?/Extra value?/Plus ingredient?/Duplicate?/Multiply?/Exaggerate? | Ballpoint with magnifier |
| 5 | Minify?<br>What to substract?/Smaller?/Condensed?/Miniature?/Lower?/Shorter?/Narrower?/Lighter?/Omit?/Streamline?/Sprit up?/Understate?/Less frequet? | Smaller inkwell ballpoint |
| 6 | Substitute?<br>Who else instead?/What else instead?/Other ingredient?/Other material?/Other process?/Other power?/Other place?/Other apprroach?/Other tone of voice?/Other time? | Contactless-type ballpoint |
| 7 | Rearrange?<br>interchange components?/Other pattern?/Other layout?/Other sequence?/Transpose cause and effect change place?/Change schedule?/Earlier?/Later? | Folding ballpoint |
| 8 | Reverse?<br>Transpose postive and negative?/How about opposit?/Turn it backward, upside down, Inside out?/reverse roles?/Change shoes?/Turn tables? Turn other cheek? | Decolosizins ballpoint for colored paper |
| 9 | Combine?<br>How about ablend alloy, an assortment, an ensemble? Combine units? | Ballpoint with radio Ballpoint with hiking compass |

Fig.4.10 Product development of ballpoint pen (Osborn's Checklist)
(Source : Sugiura, Tadashi, ed. *Konnani Yasashii Aidea Hasso ho* (*Such a Easy Idea Generating Method*), JUSE Press, Ltd., 1999.)

## Tool 4-7
# Focused Object Technique

## (1) What is the "Focused Object Technique"?

Unique ideas are not being born by only thinking around the tasks. In such a case, it is important to look into a totally different world to think. It is called as the "Focused Object Technique" because the activity of observing a analogical things with a lens and to link the result to the theme one by one resembles that the light through a large lens focus on the same point.

It is a tool to list up the related various elements and features making the quite different industry or things unrelated as cues and to link them one by one to the theme.

The "Focused Object Technique" is in many cases utilized as a technique for an individual, and in case it is used in a group, how to proceed is the same with the "Brainstorming Method" because it uses the "Brainstorming Method", or the "Brain Writing Method" when ferreting out the analogous events/ things, elements and characteristics.

## (2) How to proceed with the "Focused Object Technique"

### Step 1. Clarity the purpose
① Understand the purpose of idea generation with all the participating members.
② It help to communalization of the purpose to examine the purpose as a group.
③ If there is any limiting conditions, you should decide them.

### Step 2. Decide the theme concretely
① The more concrete the theme, the easier for the idea to come out.
② Concrete theme do not bring difference in interpretation, the direction

of thinking can be unified.

### Step 3. Choose a hint for idea generation

① Choose a thing that have unique personality or characteristics and that arouse idea generation.

② Choose a case example of quite heterogeneous world or industry, but it is better to choose things members know, those on topics, or those attracting attentions if possible.

③ Even a mechanism of goods and service, person with personality or fictions like novel and play will be acceptable. The hint can be obtained from newspapers and TV, or advertising posters.

### Step 4. List up the elements and features for idea generation

① Discuss the hint of idea generation with members frankly, and take note of the things and features from the discussion (a whim OK, a distortion OK).

② The elements and features for the hint for idea generation should not necessarily be connected to the shape, and the attributes of the hint or things associated to them will do (List up with the mind to grasp the cues to broaden the width of idea generation).

### Step 5. Generate ideas

① Generate ideas forcefully connecting the hint for ideas and the task.

② Generate ideas one item by one item. Distortion is accepted.

### Step 6. Summarize ideas.

① After fishing generating ideas, have a break about 30 minutes.

② Group them into domain or categories that are easy to group (with affinity).

③ Make group (category) with 5-6 ideas.

④ Remove those duplicated ideas.

⑤ It is recommended to regroup them further with the affinity of the categories.

⑥ If new idea appear during grouping, add them.

Tools Effective for "Planning of Measures"

**Step 7. Evaluate the ideas and narrow them down**

① Reconfirm the purpose and target of idea generation with all the members.

② Select the grouping items that match the purpose and target (ideas of lone wolf should be handled equal with the grouping items) and choose good ideas from among the extracted grouping items.

③ Inherent technologies owned should be the evaluation criteria, but evaluate with "effectiveness" and "feasibility" (Note), etc. However, when new ideas are sought, add "indigenousness/ originality" and "newness".

> (Note) In task achieving type, to evaluate with "feasibility" should be after entering the step of "Pursuing Success Scenario".

## (3) Case example of utilizing "Focus Object Technique" where the idea is arranged on a sheet (Refer to Fig.4.11)

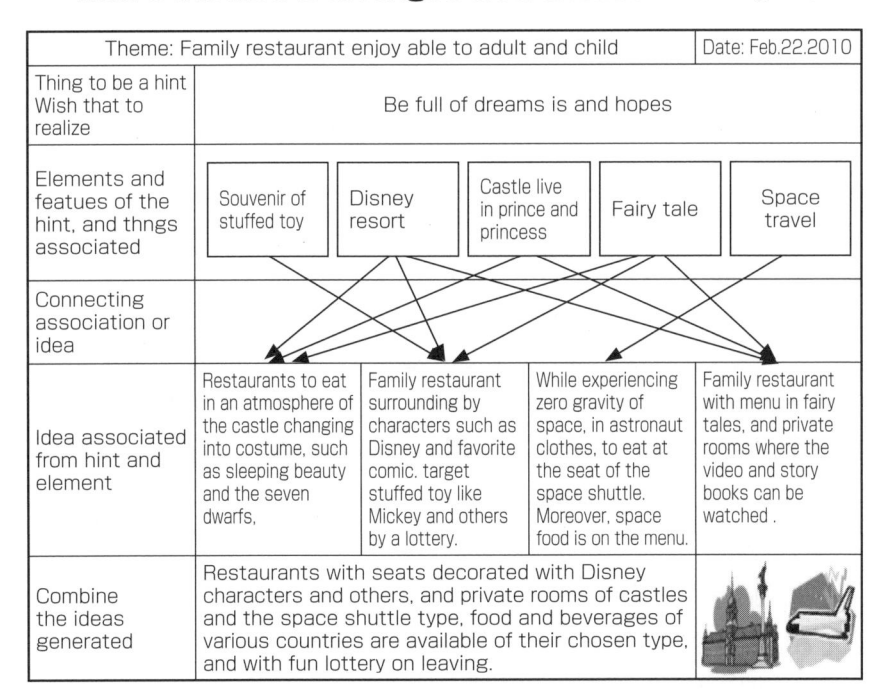

| Theme: Family restaurant enjoy able to adult and child | | | | | | Date: Feb.22.2010 |
|---|---|---|---|---|---|---|
| Thing to be a hint Wish that to realize | Be full of dreams is and hopes | | | | | |
| Elements and featues of the hint, and thngs associated | | Souvenir of stuffed toy | Disney resort | Castle live in prince and princess | Fairy tale | Space travel |
| Connecting association or idea | | | | | | |
| Idea associated from hint and element | | Restaurants to eat in an atmosphere of the castle changing into costume, such as sleeping beauty and the seven dwarfs, | Family restaurant surrounding by characters such as Disney and favorite comic. target stuffed toy like Mickey and others by a lottery. | While experiencing zero gravity of space, in astronaut clothes, to eat at the seat of the space shuttle. Moreover, space food is on the menu. | Family restaurant with menu in fairy tales, and private rooms where the video and story books can be watched . | |
| Combine the ideas generated | Restaurants with seats decorated with Disney characters and others, and private rooms of castles and the space shuttle type, food and beverages of various countries are available of their chosen type, and with fun lottery on leaving. | | | | | |

Fig.4.11 Case example of "Focused Object Technique"

Chapter 4

# Tool 4-8
# Visual Connection Technique

## (1) What is the "Visual Connection Technique"?

We believe that you understood that the idea can be easily generated with some hints or cues from the tools explained so far. This "Visual Connection Technique" is a tool to generate ideas by looking at totally unrelated drawings and pictures and forcefully connecting the impressions felt there with the theme (Connection: consolidation). It is said to be effective to generate unique ideas.

This tool aims to draw up connection giving stimuli of pictures (drawings/photographs) while members are at relaxed feeling. From this point of meaning, a room with witty interior is the best than the meeting room of a firm atmosphere, but when such environment is not available, it is recommended to air light music to relax the feeling as a background.

## (2) How to proceed with the "Visual Connection Technique"

**Step 1. Things to be prepared beforehand**
  ① 4 drawings or pictures (people/scenery/building/animal/ vehicle, etc.)
  ② Visual connection sheet (for each member) (Refer to Fig. 4.12)

**Step 2. Distribute visual connection sheets to members**

**Step 3. Leader will show the first one out of the drawings and pictures prepared for 1 to 2 minutes to members**
  ① Make sure to avoid the letters or photographs that give people who watch unpleasantness/ loathsomeness.
  ② First starting with scenery for relaxation, the sequence of town street scene, building, people, animal is effective.
  ③ It is recommended to combine distant view, near view and the middle

Tools Effective for "Planning of Measures"

| | Impression and things felt from the pictuers and drawing | Image (idea) connected to the theme |
|---|---|---|
| Picture 1 | | |
| Picture 2 | | |
| Picture 3 | | |
| Picture 4 | | |

Problems (theme):

Author:

Fig.4.12  Visual Connection Sheet

as appropriately.

④ Those that excite interests, and those usually unavailable to see will be good.

**Step 4.** Members write the impression that appeared in mind and in association from the drawing or photograph shown with short sentence into the column of impression and things felt of Photograph 1

① Member should think imaging the another world that does not come to mind usually, and not the idea generated from the drawing or photograph themselves.

② Take care because there is tendency that the ideas remain in the range of drawings and photographs.

**Step 5.** In the similar manner, members should write in their impressions after looking second through to 4th drawing or photograph

**Step 6.** Leader announce the problem (theme) after all the members finished (members will fill in the theme into the theme column)

Step 7. Members write in the ideas in the connected image column connecting the impressions and feelings (hints) after looking each of the drawings or photographs with the theme forcefully one by one

① Idea writing should spend 5 to 10 minutes for each of the drawings or photographs.
② Because it is time consuming as a total, take 30 minutes break after idea writings.

Step 8. Member announce and present each of the ideas

Step 9. Evaluate all the ideas and narrow them down

① Reconfirm the purpose and target of idea generation with the members.
② Select the grouping items that match the purpose and target
③ Choose good ideas from among the extracted grouping items.
④ Inherent technologies owned should be the evaluation criteria, but evaluate with "effectiveness" and "feasibility" (Note), etc. However, when new ideas are sought, add "indigenousness/ originality" and "newness".

(Note) In task achieving type, to evaluate with "feasibility" should be after entering the step of "Pursuing Success Scenario".

## ◻ NE POINT

### One point of the "Visual Connection Technique"

① Theme announced after : If the theme is given from the beginning, ideas are limited to those linked with theme and the unique and interesting ideas are difficult to be generated.
② Selection of drawings or photographs. : Those that give members unpleasantness and loathsomeness are NG. Devise also the sequence to show. Selection of drawings and photographs after deciding the theme will also invite worry of biased selection of photos.
③ Ideas lie out of the frame : The aim of this tool is the training of generating ideas from heterogeneous information and the information that lies faraway.

# Tools Effective for "Planning of Measures"

## (3) Case example of utilizing the "Visual Connection Technique" (Refer to Fig. 4.13)

Used photos are following 4.

① Mount Fuji with remained snow as seen from Gotemba
② Lady Movie star who triggered Korean boom in Japan
③ Parents and a child elephants walking in the ruined land
④ A300 Jetliner

Problems (theme): To convince argumentative boss

| | From the impression and things felt from the picture and drawing | Image (idea) connecting to the theme |
|---|---|---|
| Picture 1 (Mt.fuji) | ① Print of Katushika Hokusai | ① Planning a future vision, to explain the way to it. |
| | ② Great eruption | ② Explain passionately to convince |
| | ③ Views of clouds and haze | ③ Explain the unseen difficulties |
| | ④ Fresh air and looks yummy | ④ Explain with soft beautiful words |
| | ⑤ Glistening white snowcap | ⑤ Talk to each other calms "down and cool" off |
| Picture 2 (Korean actress) | ① Thin and prominent collarbone | ① Expose oneself different from usual |
| | ② Bae, Yong Joon | ② Flatter saying you looks like Korean star |
| | ③ Maybe late marriage | ③ To persuade allied with women in the workplace |
| | ④ Earrings seems large and heavy | ④ Put impact on the things talking and explaining |
| | ⑤ Nice smile beauty | ⑤ Ask beautiful colleagues to cooperate |
| Picture 3 (Parent and child of elephant) | ① Parents and children are looking for food, bathing | ① Explain over a meal |
| | ② Poaching | ② Change place to huddle in a two-person |
| | ③ Deep love | ③ Narrow the mind distance by chat and appeals to emotion |
| | ④ Ivory seal | ④ Get approved by good presentation |
| | ⑤ Wild | ⑤ Say that wild Man is cool |
| Picture 4 (Passenger plane) | ① Highjack | ① Explain saying "Emergency!" |
| | ② Passenger from packed | ② Pursuade saying "Resevation" and decision are fater the better |
| | ③ Flashy aircraft body | ③ Befog with colorful and visual data |
| | ④ Speedy and safety flight | ④ Explain carefully without hurry |
| | ⑤ Bad taste of the color of the aircraft | ⑤ Explain afterpraising the tasteful tie |

Author: Hideki Matsuzaka

Fig.4.13 Example of "Visual Connecting Technique"

# Chapter 4

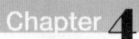

## Coffee Break

### "Let's challenge soft brain with word game"

We Japanese lives in splendid words from Nara/ Heian peiod to today. Starting with the world of 5 phrases *tanka* of 5/7/5/7/7 like "Manyoshu poetry collection" /"XX Waka collection", words are used for play as *haiku/senryu* that express the world of 5/7/5, words are enjoyed as a kind of game utilizing the expression power of words to their maximum, and it is even now widely beloved. Such "word game" became, different from the poem, general as the children plays and puns to enjoy the sounds and rhythms that words have, and to enjoy the association with homonyms. *Shiritori* (Japanese work game) and *Nazokake* (Japanese wordplay riddle), *Kaibun* (palindromes), *Goroawase* (pun), recently, entertainer divised lu-language that mingle English phrase into Japanese can often be seen on TV.

We will introduce "*kaibun* (palindromes)" that began to be introduced as a tool to deepen communication to elementary school learning, and don't you make your brain soft while enjoying it as "word game".

The "*Kaibun*" is sentence (word) that is the same read from both sides, and a word game that utilize the feature of Japanese language that has one sound for one character. When read from the beginning (ordinary) and read from the last (reverse of ordinary) are the same in the order of the appearance of the characters and syllables and still is a sentence that has some meaning to some degree as a language.

When we were children, we enjoyed "mi ga ka nu ka ga mi (unpolished mirror) ", "ta ke ya bu ya ke ta (Bush of banboo burned)", "sa ka sa no sa ka sa (reverse of reverse) " and so forth as "*sakasa kotoba* (word said backward) ", but these are one of short "kaibun". The "kaibun" that is said to be the oldest is the one found in "*Ohgisho*" (Kiyosuke Fujiwara: Poetry Text book at the end of Heian Period) in 1100 A.D and it is introduced that we can see many, not only Japanese, but those written in roman letter like "akasaka" and in English on the internet so forth.

[Chinese characters that looks like Kaibun visually]

(nichi yo bi)　(ichi kawa shi)　(ichi hara shi) (sui do sui) (karada zen tai)

　　日曜日　　　　市川市　　　　市原市　　　水道水　　　　体全体

How about making efforts to brain training while searching for the words in the QC Circle activity making these *Kaibun* that can be seen near around. Recently, it is used as one of the "Brain power training ", and even a book titled "Japanese capability training" as a drill for grown up to play with Japanese and are enjoyed on the street secretly!!

# Chapter 5

## Tools Effective for "Pursuit of Success Scenarios"

| Theme Selection | → | Clarification of Attack Points and Setting Target | → | Planning of Measures | → | **Pursuit of Success Scenarios** | → | Implementation of Success Scenarios ~ Standardization and Fixing of Control |

# Chapter 5

# Points and Tools for "Pursuit of Success Scenarios"

The "Success Scenario" indicates a script/ path that surely lead to success combining the adopted measures and considering various situations.

What should be practically implemented at the step of "Pursuit of Success Scenarios" is not only to examine the practical implementation methods and procedures but also to predict the obstacles and side effects during executing and to think preventive measures beforehand. The step of "Pursuit of Success Scenarios" is divided into 4 implementation steps (Refer to Table 5.1).

In this chapter, after introducing 2 points for the step of deployment of "Pursuit of Success Scenarios", we will introduce 6 tools for the examining the scenario (implementation practical measures), and removing the predictable obstacles and side effects in implementing them.

Table 5.1 Implementation procedures and tools effective for "Pursuit of Success Scenarios"

| 【Implementation procedures】 | 【Effective tools】 |
|---|---|
| 1. Examining the scenarios | Tool 5-1 PDPC Method |
| 2. Prediction of expected effect | Tool 5-2 Obstacles/Side Effects Exclusion Examination Table |
| 3. Prediction of Obstacles/ Side effects and Exclusion | Tool 5-3 Merits/Demerits Table |
| 4. Selection of success scenarios | Tool 5-4 FMEA |
| | Tool 5-5 Quality Table |
| | Tool 5-6 Worksheet for Pursuit of Success Scenarios |

## (1) Point of "How to Deploy Measures Plan to Success Scenarios"

There are two methods to summarize measures plan to concrete scenarios.

① The method to combine several measures to concrete levels.

## Tools Effective for "Pursuit of Success Scenarios"

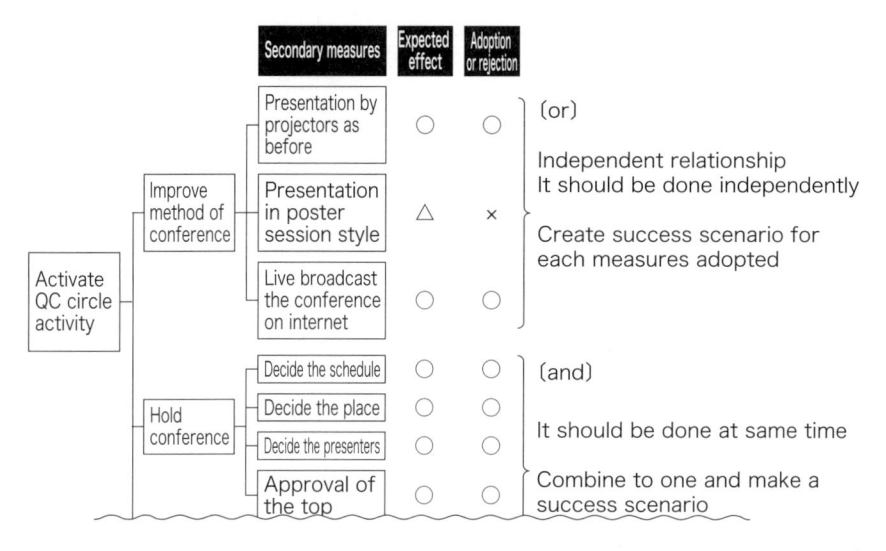

| | | Secondary measures | Expected effect | Adoption or rejection | |
|---|---|---|---|---|---|
| Activate QC circle activity | Improve method of conference | Presentation by projectors as before | ○ | ○ | (or) Independent relationship It should be done independently Create success scenario for each measures adopted |
| | | Presentation in poster session style | △ | × | |
| | | Live broadcast the conference on internet | ○ | ○ | |
| | Hold conference | Decide the schedule | ○ | ○ | (and) It should be done at same time Combine to one and make a success scenario |
| | | Decide the place | ○ | ○ | |
| | | Decide the presenters | ○ | ○ | |
| | | Approval of the top | ○ | ○ | |

Fig.5.1 How to summarize measure plan to success scenarios

② The method to break down the measures plan further and to summarize to concrete implementation plan.

To summarize some of the measures (ideas) that have been adopted at the step of "Planning of Measures", judge whether the measures are in the relationship of "and" (those should be implemented at the same time) each other or in the relationship of "or" (those are independent and to be implemented separately).

Next, those that are in the relationship of "and" are arranged in the order of implementation, and those measures that are in the relationship of "or" should be further brokendown to one step lower level and summarized to concrete implementation plan (Refer to Fig. 5.1).

## (2) Points of "Prediction of Obstacles/ Side effects and Exclusion"

At the stage of summarizing to success scenarios, the obstacles that disturb

*133*

the implementation of each success scenario or the side effects to others after the implementation should be predicted and the methods to avoid or prevent them should be examined. Generally speaking, the larger the effects of scenario plan or higher the newness of the scenario, the larger obstacles and side effects are expected.

Much of the examination of the "Prediction of Obstacles/ Side effects" are conducted on the desk, but there are many that cannot be judged only by the examination on the desk. In that case, it becomes necessary to confirm *gemba/ genjitsu* (at actual place, actual things) or to verify by actual experiments or trials.

Those scenarios which are difficult to exclude the obstacles and side effects however examinied are not adopted. However, even in the cases of the difficult exclusions, there may be the cases of exclusion with relative ease in the process of detailed examination of the steps of "Pursuit of Success Scenarios", do not exclude from the scenario easily.

## Tool 5-1

# PDPC Method

## (1) What is "PDPC Method" (Process Decision Program Chart : *Katei Kettei Keikaku Zu* )?

The "PDPC Method" is one of the new QC 7 tools and is a graphical thinking method, in the case the implementation plan to achieve the purpose has concerns that it may not proceed as originally expected, assuming such obstructive events beforehand and to cope with them (Refer to Fig. 5.2).

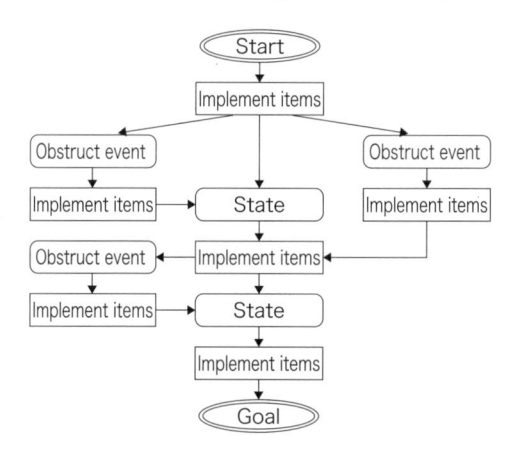

```
                    Start
                      ↓
                ┌─────────────┐
                │Implement items│
                └─────────────┘
        ┌──────────┼──────────┐
        ↓          ↓          ↓
  ┌───────────┐         ┌───────────┐
  │Obstruct event│       │Obstruct event│
  └───────────┘         └───────────┘
        ↓                       ↓
  ┌───────────────┐  ┌─────┐  ┌───────────────┐
  │Implement items│→ │State│  │Implement items│
  └───────────────┘  └─────┘  └───────────────┘
                       ↓
  ┌───────────┐   ┌───────────────┐
  │Obstruct event│← │Implement items│←
  └───────────┘   └───────────────┘
        ↓
  ┌───────────────┐  ┌─────┐
  │Implement items│→ │State│
  └───────────────┘  └─────┘
                       ↓
                ┌───────────────┐
                │Implement items│
                └───────────────┘
                       ↓
                    Goal
```

Fig.5.2 Conceptual diagram of "PDPC Method"

The "PDPC Method" is a tool in OR (Operations Research)[Note], and is devised by Jiro Kondo, a former professor at University of Tokyo getting hints from the Apollo Projects which is the first manned satellite of the United States, and its birth was in the prevention of serious cases and accidents, but recently it is utilized widely to research and technology development, new business and sales negotiations, etc.

(Note) OR (Operations Research): Mathematical Problem Solving Methods developed centered around the researches of scientists for the armed forces operations in UK and U.S.A. during the World War II.

*135*

The "PDPC Method" is useful at the step of "Pursuit of Success Scenarios", to examine the concrete scenarios of the measures of large expected effects obtained by tree diagrams, etc. and for the prediction of obstacles/ side effects and to examination of exclusion of them.

## (2) Procedures to make "PDPC Method"

### Step 1. Decide the theme

Examine if the theme is suitable for the "PDPC method" checking whether any information for the realization of the measures is lacking, or whether trial and errors are expected in the process of the implementation. In this case, do not apply problems to the tool, but choose from the viewpoint of whether the tool is suitable or not.

### Step 2. Clearly state the starting point and goal

The original state of measures, as the starting point, is put at the upper end and the state of attaining the purpose as the goal written on a card to be put on the lower end of a paper. Surround the starting point and goal card with double line and make them clearly understood. It is another method to clearly write as starting point and goal beside the card.

### Step 3. Make the preconditions clear

Make clear the preconditions and limitations such as the required quality and budget, deadline and the members.

### Step 4. Assume optimistic (basic) route

On the central line from the starting point to the goal, make optimistic route that "it seems to succeed if it is conducted in this procedures", assuming measures ☐ → state ☐ , connecting with arrows. When the implementation items are divided depending on the judgment, use ◇ (decision box) and proceed downward if it is yes, and to side if it is no.

### Step 5. Assume pessimistic routes

Predict pessimistic situations such as obstacles that seem to happen when implementing measures and side effects that seem to happen after the

Tools Effective for "Pursuit of Success Scenarios"

implementation, and write in and examine the workarounds for them as the countermeasures and return to the basic route. Finally, confirm if there is any contradictions as a whole and show the route of high success rate with red line or bold line.

### (3) Names of the Symbols and their Meanings

The symbols and their meanings used in the "PDPC Method" are shown on the Fig. 5.3. The mainly used symbols are 3 kinds of ⬜, ⬭, ➡, and ◇ and ┈┈▶ are used depending on the needs.

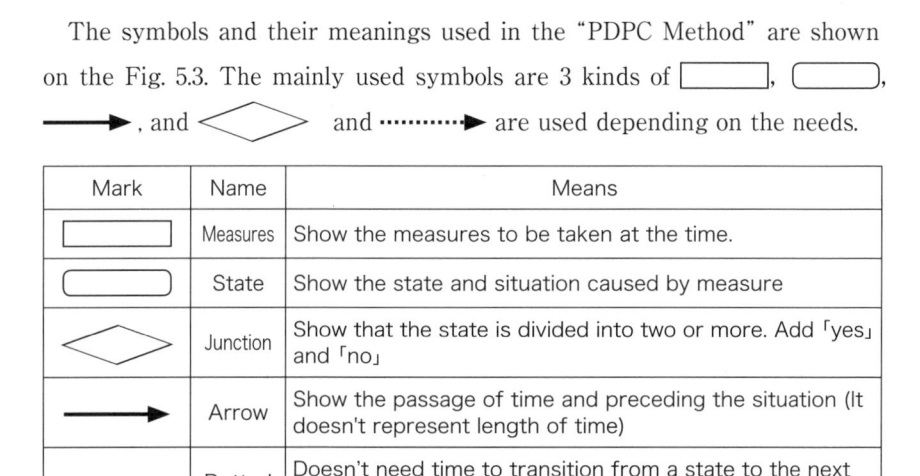

| Mark | Name | Means |
|---|---|---|
| ⬜ | Measures | Show the measures to be taken at the time. |
| ⬭ | State | Show the state and situation caused by measure |
| ◇ | Junction | Show that the state is divided into two or more. Add 「yes」 and 「no」 |
| ➡ | Arrow | Show the passage of time and preceding the situation (It doesn't represent length of time) |
| ┈┈▶ | Dotted arrow | Doesn't need time to transition from a state to the next state, and doesn't relate to counterpart response, show the sequence only. |

Fig.5.3  Names and meanings of graphical symbols

### ONE POINT

◆ At the stage of assuming obstacles and side effects, there is no limit to think of the pessimistic situations, and because there are many unknown parts and it is no meaning to describe precisely. Make the total number of cards to about 30 – 40 at the maximum.
◆ It is common practice to start with the starting point, but if it come to a deadlock, you can make it from the goal upward.
◆ After making, it is important to confirm that there is any contradiction or if any important cards are missing.

## (4) Case Example of "PDPC Method" Utilization

Fig 5.4 is a case example in QC circle activities. The "Sales Unit price Increase" as the goal, the practical procedures are clarified to two directions of "New Products Procurement" and "Distribution of Pamphlet", and the manual is made with "PDPC Method" to exclude the predictable obstacles and effects to other sections. Assuming the various situations before reaching the goal, they drew the success scenarios and made the countermeasures to corresponding events clear.

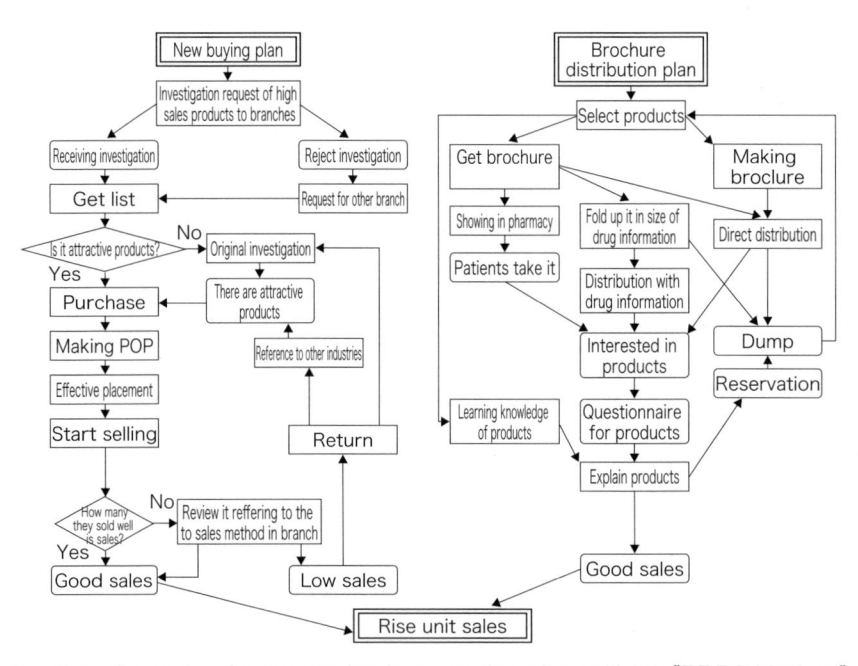

Fig.5.4  Example of concrete implementation plan utilizing "PDPC Method"
(Source : Bohsei Pharmacy, "Ayaka 3 Months Circle", *QC Circle Magazine*, Aug. 2008, Case Example 1, JUSE.)

Tools Effective for "Pursuit of Success Scenarios"

## ONE POINT

◆ Specify the important card and work out a covert plan

In case where an "irreparable pessimistic situation can be predicted if it happens" from a certain measures card, it is not a wise policy to take the workarounds after the pessimistic situation occurred. In such a case, surround the measures card with a red line or bold line and position it as an important card and it is important to examine preventive measures thoroughly beforehand so that it will not go to the worst situation.

◆ Put in a rough schedule

PDPC flow shows progress of time. Where there are target and deadline of delivery like sales and research theme, it can be used as an activity plan if the rough schedule is put in, setting the time axis along the PDPC flow.

# Chapter 5

## Tool 5-2
## Obstacles/ Side Effects Exclusion Examination Table

### (1) What is "Obstacles/ Side Effects Exclusion Examination Table"?

The "Obstacles/ Side Effects Exclusion Examination Table" is a tool to predict the obstacles in implementation with the success scenario implementation and the side effects that occur to others beforehand and to exclude them.

Table 5.2 is a case example of the "Obstacles/ Side Effects Exclusion Examination Table." In the task achieving type, the evaluation up to the step of "planning of measures" is done only with expected effects, but at this step of the "Pursuit of Success Scenario" the evaluation of feasibility is done the first time. This "Obstacles/ Side Effects Exclusion Examination Table" evaluates the feasibility with the four items of expense, man-hour, technology, and period.

Table 5.2 Example of utilizing "Obstacles/Side Effects Exclusion Examination Table"

| Classification | Scenario 1. Utilizing mixture ratio sensor | | Feasibility | | | | Possibility to exclude |
|---|---|---|---|---|---|---|---|
| | Contents | Idea for exclusion obstacles/ side effects | Cost | Man-hour | Technological | Period | |
| Obstacles | Heat-resistance limit of sensor 850°C | Eject gas from exhaust pipe | ○ | ○ | ○ | ○ | Possible |
| | Securing measure systems in each cylinder | Utilizing measuring instrument at hand | ○ | ○ | ○ | ○ | Possible |
| | | Long term borrow measurement instrument from other section | ○ | ○ | ○ | △ | |
| Side effect | Decrease of gas flow by pipe | Select pipe diameter that can stop decreasing the gas flow within limit | ○ | ○ | ○ | ○ | Possible |
| | Occupatied use measure system | Borrow from other section | ○ | △ | ○ | △ | Possible |
| | | Utilizing unused items | ○ | △ | ○ | ○ | |
| Total evaluation | There is possibility to exclude heat-resistance and decreasing flow Occupation is difficult to adjust with other section, but there is possibility to exclude | | | | | Judgment | Scenario Adopt ~~Reject~~ |

(Source : Nissan Motor Co., Ltd., "COOLS Circle" Presentation Materials at the 3940th QC Circle Convention held by the QC Circle Kanto Branch, Kanagawa District.)

Tools Effective for "Pursuit of Success Scenarios"

## (2) Procedures for Making "Obstacles/ Side Effects Exclusion Examination Table"

### Step 1. Predict obstacles/ side effects

For each scenario, predict the obstacles in implementation and the situation of side effects conceivable as the results of implementation, and list them up. For ferreting out the obstacles/ side effects, the "Brainstorming method" (Refer to Tool 4-1) is effective.

### Step 2. Generate ideas for excluding the obstacles/ side effects

Examine the ideas to exclude for each obstacle/ side effect. Here again, the "Brainstorming Method" is effective.

### Step 3. Evaluate the feasibility

Evaluate the ideas to exclude obstacles/ side effects with feasibility (expense, man-hour, technology, period, etc) and judge the possibility of excluding the obstacles/ side effects. The evaluation of feasibility is easy to understand if ○△× are used.

### Step 4. Make Total Evaluation

Arrange the series of process from the pre-examination of obstacles/ side effects, generation of ideas for exclusion to the evaluation of feasibility, and evaluate totally and judge the adoption or rejection of the scenario. In the column of total evaluation, write down the summary of evaluation with concise sentence.

## (3) Case Example of Utilizing the "Obstacles/ Side Effects Exclusion Examination Table"

Table 5.3 is a helpful case example of the "Obstacles/ Side Effects Exclusion Examination Table" in QC Circle Activity.

In this case example, the examination column is for only obstacles predictable, but actually the side effects are examined separately. For a general examination table format, like Table 5.2 it will be better to make it so

*141*

that both of the "obstacles" and "side effects" can be examined.

Table 5.3 Example of utilizing "Obstacles/ Side Effects and Exclusion Examination Table"

Raise precision of deciding card position and screw position of tools in final assembly

| Measures plan | Implement plan | Expected obstacles | Exclude obstacles | Judgment of exclusion | Adoption or rejection |
|---|---|---|---|---|---|
| Raise precision using a stand | Raise precision of protector position by raising precision of stand position | Precision of protector position can be obtained from equipment shape? | Set standard outside of equipment | Possible | Adopt |
| Correct protector position | | | | | |
| Guide by protector | Guide by protector to change screw head form like mortar | Does the same effect appear in 1.8 type screw? | Change mortar size to 1.8 type | Possible | Adopt |

Make adopter desorption method jig

| Measure plan | Implement plan | Expected obstacles | Exclude obstacles | Judgment of exclusion | Adoption or rejection |
|---|---|---|---|---|---|
| Create machine jig | Set in standard position, desorption automatically | Cover the difference in desorption mechanism? | Setting Removal Create 2 patterns | Possible | Adopt |

(Source : Hitachi Global Storage Technologies, "25TEST Circle", *QC Circle Magazine*, March 2009, Case Example 1, JUSE.)

Tools Effective for "Pursuit of Success Scenarios"

## Tool 5-3

# Merits/ Demerits Table

### (1) What is the "Merits/ Demerits Table (M/DM Table: *Ko zai hyo*)?

The "Merits/ Demerits Table" is the one which pursues the good points (merits) and the bad points (demerits) of measures and make the comparison of both in the form of table, and it is also called "*Ko zai* (Goods and Bads) table".

The "Merits/ Demerits Table" has been utilized in companies/ organizations as a decision making tool for comparison, evaluation and analysis of various policies. From this, the "Merits/ Demerits Table" is not a tool to be utilized in a limited sections like manufacturing workplace and engineering department, but it can be said to be a tool effective in all the workplaces of companies and organization.

At the step of the "Pursuit of Success Scenarios", it is useful as a tool for the prediction of expected effects and prediction of obstacles and side effects and exclusion of them. The merits of the measures are taken up as the qualitative expected effects and if there are those that correspond to obstacles and side effects in the demerits, that are used as preventive measures after enough examinations.

Also, because the "Merits/ Demerits Table" mainly utilizes language data, many of them become qualitative predictions. If it is thought that it is inappropriate to judge only with language data, it becomes necessary to investigate them actually or to confirm with experiments and trials.

### (2) Procedures for making the "Merits/ Demerits Table"

#### Step 1. Write down merits and demerits

As to the measures adopted at the step of "planning of Measures" with

*143*

large expected effects, merits and demerits are examined, for example, merit is "labor saving" and demerit is "automation budget increase", and itemize them.

Merits and demerits can be examined by one person, but the ferreting out by discussion with concerned people and QC Circle may generate more and the missing will become less.

The use of "Brainstorming method" is effective for digging up.

#### Step 2. Stratify the opinions generated

Stratify the opinions generated to merits and demerits.

#### Step 3. If the positions differ, stratify for each position

In case the merits and demerits differ depending on the positions, stratify the merits and demerits for each of the positions. If those concerned people of both (positions) are present, the differences in opinions become more clear if you can make the "Merits/ Demerits Table" for each of them.

#### Step 4. Evaluate the opinions

Evaluate the merits and demerits written out with 3 points scale like ◎○ △ or 5 points scale as needed.

## (3)　Case Example of Utilizing the "Merits/ Demerits Table"

The Table 5.4 is a "Merits/ Demerits Table" that examined the policies of development of new customer companies. It stratifies them into 2 of "Own company" and "clients companies" as customers.

When the interests are different depending on the positions like this, the difference in the opinions will become highlighted if the "Merits/ Demerits Table" is made with stratification.

Fig. 5.5 is a case example of utilizing it in QC Circle. It is very helpful in that it examined merits and demerits of "Curved Seal Work automation (NC Robotization)" and further examined the countermeasures to exclude demerits.

Tools Effective for "Pursuit of Success Scenarios"

Table 5.4  Merits/ Demerits Table that examined the policies of development of new customer companies

| Footing | Merit | Demerit |
|---|---|---|
| Own company | Increase sales<br>Be able to develop related market<br>Increase amount of sales information<br>Decrease cost in mass production | Increase development cost<br>Increase development man-hour<br>Increase office work cost<br>It makes relationship with Competitior Companies bad |
| Customers | Increase convenience<br>Shorten delivery times<br>Merit in buying from 2 companies | Increase amount of office work<br>Increase computer capacity<br>Busy to manage |

(Source : Kano, Noriaki, ed, Nitta, Mitsuru, ed., *QC Circle no tameno Kadai Tassei Gata QC Story* (*Task Achieving QC Story for QC Circles*), JUSE Press, Ltd., 1999.)

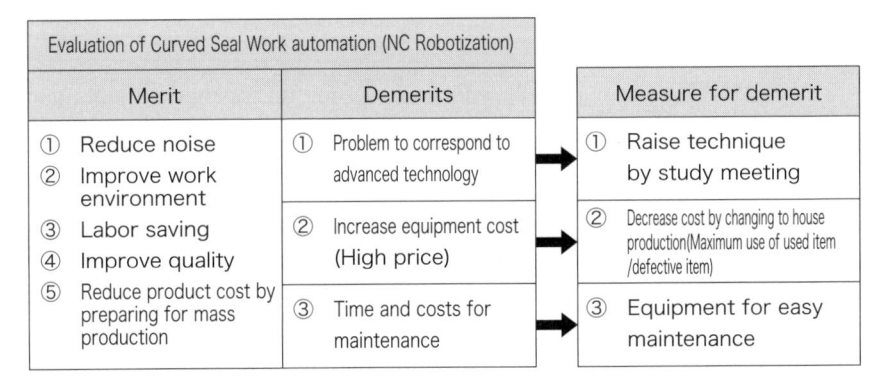

| Evaluation of Curved Seal Work automation (NC Robotization) ||||
|---|---|---|---|
| Merit | Demerits | | Measure for demerit |
| ① Reduce noise<br>② Improve work environment<br>③ Labor saving<br>④ Improve quality<br>⑤ Reduce product cost by preparing for mass production | ① Problem to correspond to advanced technology<br>② Increase equipment cost (High price)<br>③ Time and costs for maintenance | → | ① Raise technique by study meeting<br>② Decrease cost by changing to house production(Maximum use of used item /defective item)<br>③ Equipment for easy maintenance |

Fig.5.5  Merits/Demerits of "Curved Seal Work Automation (NC Robotization)" and them measures

(Source : Isuzu Motors Ltd., Hokkaido Plant (Current Isuzu Engine Manufacturing Hokkaido, Ltd.), "Dreamer Circle" Presentation Materials at the 3139th QC Circle Convention held by the QC Circle Hokkaido Branch.)

## Tool 5-4

# FMEA

## (1) What is the "FMEA (Failure Mode and Effects Analysis)"

The "FMEA" is a tool for predicting the potential failure modes a system or a product causes, evaluating the effects, and to take measures beforehand. Here, the failure modes are the condition of the failures and phenomena of failures that occur.

The "FMEA" is widely utilized as a tool for prevention in every industry like automobile, household electric products, electricity facilities, construction, and communication systems. Recently, it is also utilized for prevention of medical accidents.

The "FMEA" is an especially effective tool for technological theme and it has been utilized many in specialist sections like research and technology development of companies. Recently, it is utilized in QC Circle Activity.

There are two kind of "FMEA" that are the "Design FMEA" and the "Process FMEA".

Table 5.5 is an example of FMEA worksheet and its contents. The format of FMEA worksheet is not set uniformly and the original ones are used depending on the companies' needs.

## (2) Procedures for making the "FMEA"

The practical procedures to use are explained based on the example of worksheet in the Table 5.5.

### Step 1. Understand the target system

At first, all the team members are to understand the system of the subject of analysis and communalize. Prepare drawings of products in the case of a

Tools Effective for "Pursuit of Success Scenarios"

Table 5.5  Example of FMEA worksheet and its contents

Process/product : _____
FMEA team : _____
Team leader : _____

FMEA number _____
FMEA date (First edition) _____
Revision _____
Page _____

| FMEA process | | | | | | | | Result | | | |
|---|---|---|---|---|---|---|---|---|---|---|---|
| Part or process name | Function of part or process | Potential failure modes | Effect of failure | Potential failure cause | Severity | Frequency of occurrence | Possibility | Risk Priority Number | Implemented measure | Severity | Frequency of occurrence | Possibility | Risk Priority Number |
| | | | | | | | | | | | | | |
| Name of parts and process | Function of parts and process | Failure modes can occur (break, breakage, etc.) to list up using brainstorming method | List up the potential effect of each failure modes | Study the potential causes of occurring failure modes and enter | Evaluation in regulated evaluate standard | | | | Examine and ideal with in high risk failure modes | Re-evaluation in risk after dealing with | | | |
| | | | | Risk priority number = severity×frequency of occurrence×possibility of detecting | | | | | | | | | |
| Total of risk priority number | | | | | | | | Risk priority number after action | | | | | |

design "FMEA" and detailed flowchart of work in the case of process "FMEA", and grasp the product or system using them. Here, it is important to confirm them based on *genba/genjitsu* (at actual place/ actual thing). The results of understanding are to be filled into the columns of "Parts or Process Name" and "Function of the Part or Process" that are far left of the worksheet.

### Step 2. List up the potential failure modes

List up the potential failure modes that have possibility to affect the product quality or manufacturing process and systematize them. After systematization, fill them in to the potential failure mode column of the worksheet.

### Step 3. List up the potential effects of each failure mode

List up what happens when the failure occurs for the potential failure mode written on the worksheet.

### Step 4. Study the Potential Cause of Occurrence

Study the potential cause of occurrence of "why it fails" for the potential failure mode. For the study of potential cause of occurrence, use of FTA[Note] is effective.

> (Note) FTA (Fault Tree Analysis): Called *kosho no ki kaiseki* (Analysis of Tree of Failures) and is a top down tool to theoretically decompose the cause of severe failures that occur on a system and to subdivide, that finally dig down to the cause of failures of each part one by one.

### Step 5. Evaluate the severity (degree of effects) of each failure mode

How much effects it will give to system or human when failure occurs is called severity (degree of effects). Here, when a specific failure occurs, how severe is the effects that influence is evaluated using severity (degree of influence) in the Table 5.6 "Evaluation Criteria Table "(Note).

> (Note) It is basic to make the evaluation criteria table for each system of objective.

### Step 6. Evaluate the frequency of occurrence of each failure mode

The frequency of occurrence is the degree of possibility of occurrence the failures. To evaluate the frequency of occurrence, it is best to conduct it using the actual data that are obtained from the process. This work is evaluated using the frequency criteria of Table 5.6 "Evaluation Criteria Table".

### Step 7. Evaluate the possibility of detection for each failure mode

The degree of detection of the failures or effects of failures is called degree of detection evaluation and it is evaluated using the degree of detection criteria in the "Evaluation Criteria Table" (Table 5.6).

### Step 8. Calculate the Risk Priority Number (RPN) for each failure

The Risk Priority Number (RPN) is calculated with following formula for each item.

$$\text{Risk Priority Number} = \text{Severity} \times \text{Occurrence} \times \text{Detection}$$

The total of Risk Priority Number is obtained adding up the Risk Priority Number of each failure mode.

### Step 9. Prioritize the failure modes

The priority of failure mode is decided, ranking them by the size of Risk Priority Number. Which items to examine is decided with priority expressing

Table 5.6 Example of evaluation criteria table

| Level | Severity (Degree of effect) | Frequency of occurrence | Possibility of detecting |
|---|---|---|---|
| 10 | Fatal : Injury accident/ Property damage | Very high frequency of occurrence | Almost undetectable |
| 8 | Serious : Function Abeyance of products | High frequency of occurrence | Often undetectable |
| 6 | Function decline | Possibility of failure | Sometimes undetectable |
| 4 | Little: Little function change | Little possibility of occurrence | Mostly detectable |
| 2 | Minimum: Almost no effect | Failure rarely occurs | Most reliable detection |

on a Pareto Diagram so forth. (Refer to Fig. 5.6 Left).

### Step 10. Take action to the failure mode with high risk

Take actions to examine the elimination or reduction of failure modes with high risk utilizing the problems solving procedures like QC Story.

### Step 11. Calculate the Risk Priority Number after the action to the failure modes

After the improvement action to the product or the process, calculate the Risk Priority Number by reevaluation of the severity, occurrence and detection. When the Risk Priority Numbers are compared with Pareto diagram of before and after of actions, the effects become clear (Refer to Fig. 5.6).

## (3) Case Example of Utilizing the "FMEA"

The Fig. 5.7 is a case example of "FMEA" in QC Circle activity. In the step of "Theme Selection" of task achieving type, the "FMEA" is conducted to confirm the necessity of process improvement and the necessity of tackling is made clear. Further, after the improvement, the effects are confirmed

# Chapter 5

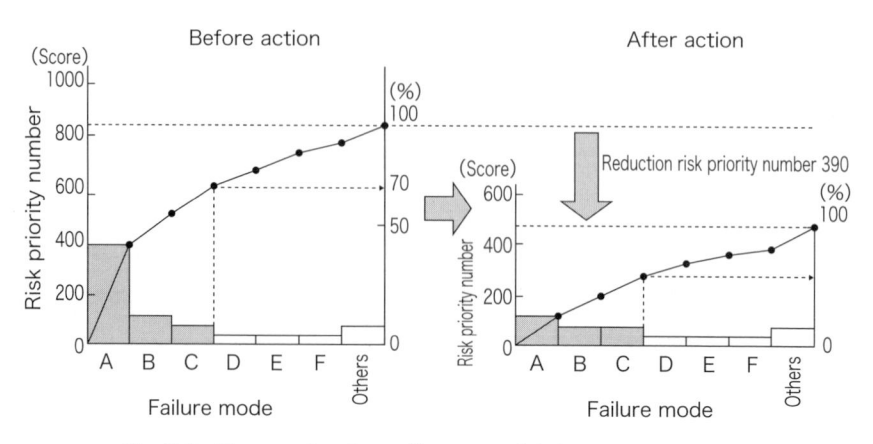

Fig.5.6  Figure of palato diagram of risk priority number

by repeating the (FMEA) analysis again. The "FMEA" can be utilized not only at the scene of "Pursuit of Success Scenarios", but also at the step of "Theme Selection", "Clarification of Attack Points", "Setting Target", and "Implementation of Success Scenarios".

| NO | Process name · Each process | Function of process · Defective item to analyze | Defective mode · Expected defect, defect in past | Effect of defect · Effect on next processes and completed car | Point of Evaluation | | | | Contents of measure · Prevention plan of recurrence |
|---|---|---|---|---|---|---|---|---|---|
| | | | | | Degree of importance | Degree of occurrence | Degree of detection | Degree of importance | |
| 1 | Visual observation | Underfill | Leaving black skin | Processing defect | 3 | 1 | 1 | 3 | Enhanced visual work |
| | | To slide mold | Processing defect | Damage processing machine | 1 | 1 | 1 | 1 | Enhanced visual work |
| 4 | Magnetic flaw detect First process | Crack | Leak in car assembly | Complaint from market | 9 | 1 | 3 | 27 | Magnetic flaw detect, guarantee second processes |
| | | Lap defect | Underfil by separation | Processing defect | 1 | 1 | 3 | 3 | Magnetic flaw detect, guarantee second processes |
| | | Damage | Underfil by separation | Processing defect | 1 | 1 | 3 | 3 | Magnetic flaw detect, guarantee second processes |
| 5 | Magnetic flaw detect second processes | Crack | Leak in car assembly | Complaint from market | 9 | 1 | 1 | 9 | Magnetic flaw detect, guarantee second processes |
| | | Lap defect | Underfil by separation | Processing defect | 1 | 1 | 1 | 1 | Magnetic flaw detect, guarantee second processes |
| | | Damage | Underfil by separation | Processing defect | 1 | 1 | 1 | 1 | Magnetic flaw detect, guarantee second processes |

FMEA evaluation standard

| Degree of effect | | Degree of occurrence | | Degree of defect | | Degree of importance |
|---|---|---|---|---|---|---|
| Evaluation | Evaluation criteria | Evaluation | Evaluation criteria | Evaluation | Evaluation criteria | Evaluation criteria |
| 10~9 | Fatal defect that lead to injury accident/ property damage | 5 | Defect rate over 3.1% | 5 | Become market claim by pass into dealer and customer | Hazard index of important defect Degree of effect × Degree of occurrence × Degree of detect = Degree of importance |
| 8~7 | Serious defect that lead to no driving and car trouble | 4 | Detect rate 2.1 ~ 3.0% | 4 | Detect before shipping | |
| 6~5 | Middle defect that causes hypofunction | 3 | Defect rate 1.1 ~ 2.0% | 3 | Detect before car assembly | |
| 4~3 | Little defect decline the outline function | 2 | Defect rate 0.6~1.0% | 2 | Detect inside that line | |
| 2~1 | Little | 1 | Defect rate under 0.5% | 1 | Defect in that process | |

> It is impossible to detect only at first process, so hazard index of leaking defects is high!

> Second process detect part that can't detect in first process

Fig.5.7  FMEA process evaluation and FMEA evaluation criteria of finishing work
(Source : Nissan Motor Co., Ltd., "Wakakusa (Young Grass) Circle", *QC Circle Magazine*, April 2008, Case Example 3, JUSE.)

*150*

Tools Effective for "Pursuit of Success Scenarios"

## Tool 5-5

# Quality Table

### (1) What is the "Quality Table"?

The "Quality Table" is a table to systematize the user required quality by language expression, to show their relationship with quality characteristics, transform the users' requirements to alternative characteristics, and to conduct quality design.

The Table 5.7 is an Example of a basic "Quality Table." The required quality of customer (In this table, "bright and good visibility" is deployed to primary, secondary and tertiary, and evaluate them in the cross section with the quality element (quality characteristics) similarly deployed, and is used for quality planning.

Table 5.7 Typical Example of "Quality Table" (Case of Head lamp)

| Quality characteristics (Alternative characteristics) / Required quality | | | Light distribution | | | | | Luminous flux | | | | Life span / Efficiency | | | Safety | |
|---|---|---|---|---|---|---|---|---|---|---|---|---|---|---|---|---|
| | | | Light distribution score | | | | | | | | | | | | ... | ... |
| Primary | Secondary | Tertiary | Light distribution score | Size of lens | Switching angle | Standard angle | Brightness of light source | Permeability | Reflectance | Color temperature | Electric power | Voltage | Airtight | Strength of filament | Characteristic of sealing gas | ... | Redundancy | Tracking angle |
| Bright and good | Good view to long distance | Bright lamp | ○ | ○ | △ | △ | ○ | ◎ | ◎ | ○ | ◎ | ○ | | | | | |
| | | Range of brightness | ◎ | | △ | | △ | △ | △ | | △ | | | | | | |
| | | Light direction is correct | | | △ | ◎ | | | | | | | | | | | ◎ |
| | | Doesn't diffuse the light | ◎ | | | | | | | | | | | | | | |
| | Good view of near place | Bright even at down light | ○ | ○ | ◎ | △ | △ | ◎ | ◎ | ○ | ◎ | ○ | | | | | |
| | | Range of brightness | ◎ | ○ | △ | | △ | △ | △ | | △ | | | | | | ◎ |
| | | Light direction is correct | ◎ | | | | | | | | | | | | | | |
| | Good view even under special conditions | Good viewing even in bad weather | ○ | | △ | | | | | | | | | | | | |
| | | Conjunction with the handle | | | | | | | | | | | | | | | ◎ |
| | | Visible even when bounding | | | | | | | | | | | | | | | ◎ |
| | | Light direction is unchanging by dry masonry | | | | | | | | | | | | | | | ◎ |
| Characteristic value | | | JIS Requirement of light distribution | 160 φ | 1° | ±4° (Up and down, left and right) | 7.5cd/mm² | 0.9 over | 0.9 over | 3000°K | 37.5/50W | 12.8V | 0.2 pa | SAE% impact | Ar80% Nt20% | ... | ... | ... |

(Source: Akao, Yoji, ed., *Hinshitsu Tenkai Katsuyo no Jissai* (*Practice of Quality Deployment Use*), JSA, 1988.)

The "Quality Table" is used to indicate only the 2 way array of required quality deployment table and quality characteristics deployment table or the one adding the planning quality setting table and design quality setting table, etc. Here, we will introduce former "quality table" in the narrow sense.

When the "Quality Table" is used in task achieving, it is considered to be used in the following three steps.

① At the step of "Clarification of Attack Points and Setting Target" to decide the attack points grasping the desired level (the shape wanted to be) from the required quality deployment and quality planning.

② At the step of "Planning of Measures", to deploy the adopted measures (ideas) to the "Quality Table" and to narrow the measures from the required quality deployment and quality element deployment.

③ To get implementation concrete measures by deploying the selected measures at the step of "Pursuit of Success Scenarios" to "Quality Table".

## (2) The Procedures to Make "Quality Table"

The procedures to make "Quality Table" are explained using the example of radio control system of Futaba Corporation.

**Step 1. Make required quality deployment**

① Collect data for required quality

Collect information from questionnaire survey, complaints and requests. These are called raw information. These are converted to language information in concise expression and written on a card one item for each card, that will become the tertiary level required quality.

② Conduct grouping of the collected language information

Gather similar language information and the language to represent the group is decided and written on a card. This card is called affinity card, and that will become the secondary level of required quality. Further, work on these affinity cards again in the same way and make affinity

## Tools Effective for "Pursuit of Success Scenarios"

Table 5.8 Converting raw information to language information

| Raw information | Language information |
|---|---|
| · I want snap roll button 1 more or over | · can control easily<br>· can do difficult works |
| · I want neutral adjustment in transmitter side | · Operation is stable<br>· can do complex operation |

(Source: Akao, Yoji, ed., *Hinshitsu Tenkai Katsuyo no Jissai* (*Practice of Quality Deployment Use*), JSA, 1988.)

cards and that will become the primary level required quality. In the quality table building, grouping cards is generally repeated 3 times like this.

③ Make affinity diagram

Arrange all the cards scattered and make an affinity diagram surrounding each group with frame line (Refer to Fig. 5.8). Clarify the primary required quality, and rearrange while adding missing items appropriately.

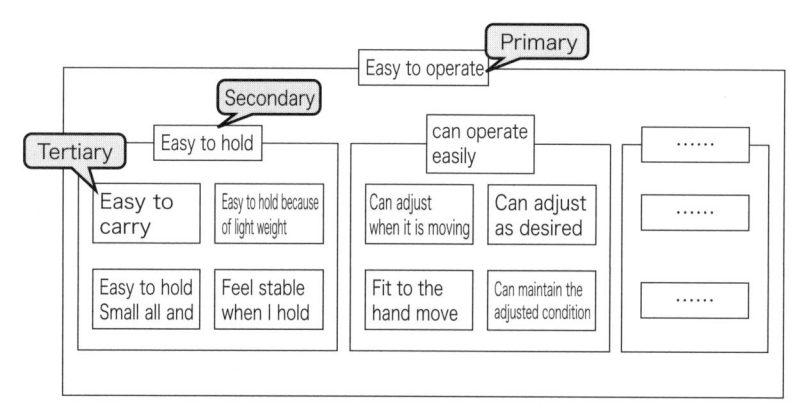

Fig.5.8 Example of grouping language information like affinity diagram

## ONE POINT

**Points of card grouping**

◆ Generally the affinity diagram is made making the level of the extracted required quality as the tertiary level. However, the abstraction level of the language is not actually clearly specified, there are many cases of that the required quality cards of high level of abstraction are made at first. When making the affinity diagram, it becomes one of the points to make the hierarchy, adjusting the abstract level of language (Refer to Fig. 5.9).

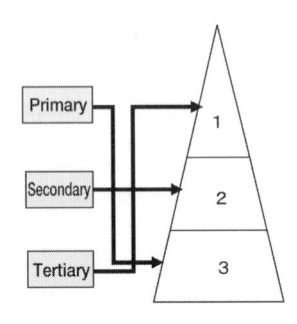

Fig.5.9 Abstract level of language and making the hierarchy

④ Complete the required quality deployment table column

After the affinity diagram is completed, put group number and arrange in the form of table and make it as required quality deployment table (Refer to Table 5.9).

**Step 2. Make quality element (quality characteristics) deployment table**

① Quality elements are selected corresponding to each item of quality requirement. In addition, collect quality element (quality characteristics) that are usually used for the theme (object) and make them as the tertiary quality elements.

② Next, make the groupings of the collected quality element with affinity diagram as the secondary quality element, and clarify the primary quality elements further grouping them. Adjust them while adding any missed items during the work and arrange them in the form of table to make it as the "quality element deployment table" (Refer to Table. 5.9 horizontal axis).

Tools Effective for "Pursuit of Success Scenarios"

Table 5.9　Example of "Quality Table"

| Quality element deployment Table | | | | Quality element | | | Operability | | | Electric performance | | |
|---|---|---|---|---|---|---|---|---|---|---|---|---|
| | | | | Secondary/Primary | | | Portability (6) | | | TRS characteristic (7) | | TS characteristic (8) |
| | | | | | Tertiary | | Size | Form | Weight | Electric current consumption | Electric temperature characteristic | Range of operating voltage | Frequency |
| Primary | Secondary | | Tertiary | | | | | | | | | | |
| 1 Easy to operate | 1 1 Easy to hold | (1) | 111 Easy to carry | | | | ◎ | ◎ | ◎ | | | | |
| | | | 112 Easy to hold because of small | | | | ◎ | ○ | | | | | |
| | | | 113 Easy to hold because of light weight | | | | ◎ | ◎ | ◎ | | | | |
| | | | 114 Feel stability when I hold | | | | ◎ | ◎ | ◎ | | | | |
| | | | 115 Stable placement | | | | ○ | ○ | ○ | | | | |
| | 1 2 No fatigue during operation | (2) | 121 Moderate weight | | | | | | | | | | |
| | | | 122 Moderate size | | | | | | | | | | |
| | 1 3 Easy to understand the operation | (3) | 131 Easy to understand in the way of using | | | | | | | | | ○ | |
| | | | 132 Easy to operate by beginner | | | | | | | | | ○ | |
| | 1 4 Easy to operate | (4) | 141 Easy to operate even it is small | | | | ○ | ○ | ○ | | | | |
| | | | 142 Easy to read ludication | | | | | | | | | ○ | |

(Source：Akao, Yoji, ed., *Hinshitsu Tenkai Katsuyo no Jissai* (*Practice of Quality Deployment Use*), JSA, 1988.)

### Step 3. Make "Quality Table" (Refer to Table 5.9)

① Combine those required quality deployment table and quality element deployment table as a L-type matrix (2 way table).

② Evaluate the strength of correspondence of the corresponding items with ◎, ○, △ and put it in at the cross section of raw (horizontal) and column (vertical).

　　◎：Strong relationship　○：Corresponding　△：Weak relationship

After the "Quality Table" is made, conduct the mechanism deployment and subsystem deployment of the product or system, and link them to the practical quality design.

### (3)　Case Example of Utilizing the "Quality Table"

The Fig. 5.10 is a case example of utilizing it in QC Circle activity. About the measures to "improve the experimental equipment for global warming", the

*155*

# Chapter 5

"Quality Table" is utilized at the step of the "Pursuit of Success Scenarios." In this case example, the "Payoff matrix" is used to get easy measures with high effectiveness and improvement measures are narrowed down, and they are deployed to the "Quality Table" to decide the "specification target" of the improved system.

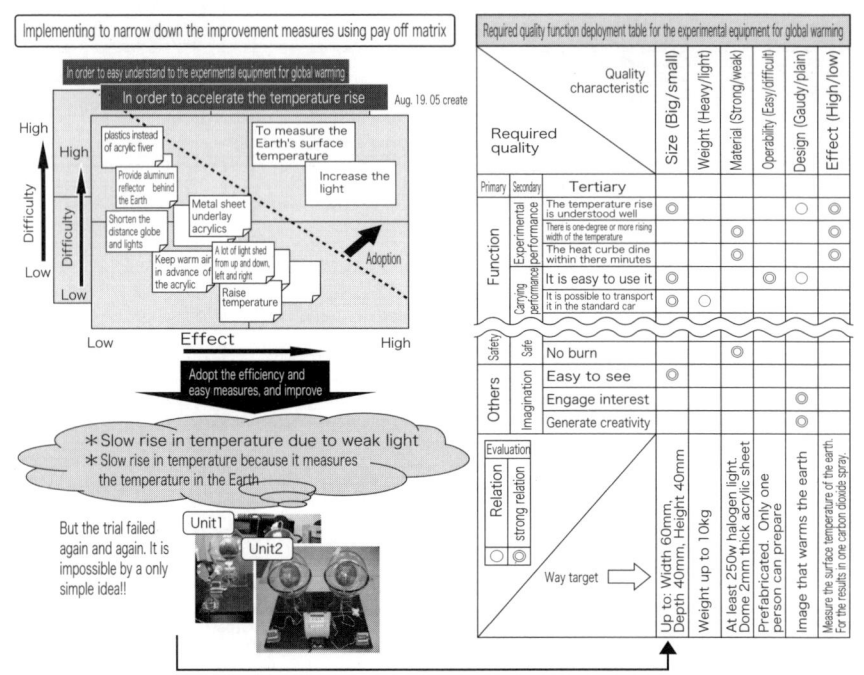

**Fig.5.10 Example of making "Quality Table" from "Payoff Matrix"**
(Source : Kansai Electric Power Co., Ltd., "Hino kuruma (Wheel of Fire) Circle" Presentation Materials at the 4970th held by the QC Circle Headquarter.)

## Tool 5-6

# Worksheet for Pursuit of Success Scenarios

## (1) What is the "Worksheet for Pursuit of Success Scenarios"

The "Worksheet for Pursuit of Success Scenarios" (Refer to table 5.10) is a worksheet to make it possible to examine the whole step of "Pursuit of Success Scenarios" at a glance. In this table, all the items that have to be examined at the "Pursuit of Success Scenarios" are covered. In the case of familiar theme or relatively easy theme, it is possible to examine directly developing on this worksheet. In the case of a big theme and the theme with high difficulty, the total picture of the step can be grasped by summarizing the results of examination at the step of "Pursuit of Success Scenarios" on this table.

By summarizing the results of examination in a table, the communalization of contents of examination becomes easy and persuasive power to the related persons including bosses will be heightened.

Table 5.10  Worksheet for Pursuit of Success Scenarios

| Measures | Concrete scenario plan | Predicted value of expected effect | Management resource | Expected effects (pros and cons) | Predicted obstacles/ side effects | Avoidance predicted obstacles/ side effects | Evaluation | Adoption or rejection |
|---|---|---|---|---|---|---|---|---|
| Measure 1 | | | | | | | | |
| Measure 2 | | | | | | | | |

## (2) Procedures to Make the "Worksheet for Pursuit of Success Scenarios"

**Step 1. Examination of Success Scenario plan**

About a measures plan adopted at "Planning of Measures", examine the

*157*

concrete scenario plan. To summarize the measures to a concrete scenario, re-confirm the "Points and Tools of Success Scenarios" explained at the beginning of this chapter. In summarizing the concrete implementation measures, more concrete success scenarios will be compiled if the scenario is summarized not only with "what" and "how" but also from the viewpoint of 5W1H such as "who" and "by when" etc.

### Step 2. Predict the expected effects

Predict the expected effects for each of the scenario plan. The expected effects should be grasped with numerical values as much as possible.

### Step 3. Predict the management resources

Predict the management resources (man/ material/ expense, etc) spent to realize the success scenario and make clear the net expected effects (gains and losses) deducting them from the predicted value of expected effects. In the case of sales theme, if certain success scenario is implemented, profit of 1 million yen is expected, but 500 thousand yen of advertising cost is anticipated, the net expected effects (gains and losses) will become the balance of 500 thousand yen.

### Step 4. Predict obstacles/ side effects and examine workarounds

Predict the obstacles in implementation and the side effects (risk) after the implementation and examine workarounds for them. In this step, the "PDPC method", the "Obstacles/ Side Effects Exclusion Examination Table" and the "Merits/ Demerits Table" are used together as needed.

### Step 5. Decide the scenario plans

Decide the adoption or rejection of the scenario plans evaluating totally the expected effects and if it is possible to work around the obstacles/ side effects. At this point, confirm if the target can be attained, totaling the expected effects of the gains and losses of adopted success scenario. When the target becomes unachievable, re-examine the scenarios that are not adopted.

## (3) Case Example of Utilizing "Worksheet for Pursuit of Success Scenarios"

Table 5.11 is a case example where the "Worksheet for Pursuit of Success Scenarios" is utilized in the theme of "30 % increase of mobilization to the QC Circle Champion Conference". In case there are those expected effects can be expressed only by language data like this case example, some devices are needed to express the expected effects (gains and losses). In this case example, evaluation is done with the priority, the priority should be made after the decision of adoption or rejections totally evaluating them as in the procedures that was explained above.

Table 5.11  Example of utilizing "Worksheet for Pursuit of Success Scenarios" on "30 % increase of mobilization to the QC Circle Champion Conference"

| Measure | Concrete scenario plans | Predicted value of expected effect | Management resource | Expected effect (pros and cons) | Predicted obstacles/ ball effects | Measures to avoid obstacles/ bad effect | Priority of implementing measures |
|---|---|---|---|---|---|---|---|
| Posting DM of championship conference on website (Ando) | Ando has a responsibility to post as soon as finishing DM | 3 persons (50×0.05) | Labor for PC input | Participants of new customer (3 peoples) | Not viewed as expected | Post website address in DM (Introduce all future event on the web, and publish DM) | 2 |
| Publish the name of participants and the on website results in DM | 1) To graph the results of a questionnaire at last year 2) Post companies participants in last year 3) Implement by conference secretariat (Murasaki manager) 4) Each secretary show to the top | Increase company interested Urcrease 20 participants | Labor to revise DM | Increase company that start delegation because of finding their delays (20 people) | Impossible to get space in DM | Mimic the DM of training leadership training | 2 |
| Place the speaker's profile | Place the profile with picture to prominent | Participants will want to join in a lot of people interested (in proportion to the popularity: 20 people) | Speaker's fee \200,000 | It is difficult to pay lecture's fee (in proportion to the popularity: 20 people) | Sudden cancellation of the speakers | List up many candidates | 2 |
| Make DM like comic | Create DM considering pictures, graphs, diagrams | Each company secretariat get interested | Labor of conference secretariat (Little) | Appeal conference | No space in DM | Strive in the range of capacity | 3 |
| | Write map as out Chiba Station (and Hon Chiba station) (from bottom to top), in the direction toward the Venue | Becomes easier to understand directions to the venue | Labor of conference secretariat | Make kind DM to participates | Nothing | Nothing | 3 |

160

Tools Effective for "Pursuit of Success Scenarios"

## Coffee Break

### "Let's Learn from the First South Pole Wintering Party"

The first South Pole Wintering Party that was conducted for one year from February 15, 1957 at the Showa base in the South Pole by the Captain Eizaburo Nishibori and other 11 people was a project using large national funds, but with the overwhelming support of the nation, it put up big result without any victim.

Mr. Nishibori had the dream to go to the South Pole some time from his young age.

The first opportunity was when he was impressed by the lecture of the Japanese first South Pole explorer Shirase First Lieutenant which his elder brother took. To realize this dream, he has said to have read many books related to the South Pole since he was young, and when he visited the USA, he met with South Pole experienced people to gather materials.

At the preliminary stage of the first South Pole Wintering Party, he obtained the things to prepare related to life and duties at the polar region by questioning many people and summarized the many information got with an affinity diagram. In this way, with self confidence as it might be said that "He believes that there is no other nation than Japanese Wintering Party with complete preparation" they left for the South Pole.

Even that, the first South Pole Wintering Party met with many hardships. The Soya that arrived at the Antarctic Ocean was blocked at once by thick ice and needed 10 days to berth at the pier of East Ongle Island. When unloading began, the load that was put on the ice began to flow with ice to the sea and became uncollectable. When transportation to the Showa Base began, snowmobiles broken sequencially, and there was real mistake to rot large amount of food at the South Pole that should have been cold.

Further, it is followed by the damage by blizzard, the failures of dynamo, and the fire at the booth.

In this way, the party has met with many sudden troubles, but with quick measures of the members trained, the damage was kept at the minimum for every one of them and accomplished the role of the wintering party wonderfully.

Among the sayings of Mr. Nishibori, there are three of them as mental attitude for conducting new things, that are "Think that sudden accidents will occur", "Important is the perfect preparation and prompt and flexible measures" and "Prompt and flexible measures should be acquired by training".

These seems to be useful as mental attitude when we tackle with the "task achieving." Especially, at the step of "Pursuit of Success Scenarios", it can be said to be important to have "complete preparation" toward the "implementation of

## Chapter 5

success scenarios", to "educate and train" sufficiently, so that "prompt and flexible measures" can be taken thinking "sudden accidents will happen".

One year later, Soya came to pick them up. However, it is blocked again by thick ice, and it was all one could do was to let the first wintering party to withdraw and the second wintering party returned to Japan together. 15 Sakhalin dogs were tied to at the Showa Base. The story of impressive Taro and Jiro.is well known in Japan.

# Chapter 6

## Tools Effective to "Implementation of Success Scenarios" ~ "Standardization and Fixing of Control"

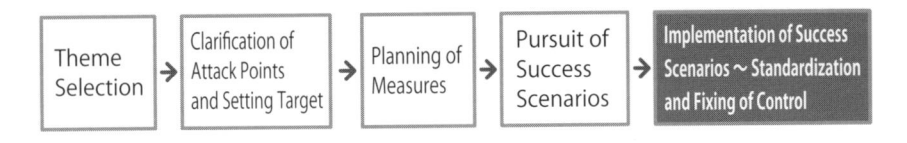

Theme Selection → Clarification of Attack Points and Setting Target → Planning of Measures → Pursuit of Success Scenarios → **Implementation of Success Scenarios ~ Standardization and Fixing of Control**

# Chapter 6

# Points and Tools for "Implementation of Success Scenarios" ~ "Standardization and Fixing of Control"

In Chapter 6, Five tools effective for remaining 3 steps of "Implementation of the Success Scenarios", "Confirmation of Effects" and "Standardization and Fixing of control" are introduced (Refer to Table 6.1). Because they are basic tools usually see often and use them well.

Table 6.1   Implementation procedures and tools effective to implementation of the success scenarios ~ standardization and fixing of control

| 【Implementation of Success Scenarios】 | 【Effective Tools】 |
|---|---|
| 1. Making Implementation plan | Tool 6-1   Gantt Chart |
| 2. Implement success scenarios | Tool 6-2   Arrow Diagram Method |
| 【Confirmation of Effects】 | Tool 6-3   PDPC Method |
| 1. Grasp tangible effect | Tool 6-4   5W1H Matrix Diagram Method |
| 2. Grasp in tangilble effect | Tool 6-5   QC 7 Tools |
| 【Standardization and fixing control】 | |
| 1. Standardization | |
| 2. Dissemination | |
| 3. Fixing of control | |

## (1)   Points of "Implementation of Success Scenarios"

In the "Implementation of Success Scenarios", it is necessary to decompose the successss scenarios into detailed implementation items, to make implementation plan, and implement them surely without omissions.

As tools for making plan, "Gantt Chart", "Arrow Diagram Method", "PDPC Method", "5W1H Matrix Diagram Method" are effective.

## (2) Points of "Confirmation of Effects"

At the step of the "Confirmation of Effects", because the confirmation of the degree of attainment of the target and side effects and the confirmation of the growth of circle and individuals are conducted, it is important to make the effects visible and to share by the all members.

As the tools, "QC 7 Tools" that can express understandably at a glance are effective. Among them, the most frequently used ones are "Pareto Diagram" and "Graphs".

## (3) Points of "Standardization and Fixing Control"

The step of "Standardization and Fixing Control" has the purpose to standardize the final success scenarios and to examine the methods for maintenance and control, and to fix them so that the implementation effects are obtained continuously. These contents are not limited to the task achieving type but should be conducted commonly to all the improvement activities. Points of this step are in the recurrence prevention and prevention before they occur of problems/ tasks by setting brake with 3 elements of standardization, dissemination (education/ training) and fixing of control, and so we will introduce the "5W1H Matrix Diagram Method" for planning for braking, and the "Graphs" in "QC 7 Tools" for continuous follow up of effects, as the effective tools.

# Chapter 6

## Tool 6-1

# Gantt Chart

## (1) What is "Gantt Chart"?

To implement success scenario without loss, it is important to decompose the scenarios into detailed implementation items, and make plan for implementation (detailed schedule), and to implement. What is most frequently used for scheduling and schedule control of operations and jobs corresponding to implementation items is the "Gantt Chart" that is also introduced in Chapter 2. It is also called as bar chart, "*yokosen koteihyo* (bar chart)" or line chart, and used in case the relatively simple rough schedule or when the number of job items are not so many (Refer to Fig. 6.1). In the task achieving type, it is frequently used as activity plan in "Selection of The Theme" and "Clarification of Attack Points and Setting Target".

| Implementation items | Role | First week in June | Second week in June | Third week in June | Fourth week in June | First week in July | Second week in July | Third week in July | Fourth week in July |
|---|---|---|---|---|---|---|---|---|---|
| Planning | a | ----► | | | | | | | |
| Adjustment of seminar lecturer | b | | ------► | | | | | | |
| Finding the place/Reservation | c | | ----► | | | | | | |
| Sorting names list | a | | ----► | | | | | | |
| Making invitation card/Sending out | b | | | | ----► | | | | |
| Summarize participants | c | | | | | ----------------► | | | |
| ⋮ | ⋮ | | | | | | | | |

(Plan -----►)　　(Implementation ———►)

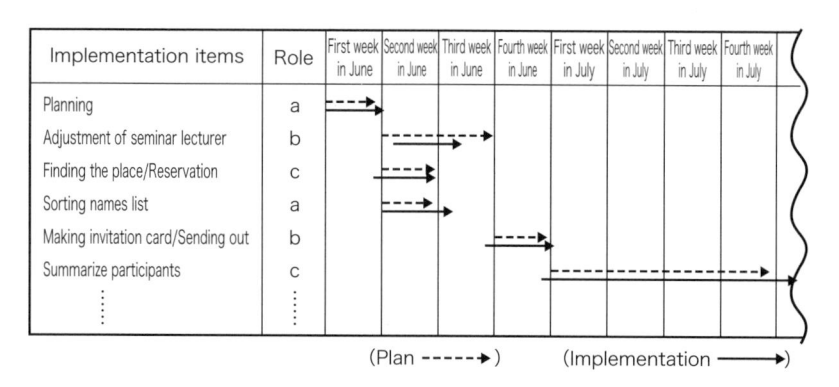

Fig.6.1 Example of "Gantt Chart" (Implementation plan of training seminar)

Because it is inappropriate in case of expressing the complex plan or mutual relation of jobs, it is recommended to use such a tool like the "Arrow Diagram Method" that will be explained later.

## (2) The Procedures to make "Gantt Chart"

### Step 1. Decompose the implementation items

Decompose the project or scenario into implementation items (jobs or work tasks).

### Step 2. Estimate time

Estimate the time (days) necessary to conduct each item.

### Step 3. Enter vertical axis/ horizontal axis

These implementation items are written on the vertical axis like the Fig. 6.1, on the horizontal axis take time like month, week, or days, and show the necessary period for each item with plan line (bar or arrow). Here, make it the beginning of the plan line shows the start of the job and the end of the so that plan line shows the end period.

Because the "Gantt Chart" shows the job period at a glance, it is easy to understand for the manager of the whole project and the person in charge of the job and it is also effective for progress management. For progress management, if the period actually needed is written under the plan line as the implementation line, one can grasp the late or early against the job plan.

## (3) Case Example of the "Gantt Chart"

Fig. 6.2 is the implementation example of the "Gantt Chart". Persons in charge are written in the table and the roles and responsibilities are made clear.

# Chapter 6

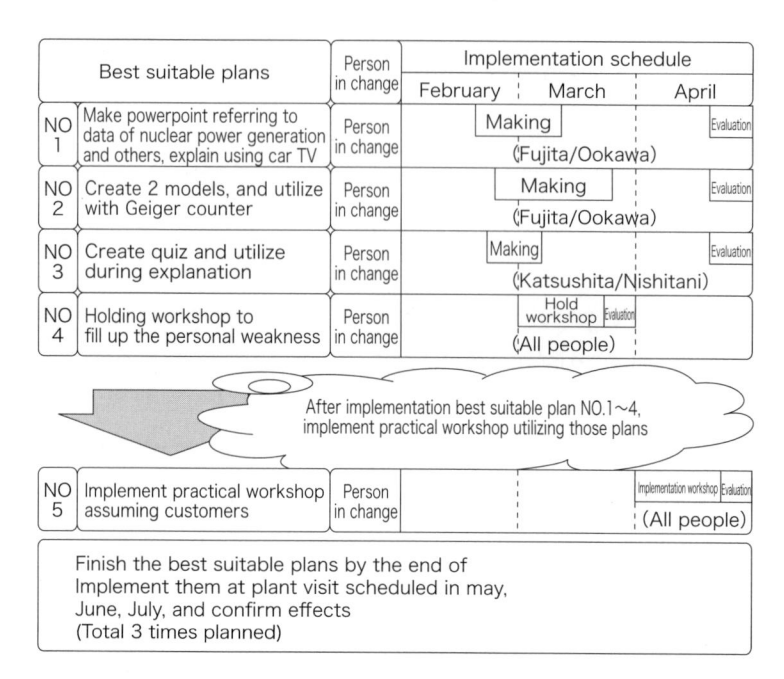

| Best suitable plans | | Person in change | Implementation schedule |||
|---|---|---|---|---|---|
| | | | February | March | April |
| NO 1 | Make powerpoint referring to data of nuclear power generation and others, explain using car TV | Person in change | Making (Fujita/Ookawa) | | Evaluation |
| NO 2 | Create 2 models, and utilize with Geiger counter | Person in change | | Making (Fujita/Ookawa) | Evaluation |
| NO 3 | Create quiz and utilize during explanation | Person in change | Making | (Katsushita/Nishitani) | Evaluation |
| NO 4 | Holding workshop to fill up the personal weakness | Person in change | | Hold workshop (All people) | Evaluation |

After implementation best suitable plan NO.1~4, implement practical workshop utilizing those plans

| NO 5 | Implement practical workshop assuming customers | Person in change | | | Implementation workshop Evaluation (All people) |

Finish the best suitable plans by the end of
Implement them at plant visit scheduled in may,
June, July, and confirm effects
(Total 3 times planned)

**Fig.6.2 Implementation plan using "Gantt chart"**

(Source : Kansai Electric Power Co., Ltd., "Challenge Up Circle", *QC Circle Magazine*, Feb., 2003, Case Example 1, JUSE.)

Tools Effective to "Implementation of Success Scenarios" ~ "Standardization and Fixing of Control"

### Tool 6-2

# Arrow Diagram Method

## (1) What is the "Arrow Diagram Method"?

When the implementation items are various and the many implementation items are intermingled complexly, it is necessary to make schedule that uses a network. The representative technique is the PERT[Note]. In the new QC 7 tools, this is called as "Arrow Diagram" (*ya sen zu*). When this is used, the dependent interrelationship among the jobs and important points of control become easy to grasp and it is useful to predict the degree of effects to the whole schedule and changes of plan when a certain job is late or early.

> (Note) PERT: A tool for scheduling and control developed in the U.S.A. It is the abbreviation of Program Evaluation and Review Technique.

The features of the "Arrow Diagram Method" lies in the following points.

① It is easy to grasp the whole image of the jobs, and the problems in the process and important points can be made clear before starting the jobs.

② When the network is drawn, one can find unexpected hints for improvement and the measures for schedule shortening.

③ It is easy to grasp the state of job progression and one can take earlier actions looking forward of the effects to others and problems in case of change in the plan.

④ It is easy to get mutual understanding and common understanding among the parties concerned.

The meanings of the symbols in the "Arrow Diagram Method" are shown in the Table 6.2. The identification numbers are given to nodes and it is called the node numbers.

Table 6.2  Meaning of symbols in "Arrow Diagram"

| Symbol | Name | Meaning |
|---|---|---|
| ──▶ | Jobs | Element work that requires time |
| ○ | Node | Separation between jobs. It is the end point of a job and the beginning of the next job |
| ----▶ | Dummy | Required time is zero, which simply indicates the sequence of the jobs involved. |

## (2) Procedures to Make the "Arrow Diagram Method"

### Step 1. Decompose to implementation items and write them on labels

Decompose success scenarios to detailed implementation items (job items) and write them on labels.

### Step 2. Estimate the days and clarify the interrelationship of dependency among the items

Estimate the necessary days (time) for each item, and clarify the interrelationship of dependency among the items like whether there is sequence among the items, are there any items that can be processed concurrently, and so forth.

### Step 3. Arrange item labels

Based on the interrelationship, arrange the item labels (jobs) along the time series from left to right direction with the relationship of preceding job and following job.

### Step 4. Position the item labels

Position the path with the most item labels that are arranged in a series on the center line.

### Step 5. Arrange the item labels at appropriate places

Arrange the item labels in the relationship of parallel to each appropriate place.

### Step 6. Write the node numbers and the days needed for the jobs

If all the item labels are able to be arranged, write the graphical symbols, and write in the node number in the order of the jobs. It will be completed when necessary days for the jobs are written under the job arrow.

Fig. 6.3 is a model for the "Arrow Diagram".

In such a way, when the days needed for each implementation items (jobs) are calculated and the earliest node time (it cannot be started by this date at the earliest) and the latest node time (it should be finished by this day at the latest) are written, schedule control can be done efficiently.

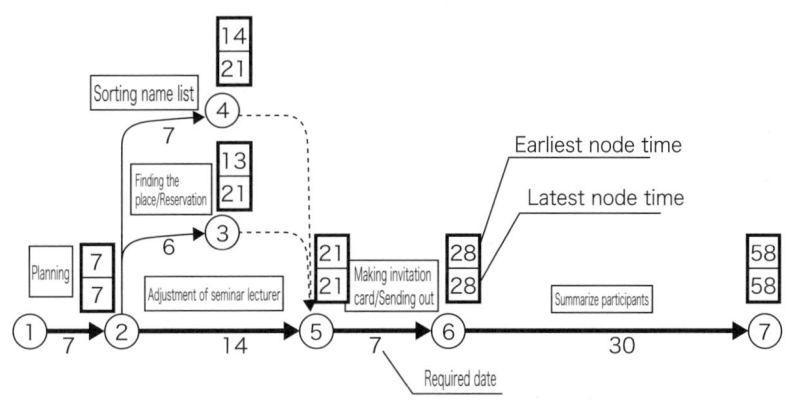

Fig.6.3 Model of "Arrow Diagram" (implementation plan for training seminar)

## (3) Case Example of Utilizing the "Arrow Diagram"

Fig. 6.4 and Fig. 6.5 are the examples of utilizing the "Arrow Diagram" by QC circles. The "Arrow Diagram" and "Matrix Diagram" is combined excellently.

## Chapter 6

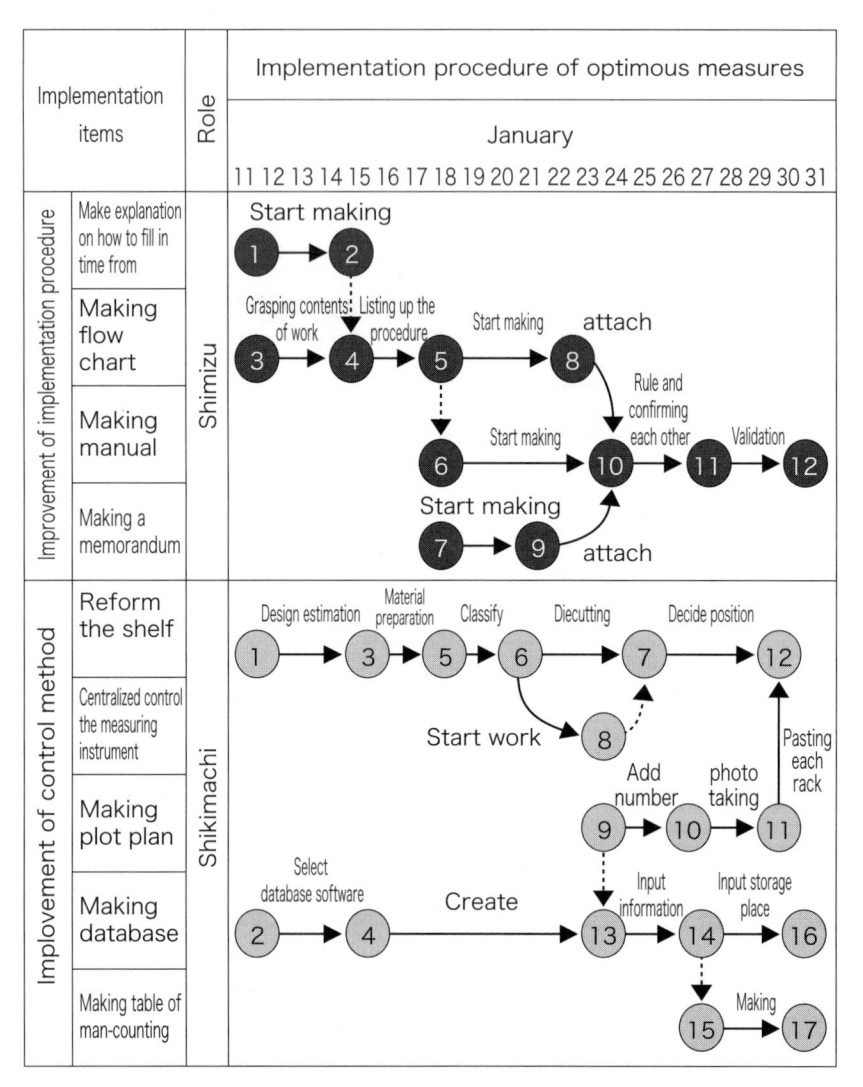

Fig.6.4  Implementation plan by "Arrow Diagram"

(Source : 2nd Air Wing, Air Self-Defense Force, "Key Point Circle", *QC Circle Magazine*, May 2006, Special Issue Case Example, JUSE.)

Tools Effective to "Implementation of Success Scenarios" ~ "Standardization and Fixing of Control"

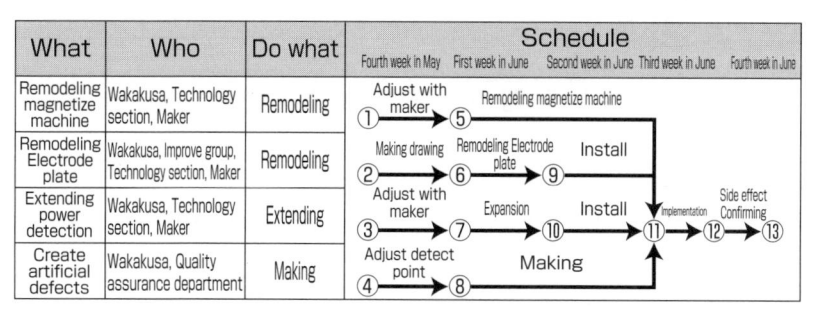

| What | Who | Do what | Schedule ||||| 
|---|---|---|---|---|---|---|---|
| | | | Fourth week in May | First week in June | Second week in June | Third week in June | Fourth week in June |
| Remodeling magnetize machine | Wakakusa, Technology section, Maker | Remodeling | Adjust with maker ①→⑤ | Remodeling magnetize machine | | | |
| Remodeling Electrode plate | Wakakusa, Improve group, Technology section, Maker | Remodeling | Making drawing ②→⑥ | Remodeling Electrode plate | Install ⑨ | | |
| Extending power detection | Wakakusa, Technology section, Maker | Extending | Adjust with maker ③→⑦ | Expansion | Install ⑩ | Implementation ⑪→⑫ | Side effect Confirming ⑬ |
| Create artificial defects | Wakakusa, Quality assurance department | Making | Adjust detect point ④→⑧ | Making | | | |

Fig.6.5 Implementing plan of Success Scenarios

(Source : Nissan Motor Co., Ltd., "Wakakusa (Young Grass) Circle", *QC Circle Magazine*, April 2008, Case Example 3, JUSE.)

## ◻NE POINT

### Story of PERT

◆ PERT is the one developed as a new technique of plan and control in the United States in 1958. It was applied to the Polaris missile manufacturing, and the development delivery date is said that two years were shortened. Because the arrow line is used to indicate the schedule, it is called "Arrow diagram method". After the introduction to Japan around 1960, it spread and it came to be used in the fields of engineering works, construction and a new product development, etc.

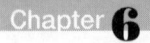

## Tool 6-3

# PDPC Method

## (1) What is the "PDPC (Process Decision Program Chart) Method"?

The "PDPC Method" is, as it is explained in the Chapter 5, a tool to be used in case, when planning and predicting the execution process, information is lacking or there is a worry that it might not go as the original plan. As a form, it is expressed as a chart that connects one or plural processes or steps with arrows along the sequence of transits of time from the start of the plan through to the final results.

## (2) Case Example of How to Use it in the "Implementation of Success Scenarios"

The uses of the "PDPC Method" in "Implementation of Success Scenarios" is, while implementing based on the "Success Scenarios PDPC" made at the "Pursuit of Success Scenarios", to add newly found implementation items and the measures to overcome the factors of new obstacles, and to keep the finally re-written "implemented PDPC" as the records.

---

**ONE POINT**

### Development Story of PDPC Method

◆ The developer is Dr. Jiro Kondo. To cope with the University of Tokyo Conflict in 1968, Professor Jiro Kondo of Engineering Department at that time developed it as a tool for problem solving/ decision making. Taking the acronym of Process Decision Program Chart, it came to be called as PDPC Method. There is almost no case that the originally made program chart maintains the original shape, and along with the development of situation, it is re-written by adding new facts and measures to exclude obstacle factors.

Tools Effective to "Implementation of Success Scenarios" ~ "Standardization and Fixing of Control"

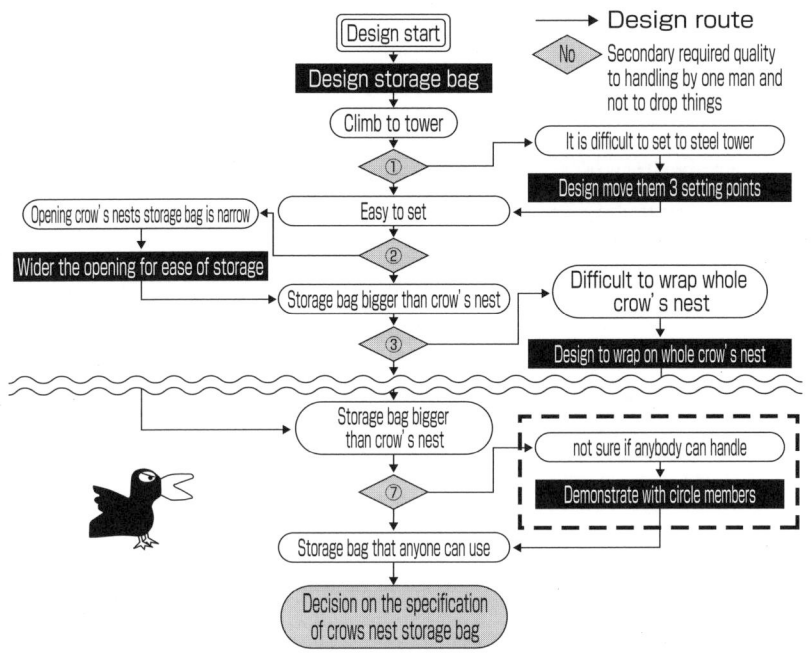

Fig.6.6 Result of examining storage bag by "PDPC"
(Source : Kansai Electric Power Co., Ltd., "Chameleon Circle", *QC Circle Magazine*, Sept. 2003, Case Example 1, JUSE.)

【Reference】 Flow Chart

There is the "Flow Chart (Flow diagram or Flow Job Chart" that is similar to the "PDPC Method". The flow chart is to arrange the job and process one by one dividing them into steps and it shows the sequence them clearly with symbols and lines, and is often used to show the process and steps of information processing or work process. Be careful not to mix them by understanding the difference between both of them. Fig. 6.7 is the case example of testing flow by a new system developed by applying success scenarios.

## Chapter 6

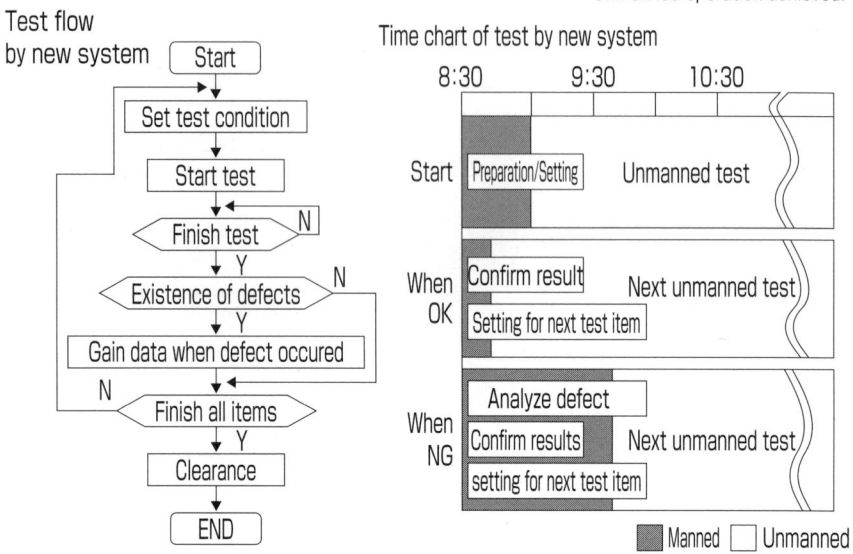

**Test flow by new system**

```
        Start
          ↓
   Set test condition
          ↓
      Start test  ←─────┐
          ↓             │
      Finish test ──N───┤
          ↓Y            │
   Existence of defects ─N─┐
          ↓Y               │
  Gain data when defect occured
          ↓            │
    ←─────┘────────────┘
    N
     Finish all items
          ↓Y
       Clearance
          ↓
        END
```

**Time chart of test by new system**　　Unmanned operation achieved!

| | 8:30 | 9:30 | 10:30 |
|---|---|---|---|
| Start | Preparation/Setting | Unmanned test | |
| When OK | Confirm result | Next unmanned test | |
| | Setting for next test item | | |
| When NG | Analyze defect | | |
| | Confirm results | Next unmanned test | |
| | setting for next test item | | |

■ Manned　□ Unmanned

Fig.6.7　Flow chart for a new system developed

(Source : Nissan Motor Co., ltd., "Denshiman (Electron Man) Circle", *QC Circle Magazine*, Feb, 2002, Case Example 1, JUSE.)

## Tool 6-4

# 5W1H Matrix Diagram Method

### (1) What is the "5W1H Matrix Diagram Method"?

In the implementation plan and standardization plan of simple success scenarios, the "5W1H Matrix Diagram Method" is often used. The "Matrix Method" is a technique to generate idea, concept, and to judge focusing on the intersection of two ways table, structured with factors that belong to row and factors belong to column. In the intersection, data or judgment symbols or contents (language) are written. The "Matrix Diagram", has many types from its shape and pattern such as L-type, T-type, Y-type, etc., but L-type is often used for implementation plan and standardization plan.

### (2) How to Use the "5W1H Matrix Diagram"

In execution plan, execution plan without missing is made by first developing implementation items (what) on the first column and by clarifying who, by when, at where, why and how on the 2nd column and after.

### (3) Case Example of Utilizing the "5W1H Matrix Diagram Method"

Table 6.3 is an example of implementation plan of success scenarios.

For the implementation plan of "Standardization and Fixing of Control", standardization plan without mission is established with 5W1H and executed (Refer to Table 6.4, 6.5).

## Table 6.3 Implementation plan of success scenario "5W1H Matrix Diagram"

### 1. Making implementation plan [Plan]

| No | What | Who | When | Where | Why | How |
|---|---|---|---|---|---|---|
| 1 | Cordinate with related sections | Chief | End May | Own group | Prevent defect occurrence | Hold meeting to adjust |
| 2 | Study meeting with in group | Chief | End May | Own group | Horizontal depelopment to members | Develop the implementing contents |
| 3 | Amount of paints added | Kawai Shinozaki | Mid-June | workshop | Decline solid content value | Adjust by changing values |
| 4 | Liquid temperature of electrodepositen lank | Shiobara Ozeki | Mid-June | workshop | Lower the temperature conducting time | Change setting values |
| 5 | Voltage/conductig time | Isobe Kasuya | Mid-June | workshop | Change voltage and conducting time | Add/change setting value |

### 2. Implementation [Do]

1) Coordination with other sections, and conduct in group study meeting

Technology section ▶ Examine predicted problems and implement adjustment
(Implementation adjustment meeting with paint manufacturers)

| No | Predicted problem | Measures |
|---|---|---|
| 1 | Incorrect operation by human error | Implementation of group study meeting / Add checkpoint for weekend and start of the week |
| 2 | Effect in quality lower film thickness | Operate at the center of control value / When setting change |

Maintenance ▶ Implement adjustment of operation method for each equipment hold study

Implementation contents ▶ Implement workshop in each equipment by 5-gen izm

(Source : Nissan Motor Co., Ltd., "PB Circle", *QC Circle Magazine*, Sept. 2001, Case Example 1, JUSE.)

## Table 6.4 Matrix Diagram for fixing of control

| Measure | Why | Who | When | Where | What | How |
|---|---|---|---|---|---|---|
| Utilizing approach-books | To recognize the need for reconstruction practically | sales in charge | As needed | Visiting place | Approach-book | Utilize and explain |
| Updating the list of owners | To suggest according to progress of the time table | sales in charge | As needed | Work place | Database of old building owner | Revised and keep the latest information |
| Role playing study meeting | To share sales skill | Hosono | Once a month | Work place | Role playing workshop | Hold and teach |
| Field study | Make field study efficient and sharing information | Each sales | As needed | At the spot | Making study report | Implement and input to database |

(Source : Polus Grand Tec Co., Ltd., "Oshare (dress up) Shisanzei (assets tax) Circle", *QC Circle Magazine*, April2006, Case Example 3, JUSE.)

## Table 6.5 Matrix Diagram of standardization and fixing of control

| Item | What | When | Where | Whi | Why | How |
|---|---|---|---|---|---|---|
| Standardization | Confirmation method of irradiation position | Dec/19 | Station | Nagaki | Confirmation of work method | Revision of work process standard |
| Education | Manual of confirming irradiation position | Dec.22 | at work place | Nagaki | Unification of work | Implementation of OJT job training |
| Maintenance control | Confirming work of irradiation position | Once a month | at work place | Worker | Assurance of precision | Implementation of periodic check |

(Source : Nissan Motor Co., Ltd., "Clean World Circle", *QC Circle Magazine*, June, 2005, Case Example 2, JUSE.)

Tools Effective to "Implementation of Success Scenarios" ~ "Standardization and Fixing of Control"

In the case example in Fig. 6.8, the standardization and fixing of control plan with 5W1H and the state of maintenance control of effects by line chart of "QC 7 Tool".

Implement 5W1H                               Author: Shinozaki

| NO | Why | What | Who | When | Where | How |
|----|-----|------|-----|------|-------|-----|
| 1 | Standardization | Amount of supplied paints Table of changes | Advisor | Until Jun.16 | Office | Make a fresh |
| 2 | Standardization | Setting point of liquid temperature Table of changes | Advisor | Until Jun.16 | Office | Make a fresh |
| 3 | Standardization | Standard work manual | Advisor | Until Jun.16 | Office | Make a fresh |
| 4 | Recording | Contents of changes | Worker | When conditions change | Shopfloor | Write in table of changes |
| 5 | Prevent omission | Table of changes | Chief Advisor | When conditions change | Shopfloor | Confirm/Check |
| 6 | Maintain and continue effect | Condition of liquid | Leader Advisor | Once in week | Shopfloor | Coordinate with maker |
| 7 | Disceminete | Provision of information | Chief | Once in week | Rest area | Hold group meeting |

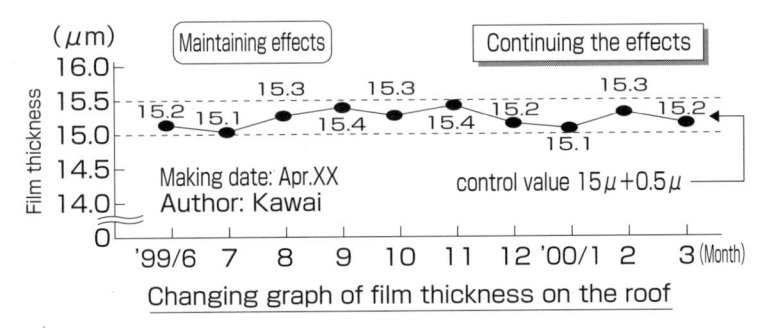

Fig.6.8 Standardization and fixing of control

(Source : Nissan Motor Co., Ltd., "PB Circle", *QC Circle Magazine*, Sept. 2001, Case Example 1, JUSE.)

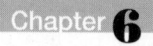

## Tool 6-5

# QC 7 Tools

## (1) What is "QC 7 Tools"?

At the step of the "Confirmation of Effects", it is usual to use the "QC 7 Tools" to show the effects of before and after the improvement for ease of understanding.

As the representative ones, there are "Pareto Diagram", "Graph" (bar chart, line chart, radar chart), "Histogram", "Control Chart" and so forth.

## (2) How to Use the "QC 7 tools"

What is important in using the "QC 7 Tools" is to choose the most appropriate one to show the data of activities among the many tools.

To visualize, by putting making the data and results into diagram and chart using the "QC 7 Tools", is useful not only to share information among the members but also to make it understandable and persuasive when explaining to the boss and others.

## (3) Case Example of utilizing the "QC 7 Tools"

4 typed of case examples are introduced in Fig. 6.9 (Pareto Diagram), Fig. 6.10 (Histogram), Fig. 6.11 (Bar Chart), Fig. 6.12 (Line Graph).

Fig. 6.10 is, in the process of heat processing with the parts attached on a tray, a case example of reduction of distortion by ascertaining that the distortion occurs to the part shape by the difference in pre-heating, and by changing the temperature setting.

Tools Effective to "Implementation of Success Scenarios" ~ "Standardization and Fixing of Control"

Comparison of man hours for multi link front assembly before and after the countermeasures

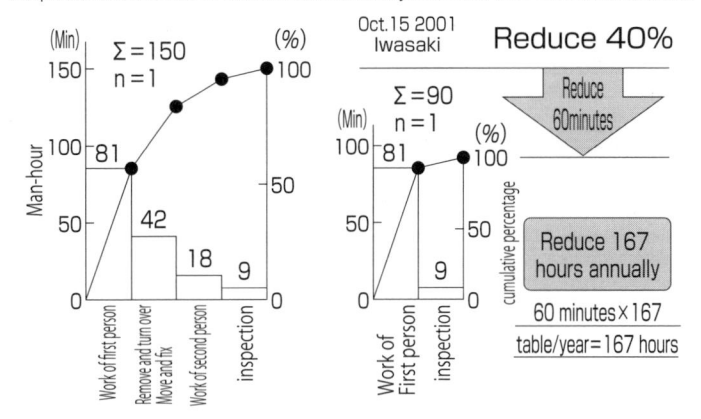

**Fig.6.9  Confirming Effect by "Pareto Diagram"**

(Source：Nissan Motor Co., Ltd., "Climb Circle", *QC Circle Magazine*, April 2004, Case Example 1, JUSE.)

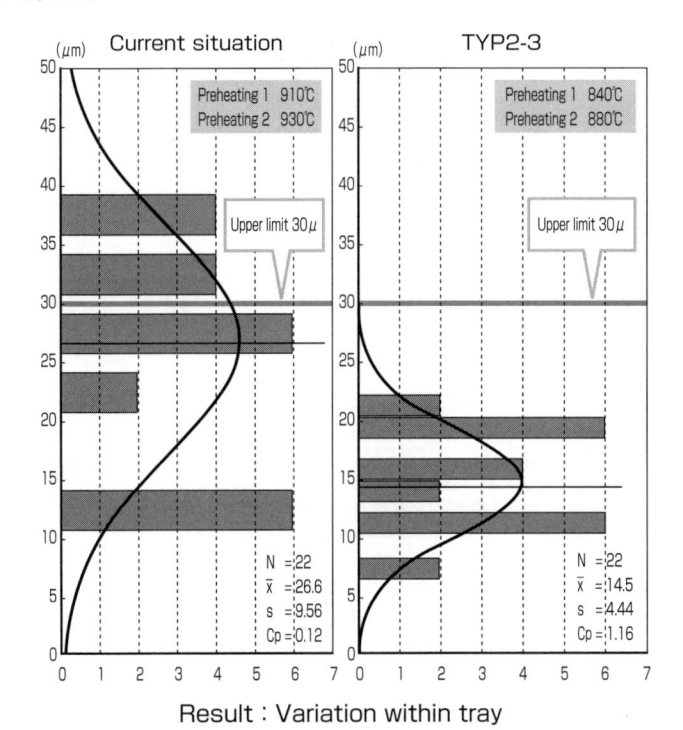

Result：Variation within tray

**Fig.6.10  Confirming Effect by "Histogram"**

(Source：Honda Co. Ltd., "Kamataki (Boiler) man Circle", *QC Circle Magazine*, May 2004, Special Feature Case example, JUSE.)

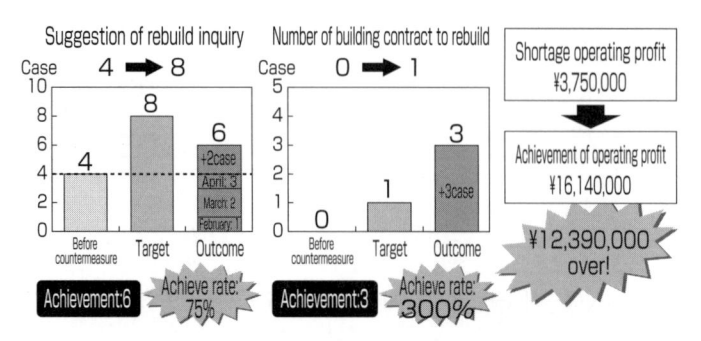

**Fig. 6.11 Confirming effect by Bar Chart**

(Source : Polus Grand Tec Co., Ltd., "Oshare (dress up) Shisanzei (assets tax) Circle", *QC Circle Magazine*, April2006, Case Example 3, JUSE.)

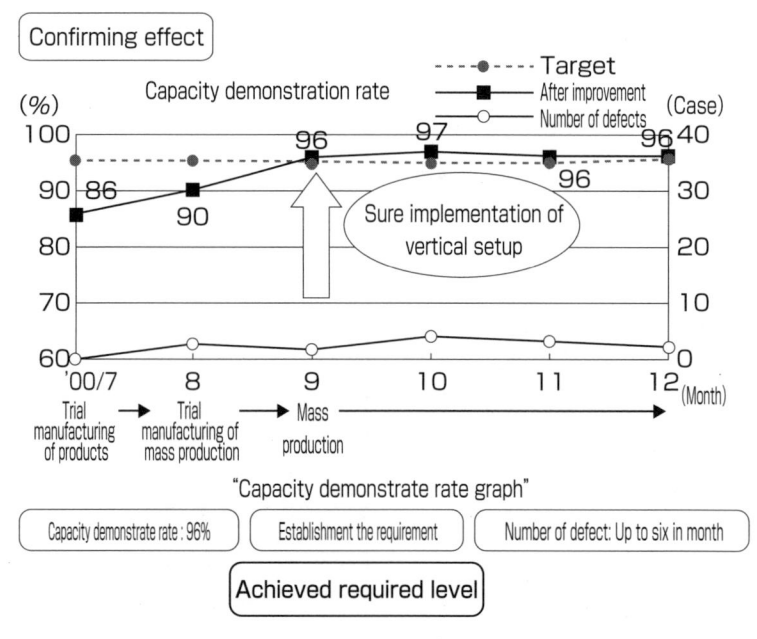

**Fig.6.12 Confirming Effect by "Line Graph"**

(Source : Konica Co., ltd. "AP-50 unite Circle", *QC Circle Magazine*, Jan. 2002, Case Example, JUSE.)

Among the graphs, the "radar chart" is most frequently used when showing the intangible effects. The "radar chart" is where lines are extended from the center of the circle as many as the number of classification items that you want to show, and to express the size of the quantity by the length of bar from the center, and the plot points are connected by straight line. When the before activity (dotted line) and after activity (solid line), or data with different element are written on the same chart, the bias among the evaluation items or the judgment of the size of effects of activity can be grasped at a glance. Fig. 6.13 is a case example of intangible effects of comparison of circle diagnosis between before and after on a "Radar Chart".

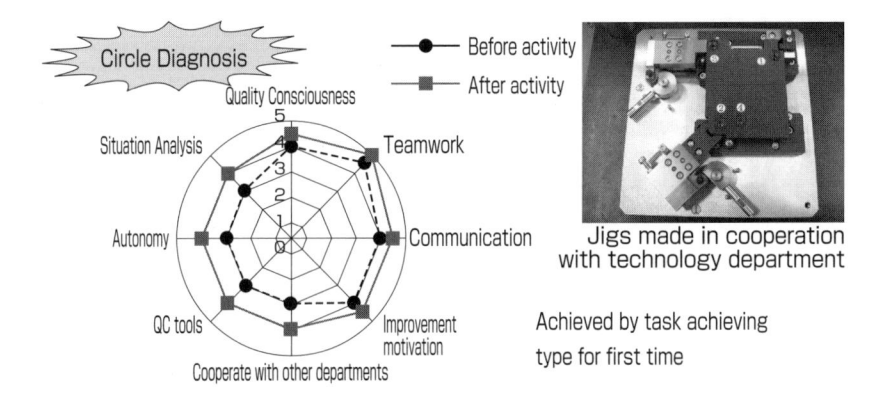

Fig.6.13 Confirming Intangible Effects by "Radar Chart"
(Source : Hitachi Global Storage Technologies, "25TEST Circle", *QC Circle Magazine*, March 2009, Case Example 1, JUSE.)

# Chapter 7

## To Utilize "Task Achieving" Effectively

## 7-1

# Let's Become an Expert of Tools

Since the approach of task achieving has big freedom, it may be difficult to tackle with, but one could proceed the activity effectively/ efficiently if the tools studied up to the Chapter 6 are used well.

Here, let's review the importance of tools again.

For example, first class dishes are made possible because first class cock cooks by the best cooking method, preparing necessary materials (vegetables, meat, seasonings), using appropriate tools (knife, cutting board, pot).

Similarly to this, the improvement activities that generate big effects are realized by conducting an activity where well studied members gather necessary data and information, using appropriate tools and with appropriate procedures (problem solving and task achieving).

The tools taken up in this book correspond to these appropriate equipment/ tools. To utilize tools, following two things are important. The first is to master how to use the basic tools recommended and the tools taken up in this book. The second is to look to the new tools developed/ introduced along with the progress of management techniques, and to find out the tools that most appropriate to you. There are many tools other than the tools taken up in this book.

From the ancient times, it is said the masters in one field obtained good tools and used well to the extent they fit to their hands. Tools become the sharper when used more, and will get rusted if not used. We hope you too become masters and solve the important tasks in your workshop deftly! The tools/ techniques effective to task achieving is summarized in Table 7.1. Those who want to know each of them in details, please refer to the books in the special field.

## To Utilize "Task Achieving" Effectively

### Table 7.1 Tools Useful for Task Achieving

| Group | Tool, Method | Chapter in this book | Group | Tool, Method | Chapter in this biik |
|---|---|---|---|---|---|
| QC 7 tools | Check sheet | Chapter 3 | Creativity technique | Brainstorming method | Chapter 4 |
| QC 7 tools | Graph | Chapter 3,6 | Creativity technique | Brain writing method | Chapter 4 |
| QC 7 tools | Histogram | Chapter 6 | Creativity technique | Wish-points listing method | Chapter 4 |
| QC 7 tools | Pareto diagram | Chapter 3,6 | Creativity technique | Defects listing method | Chapter 4 |
| QC 7 tools | Cause and effect diagram | | Creativity technique | Checklist method | Chapter 4 |
| QC 7 tools | Scatter diagram | | Creativity technique | Attribute listing method | |
| QC 7 tools | Control chart | | Creativity technique | Morphological analysis | |
| QC 7 tools | Stratification | Chapter 3 | Creativity technique | What if? technique focused object technique | |
| New QC 7 tools | Affinity diagram | | Creativity technique | Object technique | Chapter 4 |
| New QC 7 tools | Relation diagram | | Creativity technique | Visual connection technique | Chapter 4 |
| New QC 7 tools | Tree diagram | Chapter 4 | Creativity technique | Gordon technique | |
| New QC 7 tools | Matrix diagram | Chapter 6 | New product planning & management | Group interview | |
| New QC 7 tools | Arrow diagram | Chapter 6 | New product planning & management | Questionnaire survey | Chapter 3 |
| New QC 7 tools | PDPC | Chapter 5,6 | New product planning & management | Positioning analysis | |
| New QC 7 tools | Matrix data analysis | | New product planning & management | Table type conceptualization | |
| SQC | Test · estimate of variables of attribute | | New product planning & management | Conjoint analysis | |
| SQC | Test · Inspection of enumerated data | | New product planning & management | Quality table (QFD) | Chapter 5 |
| SQC | Correlation and regression analysis · multiple regression analysis | | New product planning & management | Fault Tree Analysis | |
| SQC | Analysis of variance | | New product planning & management | Failure mode and effect analysis | Chapter 5 |
| SQC | Multivariate analysis | | New product planning & management | SWOT analysis | Chapter 3 |
| SQC | Experimental design | | New product planning & management | KT method | |
| SQC | Reliability analysis | | New product planning & management | Benchmarking | Chapter 3 |
| IE | Motion study: Motion analysis | | The tools/techniques specific to task achieving | Gantt chart | Chapter 2,6 |
| IE | Motion study: Principles of motion economy | | The tools/techniques specific to task achieving | Problems/Tasks digging up checksheet | Chapter 2 |
| IE | Time study: Time analysis | | The tools/techniques specific to task achieving | Problems/Tasks selection sheet | Chapter 2 |
| IE | Time study: Operation analysis | | The tools/techniques specific to task achieving | Problems/Tasks narrowing down evaluation table | Chapter 2 |
| IE | Method study: Process analysis | | The tools/techniques specific to task achieving | Kaizen(improvement)procedures selection method | Chapter 2 |
| IE | Method study: Flow analysis | | The tools/techniques specific to task achieving | Investigation Items Selection Table | Chapter 3 |
| IE | Method study: Material handling analysis | | The tools/techniques specific to task achieving | Attack Points Selection Sheet | Chapter 3 |
| | | | The tools/techniques specific to task achieving | Obstacles/ Side effects exclusion examination table | Chapter 5 |
| | | | The tools/techniques specific to task achieving | Merit/Demerit table | Chapter 5 |
| | | | The tools/techniques specific to task achieving | Worksheet for pursuing success scenarios | Chapter 5 |

*187*

## 7-2

# Let's Learn from Case Examples of Task Achieving Activities

> Case Example of JHS (Jimu : work, Hanbai : Sales, Service Department)

## A Challenge to the Attractive Delivery Lectures to Next Generation Group

Kansai Electric Power Ltd. Naniwa Business Office, Director's Room
"Hinokuruma Circle"
(Derived from Proceeding of 4970th QC Circle Conference sponsored by the QC Circle Headquarter)

Naniwa Business Office of Kansai Electric Power is supplying electricity to the South of Osaka city where the sightseeing spots like Shinsai Bridge and Tsuten Kaku are located. Since the year 2000, the director's office, where the circle belongs, is working on the activity to increase KEPCO fans of the future by conducting the "delivery lectures to next generation group" (delivery lectures, hereafter) mainly to 5th year student of elementary school to let them have correct knowledge and interest to energy and global environmental problems.

This is the case example of getting great results by taking in rich ideas to teaching contents, texts, and programs utilizing customers' voices and many techniques and tools of task achieving type approach, to enhance the evaluation of the students and teachers on the delivery lectures further. It can be said the case example of "breakthrough".

To Utilize "Task Achieving" Effectively

## Step 1  Selection of the Theme

Utilizing "Problems/ Tasks Digging out Checklist" and "Problems/ tasks Selection Sheet", they ferreted out the things concerned, and for each of them, what is known and what is unknown are confirmed and the tentative themes were decided (Refer to Fig. 7.1). On the tentative themes, evaluation items of importance, urgency, desired level, cost, boss's policy and effects are set and weighted, and evaluation were done, and decided the theme to tackle as the "Challenge to the Attractive Delivery Lectures to Next Generation Group" (Refer to Fig. 7.2). The activity period was set to 11 months, and the activity plan with primarily responsible person for each step was made and entered the activity (Refer to Fig. 7.3).

### ONE POINT

◆ When digging out and ferreting out problems/ tasks, many tentative themes can be ferreted out if they are done carefully from the 4 checkpoints of using the recommended tools.

Making: Jun.2.2005

| Checkpoint | What concerns you | What is known | What is unknown | Tentative theme |
|---|---|---|---|---|
| What is upper policy? | Does safety have priority over other things in work place? | Safety awareness is still low | If safety rules are observed | How to let them observe the safety rules perfectly |
| | Self-development is low | Personal motivation for self actualization is low | If they knows the means of self development | How to activate self-development |
| | QC circle activity is inactive | Purpose of QC circle activity become to only for presentation | If methods and technique are understood | How to activate QC Circle activity |
| | | There is no time to join in QC circle activity | | |
| | Work improvement suggestion in inactive | There is no time to revise idea to propose and to be modified | | How to activate work improvement suggestion |
| What is customer's demands? | Doesn't customer service suffice in director office? | There is some complaint in branch office | Are the other department satisfied | How to improve satisfaction in customer service |
| What are problems and tasks expected in the future? | Resolution rate of charge payable on site utility pole | It goes left worse if | Lack of land owner information | How to raise resolution rate of charge on site utility pole |
| What are the things desired higher than current level? | There are complaints to some of delivery lectures for next generation | Demand for class contents become higher | What are the demand | How to improve quality of delivery lectures for next generation |

Fig.7.1 Ferreting out the theme by "Problems/Tasks Digging out/Selection Sheet"

(Point allotment) ○:3pt. △:2pt. ×:1pt.　05/06/02

| No. | Problems and Tasks | Importance | Urgency | Possibility | Cost | Boss's policy | Effects | Overall evaluation |
|---|---|---|---|---|---|---|---|---|
| 1 | How to let them observe the safety rule perfectly | ○ | △ | △ | △ | ○ | △ | 144 |
| 2 | How to activate self-development | △ | × | × | ○ | ○ | × | 18 |
| 3 | How to activate QC Circle activity | △ | △ | × | ○ | ○ | △ | 72 |
| 4 | How to activate work improvement suggestion | △ | △ | × | ○ | ○ | △ | 72 |
| 5 | How to improve satisfaction for customer service | ○ | △ | △ | △ | ○ | △ | 144 |
| 6 | How to raise resolution rate of charge on site utility pole | ○ | ○ | △ | × | ○ | ○ | 162 |
| 7 | How to improve quality of delivery lectures for next generation | ○ | △ | ○ | △ | ○ | △ | 216 |

'Decided the theme to "Challenge to the attractive delivery lectures to next generation group"

Fig.7.2　Deciding the theme by "Problems/Tasks narrowing down evaluation table"

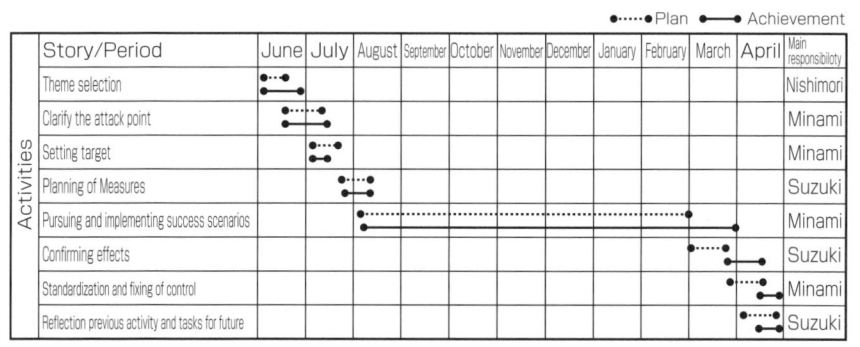

●·····● Plan　●——● Achievement

| Activities | Story/Period | June | July | August | September | October | November | December | January | February | March | April | Main responsibility |
|---|---|---|---|---|---|---|---|---|---|---|---|---|---|
| | Theme selection | ●·●| | | | | | | | | | | Nishimori |
| | Clarify the attack point | ●···● | | | | | | | | | | | Minami |
| | Setting target | ●···● | | | | | | | | | | | Minami |
| | Planning of Measures | | ●···● | | | | | | | | | | Suzuki |
| | Pursuing and implementing success scenarios | | | ●·················● | | | | | | | | | Minami |
| | Confirming effects | | | | | | | | | ●···● | | | Suzuki |
| | Standardization and fixing of control | | | | | | | | | | ●···● | | Minami |
| | Reflection previous activity and tasks for future | | | | | | | | | | | ●···● | Suzuki |

Fig.7.3　Activity plan

## Step 2　Clarification of the Attack Points and Setting Target

According to the questionnaire done after the delivery teachings, 74 % of the teachers are satisfied, but to make it to the 100% is the desire of all the circle members. Clarifying the desired state and current state with the investigation items from the aspects of man/ materials/ environment/ methods, and thought the candidates of attack points.

As the results of weighted evaluation, 5 items of the highest points,

To Utilize "Task Achieving" Effectively

"improvement of teaching methods", "Review/ improvement of Experimental equipments", "Improvement of the method of experiment", "Review/ improvement of text" and "improvement of the program of delivery teaching" were adopted as the "attack points". (Refer to Fig. 7.4).

(Point allotment) ○:3pt. △:2pt. ×:1pt.  Jul.7.05

| Characteristic/Items | Vision to reach | Current vision | Gap | Attacking point (candidates) | Evaluation items | | | Overall evaluation | Adoption or rejection |
|---|---|---|---|---|---|---|---|---|---|
| | | | | | Expected effect | Importance | Upper policy | | |
| (Quantitative Characteristics) Satisfaction in questionnaire | Gain 100% satisfaction in all schools | 74% satisfied by schools done | Teachers are frustrated by 26% | | | | | | |
| (Man) Level/Method of lectures | Gain understanding of all students by easy explanation | Some teacher says 'difficult to understand are to elementary school students' | The course content is not understood by all students | Level up of explaining | △ | △ | △ | 8 | △ |
| | | | | Improvement in teaching methods | ○ | △ | ○ | 18 | ○ |
| (Material) Equipment and text for explanation | Each equipment/texts are easy to understand for all students | Heard voice that some equipment/texts are confusing | Review/ improvement has not been done on equipment/texts | Review/ improvement experimental equipment | ○ | △ | ○ | 18 | ○ |
| | | | | Improvement in experimental method | ○ | ○ | ○ | 27 | ○ |
| | | | | Review/ improvement in text | ○ | △ | ○ | 18 | ○ |
| (Environment) Facility for visit | Want to be told good visiting | Not all sudents are satisfied | Has been left up to the PR institution | Improvement the institution like PR institution | △ | × | △ | 4 | △ |
| (Method) Curriculum | Make the classes to meet the needs of all schools | Little variety of program | Programs are not improved | Improvement of the program of delivery teaching | ○ | ○ | ○ | 27 | ○ |

| Target object | Result of questionnaire for the teacher after implementing the attractive delivery teaching of next generation group |
|---|---|
| Target Value | Degree of satisfaction 74% → OVER 90% |
| Time limit | 8 months later (05 Year-end) |

Fig.7.4 "Attacking Points Selection Sheet" and Setting Target

The target was set to make the teachers' satisfaction by the questionnaire after delivery teachings to more than 90% by 8 month later (Refer to Fig. 7.4).

## ONE POINT

◆ The desired state and current state and the gaps should be quantified as much as possible, but because it tends to become language expression in JHS sections, it might be a good idea to use questionnaire like this case example. Feasibility is not included in the evaluation items for narrowing down the attack points, and the possibility to lead to innovative measures is high.

*191*

## Step 3  Establishing Measures

Focusing on the attacking points adopted by "Attacking Points Selection Sheet", many measures ideas have been decided to be generated together. To deploy the measures to practical level, the information analysis of the improvement desired items in questionnaire survey was conducted. When summarized as a Pareto diagram by items, two items of each of the experiment contents and the teaching contents were found to be the focus points. (Refer to Fig. 7.5).

The practical measures were generated together referring to the results of the analysis, and they were arranged in a tree diagram, and as the results of evaluation, it is decided to proceed to the "Pursuit of Success Scenario" on the 4 items of the Fig. 7.6.

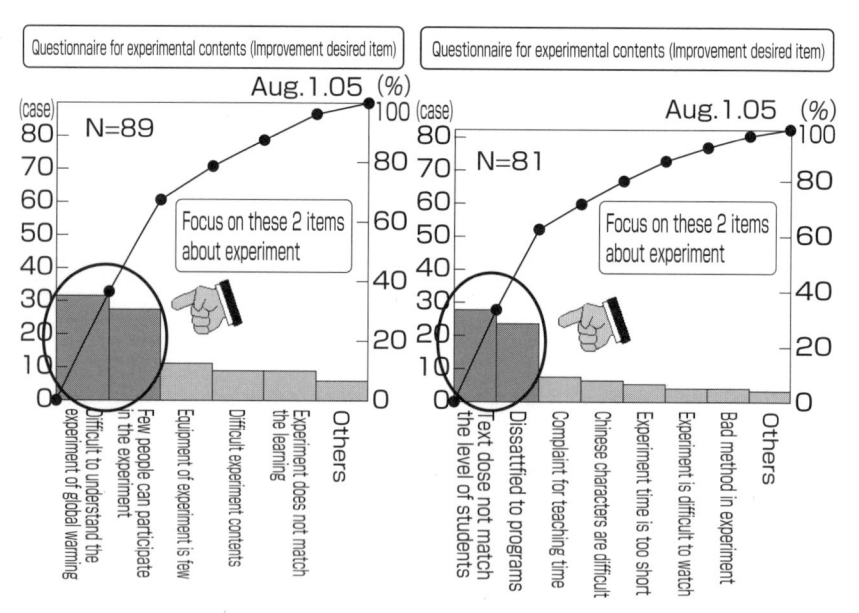

Fig.7.5  Extraction of Improvement Items by Pareto Diagram

To Utilize "Task Achieving" Effectively

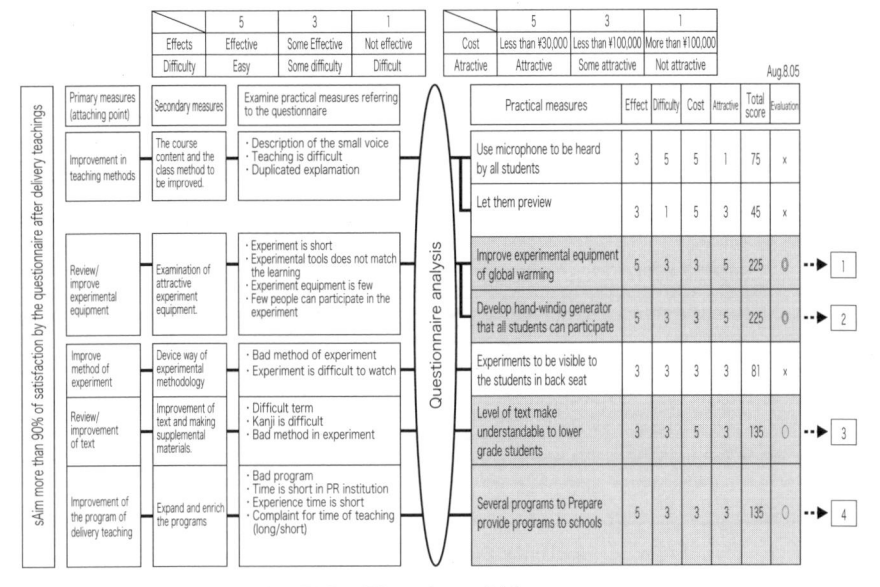

| | | | | 5 | 3 | 1 | | 5 | 3 | | 1 | |
|---|---|---|---|---|---|---|---|---|---|---|---|---|
| | | | Effects | Effective | Some Effective | Not effective | Cost | Less than ¥30,000 | Less than ¥100,000 | More than ¥100,000 | | |
| | | | Difficulty | Easy | Some difficulty | Difficult | Atractive | Attractive | Some attractive | Not attractive | | Aug.8.05 |

| | Primary measures (attaching point) | Secondary measures | Examine practical measures referring to the questionnaire | | Practical measures | Effect | Difficulty | Cost | Attractive | Total score | Evaluation | |
|---|---|---|---|---|---|---|---|---|---|---|---|---|
| sAim more than 90% of satisfaction by the questionnaire after delivery teachings | Improvement in teaching methods | The course content and the class method to be improved. | · Description of the small voice<br>· Teaching is difficult<br>· Duplicated explamation | Questionnaire analysis | Use microphone to be heard by all students | 3 | 5 | 5 | 1 | 75 | x | |
| | | | | | Let them preview | 3 | 1 | 5 | 3 | 45 | x | |
| | Review/improve experimental equipment | Examination of attractive experiment equipment. | · Experiment is short<br>· Experimental tools does not match the learning<br>· Experiment equipment is few<br>· Few people can participate in the experiment | | Improve experimental equipment of global warming | 5 | 3 | 3 | 5 | 225 | ◎ | ··▶ 1 |
| | | | | | Develop hand-windig generator that all students can participate | 5 | 3 | 3 | 5 | 225 | ◎ | ··▶ 2 |
| | Improve method of experiment | Device way of experimental methodology | · Bad method of experiment<br>· Experiment is difficult to watch | | Experiments to be visible to the students in back seat | 3 | 3 | 3 | 3 | 81 | x | |
| | Review/improvement of text | Improvement of text and making supplemental materials. | · Difficult term<br>· Kanji is difficult<br>· Bad method in experiment | | Level of text make understandable to lower grade students | 3 | 3 | 5 | 3 | 135 | ◎ | ··▶ 3 |
| | Improvement of the program of delivery teaching | Expand and enrich the programs | · Bad program<br>· Time is short in PR institution<br>· Experience time is short<br>· Complaint for time of teaching (long/short) | | Several programs to Prepare provide programs to schools | 5 | 3 | 3 | 3 | 135 | ◎ | ··▶ 4 |

Fig.7.6 Planning of Measures

## ONE POINT

◆ It is to be referred that, when thinking about the measures plan, the language informations of the questionnaire survey are quantified and they are used for finding out the focus points of idea generation and for ferreting out practical measures. Because evaluation from many perspectives is conducted, the final narrowing down of measures is appropriate.

## Step 4　Pursuit of Success Scenarios

To pursue the success scenarios, activity plan was made and tackled (Refer to Fig. 7.7)

| | Success scenario | | Implementation period | | | | | Representative |
|---|---|---|---|---|---|---|---|---|
| | | Date | 8/1 | 8/15 | 9/1 | 9/15 | 9/30 | |
| 1 | Improve experimental equipment of global warming | Plan | ◀----------▶ | | | | | Minami |
| | | Achievement | ◀━━━━━━━━━━━━━━━━▶ | | | | | |
| 2 | Develop hand-winding generator that all students can participate | Plan | ◀---------▶ | | | | | Suzuki |
| | | Achievement | ◀━━━━━━━▶ | | | | | |
| 3 | Make the text level understandable to lower grade students | Plan | | | | ◀---▶ | | Minami Suzuki |
| | | Achievement | | | | ◀━━━━━▶ | | |
| 4 | Prepare programs to provide to schools | Plan | | | | ◀---▶ | | Minami |
| | | Achievement | | | | ◀▶ | | |

◀---▶ Plan　　◀━━▶ Achievement

Fig.7.7　Activity plan of Success Scenarios

【Measures 1】 The development of "new experimental equipment for global warming"

Practical measures like "change the color of the inside of the earth depending on the temperature", "making the model georama of the earth" have been generated the members together and narrowed down utilizing the "pay-off matrix" of "workout technique" (Refer to the left of Fig. 7.8). After the trial of the 1st and 2nd prototype, new issues like "the temperature rise is weak because of the weak light" have arisen and detailed specification targets arrived through "Quality Function Deployment (QFD)" were decided to be reflected to the revised one (Refer to the right of Fig. 7.8).

【Measures 2】 The development of "hand winding electric generator" that all the students can participate

Ideas are generated together to solve the weak point of the current generator that only one student can rotate, and decided to apply the ideas like "a method that will not light on if all the students cooperate utilizing the group activity psychology of 4th to 5th elementary students", "the size even elementary students can rotate", "the amount of generated electricity is visible in proportion to the power of rotation".

**【Measures 3】Text book easy to understand even to elementary students**

The defects/ unsatisfactory points of current texts were ferreted out using "Defects Listing Method" and 6 main defects were summarized. Taking in the advices from teachers and the opinions of the families of the circle members, final solution measures were found out for each of them (Refer to Fig. 7.9).

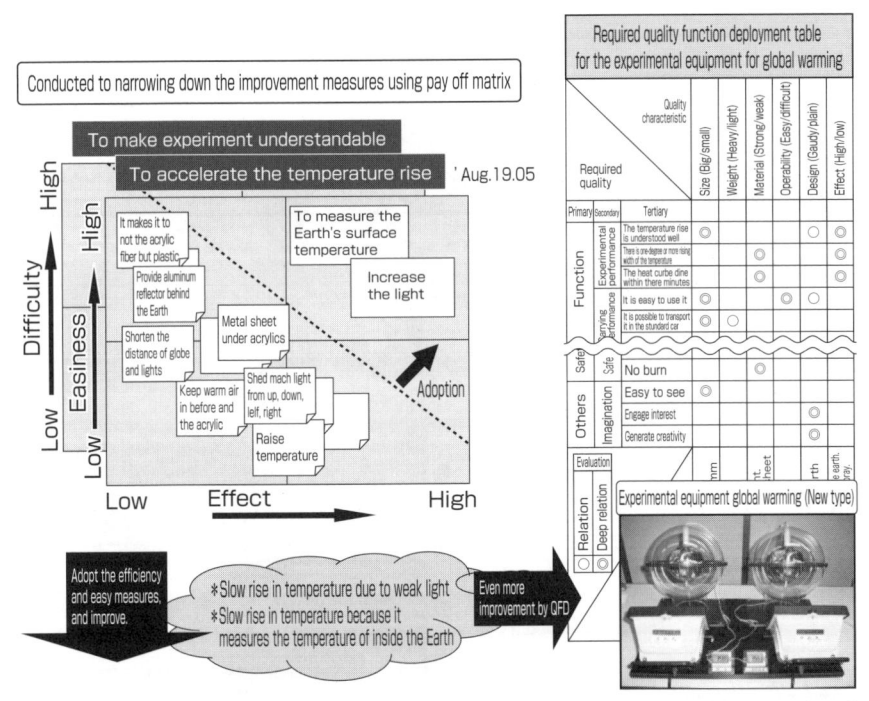

Fig.7.8 Development to experimental equipment of global warming by "Pay-off Matrix" and "QFD"

**【Measures 4】Provision of Several Programs**

Expanding the ideas to beyond inside school and the electricity generating stations, many programs like set menus and options were considered, and as results of conducting matrix evaluation with the conditions of place/

environmental conditions to conduct the teaching/ cost/ time, 6 programs were decided to adopt (Refer to Fig.7.10).

## ONE POINT

◆ It is highly recommended to refer to the process of measures are led to success scenario utilizing many organizing methods/ idea generating methods" like the "pay off matrix", "Quality Function Deployment (QFD), and "Defects Listing Method" for the generation of ideas and development of the equipments.

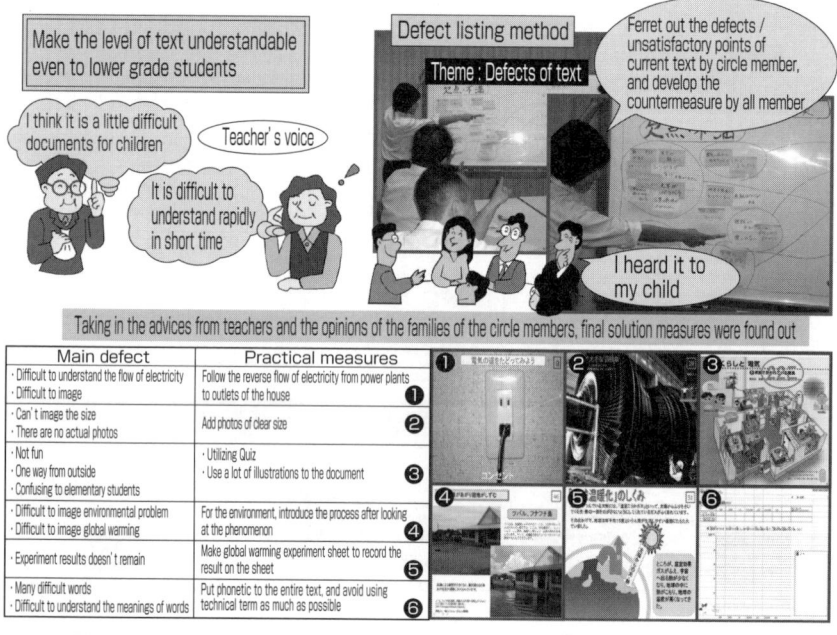

| Main defect | Practical measures | |
|---|---|---|
| · Difficult to understand the flow of electricity<br>· Difficult to image | Follow the reverse flow of electricity from power plants to outlets of the house | ❶ |
| · Can't image the size<br>· There are no actual photos | Add photos of clear size | ❷ |
| · Not fun<br>· One way from outside<br>· Confusing to elementary students | · Utilizing Quiz<br>· Use a lot of illustrations to the document | ❸ |
| · Difficult to image environmental problem<br>· Difficult to image global warming | For the environment, introduce the process after looking at the phenomenon | ❹ |
| · Experiment results doesn't remain | Make global warming experiment sheet to record the result on the sheet | ❺ |
| · Many difficult words<br>· Difficult to understand the meanings of words | Put phonetic to the entire text, and avoid using technical term as much as possible | ❻ |

Fig.7.9  Revision of several texts by "Defect Listing Method"

# To Utilize "Task Achieving" Effectively

**Prepare multiple programs and providing to school**

◎: Possible　○: Possible in conditional　△: Difficult　×: Impossible

| Program \ Condition of expanding the program | Place | | | Environmental conditions of teaching | | | | Cost | Time | | |
|---|---|---|---|---|---|---|---|---|---|---|---|
| | Accommodate about 40-160 people flexibly | Possible to teach in school system | Experimental tools can be used (Meeting fire restrictions and other conditions) | Environment that students can take classes (Quiet, Not the others) | Easy to hear the voice of lecturers. And Material is visible on the screen | Can be implemented between 9 to 15 (one day at school) | Take enough time to explain and understand | Meet the budget and can be implemented within budget | Moving time within 60 minutes in campus | Can be ensured to take place of Lunch (lunchbox) | |
| Energy (45 min), environment (45 min) 90 minute classes (conduct of class by class in the school) | ◎ | ◎ | ◎ | ◎ | ○ | ◎ | ◎ | ◎ | ◎ | ◎ | In school |
| About 60 minutes teaching a set of energy and the environment (in school) | ◎ | ◎ | ◎ | ◎ | ○ | ◎ | ○ | ◎ | ◎ | ◎ | |
| Teaching utilizing conference room in our office | × | ○ | ○ | ○ | ○ | ○ | ◎ | ◎ | △ | ○ | |
| One-day teaching (AM) Energy and environmental lessons (PM) The power plant tour | ◎ | ◎ | ◎ | ◎ | ◎ | ◎ | ◎ | ◎ | ◎ | ◎ | A set with power plant |
| Half-day classes that a set of energy/environmental class and power plant tour | ◎ | ◎ | ◎ | ◎ | ◎ | ◎ | ○ | ◎ | ◎ | ◎ | |
| Implement in a set of our facilities tour (municipal science museum, science technology museum), | ◎ | ○ | ◎ | ◎ | ○ | ◎ | ◎ | ◎ | ◎ | ◎ | Options |
| Implementation of extra-curricular learning programs in non-per-class | ○ | ○ | ○ | ○ | ○ | ○ | ◎ | ◎ | ◎ | ◎ | |
| Teaching in the with a set with nuclear power plant tour | △ | ○ | ○ | ○ | ○ | ○ | △ | × | × | × | |
| Program in combination with other company | △ | ○ | ○ | ○ | ○ | ○ | ○ | × | △ | △ | |

Fig.7.10　Examination of Multiple Programs by "Matrix Diagram"

## Step 5　Implementation of the Success Scenarios

The developed measures (success scenario) were implemented one by one, and final menu for the delivery lectures were prepared and the opinions of teachers and the responses of students were confirmed. New experiment equipment for global warming finally completed which had (Refer to Fig. 7.11) the features of "temperature increases in short time with 2 halogen lumps", "air and $CO_2$ are increased with smaller globe", and the "collapsible and portable." Voices like "It raises the image of global warming and easy to understand" from teachers were heard and the shortening of the cycle time has been recieved.

The hand rotating electricity generator invited the opinions like "Final result is like hanamaru (flower circle: equivalent to gold stars given to children and well done feeling" have raised and it has been named as the

*197*

"hand rotating electricity generator "hanamaru kun". When the new electric generator was tried by children, the smiling face during the experiment became the same when they were given "hanamaru". The "new texts" (Refer to Fig. 7.12) were made with easy to understand rich contents and the "Several Programs" came to be selectable with increased guide menu for schools.

Fig.7.11　Completed new experimental equipment of global warming

Fig.7.12　Revised new text

## Step 6　Confirmation of Effects

Implementing the newly improved/ developed delivery teaching, the confirmed result of satisfaction by questionnaire was 91% and the target was cleared. Above all, the sense of achievement has been tasted by the shining eyes and cheers of students during the class and the response like the letter of gratitude. It was also well received by the teachers like "Talk and experiment, both were very easy to understand", "It was good that the experiment was done that is not possible at school", "It was good because it was experiential learning."

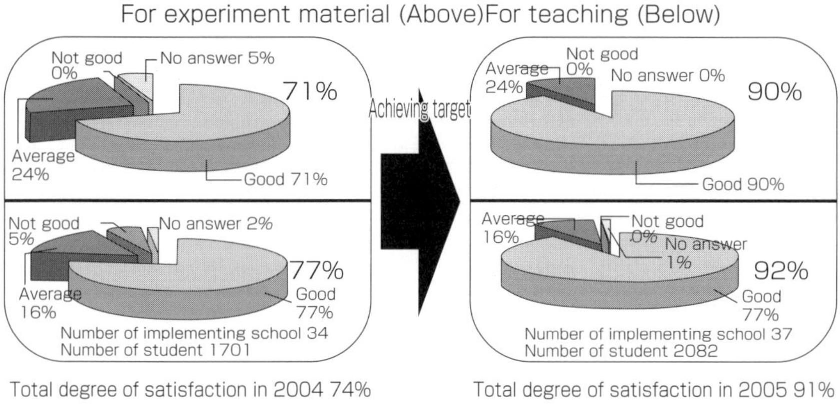

For experiment material (Above)For teaching (Below)
Not good 0%
No answer 5%
71%
Average 24%
Good 71%
Not good 5%
No answer 2%
77%
Average 16%
Good 77%
Number of implementing school 34
Number of student 1701
Total degree of satisfaction in 2004 74%
Achieving target
Not good 0%
Average 24%
No answer 0%
90%
Good 90%
Average 16%
Not good 0%
No answer 1%
92%
Good 77%
Number of implementing school 37
Number of student 2082
Total degree of satisfaction in 2005 91%


Fig.7.13 Confirm Effect

## Step 7 Standardization and Fixing the Control

Contents of the implementation was reflected to the revision of "Delivery Lectures Manual, and it was made possible to utilize the "Delivery Lectures Role Play" VTR for in-house training/ communicating tool to the newly assigned people. We will continue the questionnaire survey and to maintain/ confirm the degree of satisfaction and we will also make efforts to continue timely improvement utilizing the raw voices hereafter.

Later, toward the company-wide deployment of delivery Lectures, we provided the information to "Working group on presentation materials for next generation group", and the results of activities were able to be reflected to the standard text.

## Chapter 7

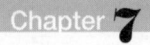

### ONE POINT

◆ The result of activity came to be not only horizontally deployed but also adopted/ reflected to the company-wide delivery Lectures activity implies the high quality of this task achieving. When great results were achieved with task achieving, such an encouragement and deployment to vertical/ horizontal direction are important.

To Utilize "Task Achieving" Effectively

Case Example of PN (Production Network) Department

## Realization of Man-hour reduction by Enhancing Detection Power of Magnetic Flaw Detector

Nissan Motor Co., Ltd. Yokohama Plant 2nd Manufacturing Department Hot Forming Section
"Wakakusa (Young Grass) Circle"
(Derived from Case Example 3, QC Circle Magazine. April 2008.)

Yokohama Plant of the Nissan Motor Co., Ltd. is a general unit plant that manufactures engine/ axle/ formed and fabricated materials for passenger cars. The workshop of the Circle is the material finish process of forged parts, and in charge of the quality inspection of knuckle spindle and knuckle steering (knuckle parts, hereafter) and the members are composed of veterans and youngsters.

In this case example, to achieve the man-hour reduction target of the team to which the circle belongs, aiming at the breakthrough of the difficult task of man-hour reduction of magnetic flaw detector, it tackled with the task achieving to get half reduction of the man-hour by involvement of many related peoples and utilization of the techniques/ tools learned, and at the same time achieved the fostering young members and enhancement of analytic skills.

It is a case example which can be referred to in various aspects like how to proceed with task achieving and the utilization of many tools and devises for operation.

(Note) Knuckle parts are important security parts to transmit the steering power that is attached to front suspension of automobile.

## Step 1 Selection of the theme

Because there was a concern of failure to attain the teams activity plan to reduce man hour, we ferreted out the themes concerning the quality cost, and

## Chapter 7

as a result of evaluation with "Theme Selection Matrix ("Problems/ Tasks Narrowing Down Evaluation Table"), it is decided to tackle with "Man-hour Reduction by enhancement of the Detect Power of Knuckle Parts Magnetic Flaw Detector" with task achieving (Refer to Fig. 7.14).

**Quality cost review item**

Evaluation score ◎=3 ○=2 △=1

| Item (prevention cost) | Measure (Evaluation cost) | Effect (Correction cost) | Activities | Boss's policy | Urgency | Importance | Contribution for quality loss | Score | Rank |
|---|---|---|---|---|---|---|---|---|---|
| Increasing quality of side gear and pinion mate | Abolishing process of magnetic flaw detector | Reduce 1.0 man-hour | Implementation planned in September | Now in activity | | | | | |
| Prevention slppege bend defect of in curve of side flange | Curve measurement by sensor | Reduce 0.2 man-hour | Reviewing with technology section | ◎ | ○ | ◎ | ○ | 10 | 3 |
| Increase quality of housing with shaft | Abolishing process of magnetic flaw detector | Reduce 0.3 man-hour | Investigating the source | ◎ | ◎ | ◎ | ○ | 11 | 2 |
| Enhancement of the detect power of knuckle parts magnetic flaw detector | Magnetic flaw single process detecton | Reduce 2.0 man-hour | No implementation | ◎ | ◎ | ◎ | ◎ | 12 | 1 |
| Shortening lead time of connecting rod cap | Inline visual work | Reduce 0.2 man-hour | Considering the layout of the equipment | ◎ | ○ | ◎ | ○ | 10 | 3 |

Fig.7.14 Narrowing down the theme by "Theme Selection Matrix"

Knuckle parts for Caravan are alternatively produced between knuckle spindle and knuckle steering line, and since the Magnetic Flaw Detect Inspection (Refer to Fig. 7.15) is conducted for 2 processes (2 times), the man-hours needed is 4 man-hours. The finishing operation was evaluated why 2 processes are needed, with "FMEA (Failure Mode and Effects Analysis)", it was re-acknowledged that the magnetic flaw detection inspection needs 2 man-hours because the knuckle parts are large in size and with complex shape, and with high risk index of important failures slippage. (Refer to Fig. 7.16)

When benchmarked with other companies in the same industry, it was found that G company is able to assure with one process. Such necessity to tackle with was summarized in the Table 7.2 with the results of investigation/ arrangement from the aspects of urgency and importance.

To Utilize "Task Achieving" Effectively

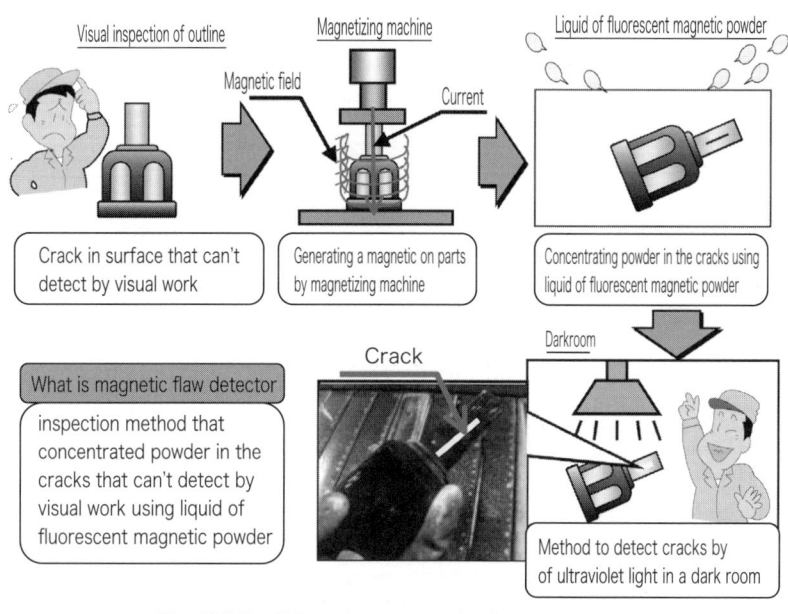

### Visual inspection of outline
Crack in surface that can't detect by visual work

### Magnetizing machine
Magnetic field / Current
Generating a magnetic on parts by magnetizing machine

### Liquid of fluorescent magnetic powder
Concentrating powder in the cracks using liquid of fluorescent magnetic powder

**What is magnetic flaw detector**
inspection method that concentrated powder in the cracks that can't detect by visual work using liquid of fluorescent magnetic powder

Crack

Darkroom

Method to detect cracks by of ultraviolet light in a dark room

Fig.7.15　What is magnetic flaw detector

| NO | Process name · Each process | Function of process · Defective item to analyze | Defective mode · Expected defect, defect in past | Effect of defect · Effect on next processes and completed car | Point of Evaluation | | | | Contents of measure · Prevention plan of recurrence |
|---|---|---|---|---|---|---|---|---|---|
| | | | | | Degree of importance | Degree of occurrence | Degree of detection | Degree of importance | |
| 1 | Visual observation on outline | Underfill | Leaving black skin | Processing defect | 3 | 1 | 1 | 3 | Enhanced visual work |
| | | To slide mold | Processing defect | Damage processing machine | 1 | 1 | 1 | 1 | Enhanced visual work |
| 4 | Magnetic flaw detect First process | Crack | Leak in car assembly | Complaint from market | 9 | 1 | 3 | 27 | Assure 2 processes for magnetic detection flow |
| | | Lap defect | Underfil by separation | Processing defect | 1 | 1 | 3 | 3 | Assure 2 processes for magnetic detection flow |
| | | Damage | Underfil by separation | Processing defect | 1 | 1 | 3 | 3 | Assure 2 processes for magnetic detection flow |
| 5 | Magnetic flaw detect second processes | Crack | Leak in car assembly | Complaint from market | 9 | 1 | 1 | 9 | Assure 2 processes for magnetic detection flow |
| | | Lap defect | Underfil by separation | Processing defect | 1 | 1 | 1 | 1 | Assure 2 processes for magnetic detection flow |
| | | Damage | Underfil by separation | Processing defect | 1 | 1 | 1 | 1 | Assure 2 processes for magnetic detection flow |

**FMEA evaluation standard**

| Degree of effect | | Degree of occurrence | | Degree of defect | | Degree of importance |
|---|---|---|---|---|---|---|
| Evaluation | Evaluation criteria | Evaluation | Evaluation criteria | Evaluation | Evaluation criteria | Evaluation criteria |
| 10~9 | Fatal defect that lead to injury accident/ property damage | 5 | Defect rate over 3.1% | 5 | Become market claim by pass into dealer and customer | Hazard index of important defect<br>Degree of effect×<br>Degree of occurrence×<br>Degree of detect=<br>Degree of importance |
| 8~7 | Serious defect that lead to no driving and car trouble | 4 | Detect rate 2.1~3.0% | 4 | Detect before shipping | |
| 6~5 | Middle defect that causes hypofunction | 3 | Defect rate 1.1~2.0% | 3 | Detect before car assembly | |
| 4~3 | Little defect decline the outline function | 2 | Defect rate 0.6~1.0% | 2 | Detect inside that line | |
| 2~1 | Little | 1 | Defect rate under 0.5% | 1 | Defect in that process | |

It is impossible to detect only at first process, so hazard index of leaking defects is high!

Second process detect part that can't detect in first process

Fig.7.16　FMEA process evaluation and FMEA evaluation of finishing work

203

Table 7.2  Investigation result of necessity to tackle with

| Classify | Item | Investigation result |
|---|---|---|
| Urgency | Personnel placement to knuckle | 4 people work on 2 process of magnetic flaw detector |
| | Comparative investigation on required man-hour | Knuckle process takes to 4 people |
| Importance | Investigation of each important safety parts | Implementation 2 process of magnetic flaw detector in only knuckle parts |
| | Investigation of benchmarking | Assure magnetic flaw detector in 1 process in other companies in the same industry |
| | FMEA process evaluation | High risk of serious failures in 1st process magnetic flaw detector |

The activity plan was made with "Gantt Chart" weaving that it would be worked on in cooperation with related departments (quality assurance department, technology section, and the supplier) and that young member Terada to be assigned as the sub leader of all the steps.

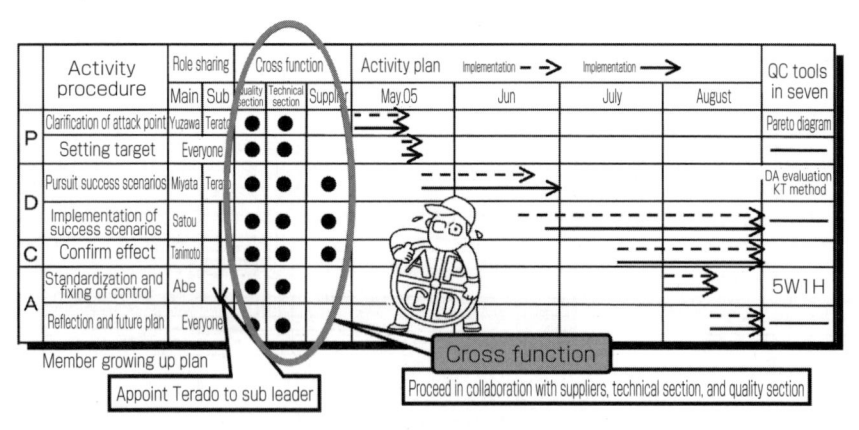

Fig.7.17  Making activity plan

## To Utilize "Task Achieving" Effectively

> **ONE POINT**
> 
> ◆ In the clarification of the needs to tackle with, it is highly helpful that the urgency and importance, and especially the setting of the required target level is done with "benchmarking" of other companies in the same industry. In addition, that they have done process evaluation with "FMEA" and extracting the failure modes in the process and confirmed the reliability of the finishing process considering their effects and evaluation and countermeasures, gives the impression of the high quality of the circle that is tackling with the man-hour reduction with consciousness of the quality assurance.

## Step 2  Clarification of Attack Points and Setting Targets

To ferreting out the attack points, it is investigated/ grasped from the viewpoints of 4M. Although there is no cracking failure spill over, most of the nonconformance were found in the 1st process, 13% was also found in the 2nd process (2nd round). The positions found in the 2nd process are where the florescent sharpness was thin and it seemed to make the detection difficult. When we investigated its factor, the electricity focusing on the positions of the thin sharpness, it was found the possibility of existence of positions of insufficient electricity due to "Electrode board was not touched" in the case of knuckle spindle, and due to "Magnetized cable is not independent and lines were connected" in the case of knuckle spindle.

For each investigation item, the current level and required level were organized and the candidates for attack points were ferreted out from the gaps, and it was summarized in the "Attack Points Selection Sheet". Evaluating the attack points candidate, 3 items of attack points were selected, and the target was decided as "To make the magnetic flaw detector of knuckle parts 1 process assurance by October 2005" (Refer to Fig. 7.18).

# Chapter 7

◎ =3point ○ =2point △ =1point

| Theme characteristic | Current level | Required level | Achievement level | Possibility of eliminate gap | Expected effect | Ability to respond in the workplace | Score | Rank |
|---|---|---|---|---|---|---|---|---|
| Magnetic flaw detector inspection | 2 process assurance | 1 process assurance | 1 process assurance | | | | | |

| | Grasping item | Current level | Required level | Gap | Candidate of attacking point | Possibility of eliminate gap | Expected effect | Ability to respond in the workplace | Score | Rank |
|---|---|---|---|---|---|---|---|---|---|---|
| Attack point selection sheet | Investigation defective rate in previous process | Defect rate 0.5% | Defect rate less than 0.5% | No gap | — | — | — | — | — | — |
| | Defect investigation of defection past 3 year | Defect continuing 0 magnetic flaw detector | 0 defect in magnetic flaw detector | No gap | — | — | — | — | — | — |
| | Investigation detection by worker | Detect defect by worker | Exhaustive detection by all workers | No gap | — | — | — | — | — | — |
| | Investigate detection capability by worker | Exhaustive detection in all workers | Exhaustive detection by all workers | No gap | — | — | — | — | — | — |
| | Investigate defectives by part | Detect in 2 process of magnetic flaw by | Exhaustive detection in1 process of magnetic flaw detector | miss detection | Review assurance position | ◎ | ◎ | ◎ | 9 | 1 |
| | Investigate sharpness of defect positions | Rank of sharpness exist 1 or 2 | More than rank 3 of sharpness | Parts that rank of sharpness is 1 or 2 | Improve crack sharpness | ◎ | ◎ | ◎ | 9 | 1 |
| | Investigation of magnetizing current flow | Unclear it fl to whole part | To flow whole part | Current flow | Improvement method assurance posithion | ◎ | ◎ | ◎ | 9 | 1 |
| | by method of Knuckle part | 4.0 man-hour in 2 processes of magnetic flaw detector | 2 man-hour in 1 process assurance | 2 man-hour | Review assurance posithion | ◎ | ◎ | ◎ | 9 | 1 |

Fig.7.18 "Attack Points Selection Sheet"

## ONE POINT

◆ They decided the investigation items from 4M (man, material, machine/equipment, work methods), clarified the current level and required (desired) level carefully and the attack points candidates are thought from the gaps grasping from big view. In the evaluation and narrowing down the attack points, it is the point that evaluation items were set that were not tied up with feasibility so that it will lead them to the measures with rich ideas.

## Step 3  Planning of Measures

As the result of idea generation in the "measures family meeting" attended by facilitators and technical experts, it was almost decided that for the knuckle spindle "to increase the electrode of magnetizing machine to flow magnetic current evenly" and for the knuckle steering "to disperse the

To Utilize "Task Achieving" Effectively

Table 7.3  Selection of part aggregation lines by "KT Method DA Evaluation"

| Select line<br>Examination items | | Plan 1<br>Part aggregation in knuckle spindle line | | | Plan 2<br>Part aggregation in knuckle steering line | | |
|---|---|---|---|---|---|---|---|
| Must item | | Possible? | GO / NO | | Possible? | GO / NO | |
| Doesn't overload if part even after aggregation | | No problem because total load factor in 2 line is 98% | GO | | No problem because total load factor in 2 line is 98% | GO | |
| WANT item | W Weight | Consideration result | S Score | S×W | Consideration result | S Score | S×W |
| Improvement cost | 5 | More than ¥10 million | 2 | 10 | ¥2 million | 5 | 25 |
| Models producible | 3 | 6 models out of 31 | 1 | 3 | 25 models | 3 | 9 |
| Cycle time | 2 | 0.245 minutes | 2 | 4 | 0.245 minutes | 2 | 4 |
| Total score | | | | 17 | | | 38 |

Consideration involving related departments
Participating members: Circle member, the quality assurance department, technical expert

◎=3　○=2　△=1

| Realization 1 process assurance of magnetic flaw detector | | | | Expected effect | Responsability | Cost | Score | Rank |
|---|---|---|---|---|---|---|---|---|
| Review assurance positions | Review assurance of crack | Assure of next process | | ○ | △ | △ | 4 | 11 |
| | | Improve of source | | ○ | ○ | ◎ | 7 | 5 |
| | Review assurance of 1 process method | Standardization of crack spec. | | △ | △ | ◎ | 5 | 9 |
| | | Change fluorescent magnetic particle | | △ | ○ | △ | 4 | 11 |
| Improve method of magnetizing electrification | Change current flow | Change the currency circuit to 6 electrodes | | ◎ | ◎ | ◎ | 9 | 1 |
| | | Change way of electrification | | ○ | △ | ◎ | 6 | 7 |
| | Disperse the connecting parts | Change electrode board to 6 electrodes | | ◎ | ◎ | ◎ | 9 | 1 |
| | | Change the current flow by independence cable | | ◎ | ◎ | ◎ | 9 | 1 |
| Improve crack sharpness | Improve sharpness rank | Change the current flow | | ◎ | ◎ | ◎ | 9 | 1 |
| | | Change electrification time | | △ | △ | ◎ | 5 | 9 |
| | Flow the current in unsharp part | Change the way of magnetizing | | ◎ | △ | ◎ | 7 | 5 |
| | | The current value is improved | | ◎ | △ | ○ | 6 | 7 |

Fig.7.19  Planning of Measures by "Measures Deployment Type Tree Diagram"

connecting parts to flow the current to whole the part", but it was indicated by technical expert that it was not possible because of the large modification cost. Then, the boss gave an advice "How about aggregate the parts to one of the line, ···" and as the result of immediate investigation utilizing the "KT method DA evaluation" (Kepner-Trego Method Decision Analysis Evaluation), it was decided to enhance the detection power by aggregation to knuckle spindle line that can cope with 25 models of cars and which the modification cost is cheaper.

Further, as a result of ferreting out the measures by measures deployment type tree diagram involving related departments, "to change the secondary currency circuit and electrode board of magnetizing machine to 6 electrodes from 4 electrodes" and "to change the currency of electricity by dispersing the connecting points of electrode board" became high scores and were decided to be adopted (Refer to Fig. 7.19). During the investigation of the implementation of the measures, we were hit by the issue that the current ampere meter indicated total ampere of each positions, and because the currency value of each position cannot be known, "it cannot be confirmed if the electric currency is really flowing". During such examination, a circle member with enthusiasm had proposed an idea "Why don't we install ampere meters to each position?" and all agreed with it, the technical expert proposed to the supplier and as the result of consultation, it concluded with the increase installation of electric power detectors.

## ONE POINT

◆ It is really a step of planning of measures that fit to task achieving such as the devised ide ageneration meeting, utilization of "KT method", "Tree Diagram", the member on idea generation that broke the walls. Especially, the utilization of "KT Method DA Evaluation", a methodology for thinking/ decision where the best measures are decided from many ideas, was effective/ efficient. The narrowing down the measures should be evaluated focusing only on the effects of various viewpoints.

## Step 4  Pursuit of Success Scenarios

The stream of the success scenarios was decided that first make the knuckle steering to 1 process assurance, aggregate knuckle spindle,

# To Utilize "Task Achieving" Effectively

horizontally deploy to knuckle spindle, and finally realize the 1 process assurance of all the knuckle parts. To speed up the improvement, 2 teams were organized involving related sections, and the procedures were clarified with the "PDPC Method" as in the Fig. 7.20.

It is decided to confirm the improvement effects by making the implementation plan of enhancing the crack detection by ① modification of magnetizing machine itself, ② modification of electrode board, ③ optimum setting of electricity detector, ④ making of artificial defects sample reproducing the trend of cracks (Refer to Fig. 7.21).

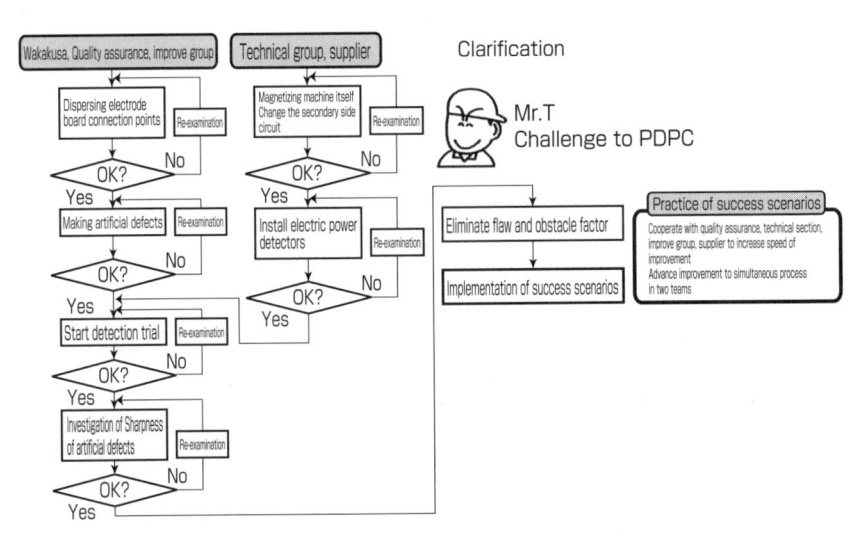

Fig.7.20 Pursuit of Success Scenarios by "PDPC"

| What | Who | How | Date | | | | |
|------|-----|-----|------|---|---|---|---|
| | | | May fourth week | June first week | June second week | June third week | June fourth week |
| Modification of magnetizing machine | Wakakusa, technical section, supplier | Modification | Adjust with supplier ① → ⑤ | | Modification of magnetizing machine | | |
| Modification of electrode board | Wakakusa, improve group, technical section, supplier | Modification | Making drawing ② → ⑥ | Modification of electrode board → ⑨ | Set | | |
| Increase electric power detectors | Wakakusa, technical section, supplier | Increase | Adjust with supplier ③ → ⑦ | Increasing construction → ⑩ | Set | Implementation ⑪ → ⑫ | Confirm side effect → ⑬ |
| Making of artificial defects | Wakakusa, Quality assurance department | Making | Adjustment of detection point ④ → ⑧ | Making | | | |

Fig.7.21 Implementation plan of defection power improvement in knuckle steering line

209

Table 7.4 Obstacles Exclusion Examination Table

| Improvement items | Obstacles | Obstacles exclusion | Judgment |
|---|---|---|---|
| Electrode board | Increase secondary side electrode Obstacle causes in the working arrangements | No problem verifved | ○ |
| Electric power detection | Current value does not rise up in other areas, so electric power failures happen | Pole has already set up to implement based on a review of the whole electrode board | ○ |
| Crack detecting power | Can't detect the crack because of unaware troubles | Confirm crack by master check before work | ○ |

While suffering the obstacles like electric power failures, we could see the ways to exclude all the obstacles (Refer to Table 7.4).

## ONE POINT

◆ It is a good idea to have pursued the success scenarios forming plural teams borrowing the outside expective of the circle aiming at the early solution of the improvement, Here again, they have done their activities efficiently utilizing the tools such as "PDPC Method", "Arrow Diagram Method" and "Obstacles Exclusion Examination Table."

## Step 5  Implementation of the Success Scenarios

Implementation plan of the success scenarios has been made like Fig. 7.22 and the result of trials, we could start as in the plan without any electricity power failures. We could verify the enhancement of magnetic flaw detection with 1st process without any detection of nonconformance in the 2nd process for the 4 months after the implementation. We confirmed that there were no side effects to all the items (Refer to Table 7.5).

In the November of 2005, 7 months later after the start of the activity, we could realize the 1 process assurance by abolishing the magnetic flaw 2nd inspection process for the knuckle steering and in February 2006, for the knuckle spindle.

## To Utilize "Task Achieving" Effectively

> **ONE POINT**
>
> ◆ Like this circle, even in the step of implementation of the success scenarios, if new obstacles or side effects are worried, it is necessary to examine well the measures to exclude them.

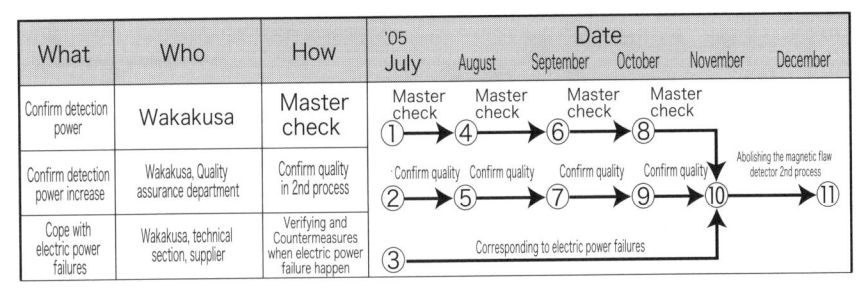

| What | Who | How | '05 July | August | September | October | November | December |
|---|---|---|---|---|---|---|---|---|
| Confirm detection power | Wakakusa | Master check | Master check ① | | Master check ④ | Master check ⑥ | Master check ⑧ | |
| Confirm detection power increase | Wakakusa, Quality assurance department | Confirm quality in 2nd process | Confirm quality ② | Confirm quality ⑤ | Confirm quality ⑦ | Confirm quality ⑨ | ⑩ | Abolishing the magnetic flaw detector 2nd process ⑪ |
| Cope with electric power failures | Wakakusa, technical section, supplier | Verifying and Countermeasures when electric power failure happen | ③ | | Corresponding to electric power failures | | | |

Fig.7.22 Implementation plan of Success Scenarios

Table 7.5 "Side Effect Confirming Investigation Sheet"

| Improvement item | Confirming item | Confirming result | Judgment |
|---|---|---|---|
| Magnetic machine itself | Failure due to load that is caused to increase secondary side magnetic machine | Verified result : there are no unusual loads in equipment | No problem |
| Electrode board | Faster wear of electrode board because of setting electrode board curve prevention pole | Cushion is attached to the electrode board, so there are no unusual wear | No problem |
| Electric power detection equipment | Electric power detection equipment are crashed when the over current flow | No problem because current setting is done with old one currency setting | No problem |

Moreover! Verify and cope with defect expected

## Step 6  Confirmations of Effects

The 1 process assurance of knuckle parts was realized and finally man hour reduction of 3 was attainted over the target. The tangible effects were ¥5.75 million and the intangible effects were enhancement of the quality reliability through addition of the ampere meters, etc. (Refer to Fig. 7.23). At the FMEA process evaluation after the activity, we could confirm the big improvement of the nonconformance slippage risk number by the detection power increase of 1 process. As the results of circle diagnosis, young members grew and the improvement consciousness and analytic power has been enhanced.

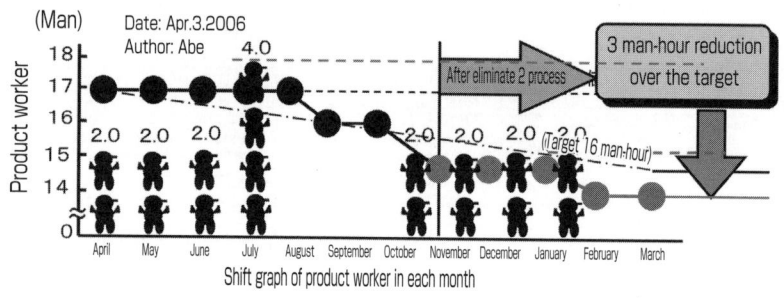

## Man-hour reduction activity in 2005

Date: Apr.3.2006
Author: Abe

After eliminate 2 process

3 man-hour reduction over the target

(Target 16 man-hour)

Shift graph of product worker in each month

Tangible effects ¥1,912,965 in year
(¥5,749,125 in year in total the knuckle spindle)
Intangible effects Improve production by realization of 1 process of ensuring magnetic flaw detector (100%)!
Improve quality reliability by increasing current ampere meter

Fig.7.23 Confirming Effects

## Step 7 Standardization and Fixing of the Control

The maintenance control by the revision of the control process chart/process table, one point lesson, and master check, etc. have been implemented in planned manner with 5W1H. Aiming at the enlargement of the effects, we are now horizontally deploying the electric power detection equipment set this time to all the magnetic flaw detection line of the finishing plant.

To Utilize "Task Achieving" Effectively

5W1H    Author: Satou

| What | Why | Who | Where | When | How |
|---|---|---|---|---|---|
| Control process chart/ process table | Abolishing the magnetic flaw inspection 2nd process | Technical expert | Technical section | 05.11.29 | Revision |
| One point lesson | Change magnetize method | Abe | workshop | 05.7.03 | Making |
| Quality assurance | Defect prevention | Satou | ↑ | 05.07.04 | Re-teaching |
| Master check | ↑ | | Worker | ↑ | When parts changes | Check sharpness of artificial defects |

Horizontal deployment of electronic power detection equipment

Fig.7.24  Standardization and Fixing of the Control by 5W1H

## 7-3

# Do's and Don'ts of Task Achieving

Along with the dissemination of task achieving type, there are many excellent helpful case examples. On the other hand, there are some case examples that are deviated from the basic usage and used in misunderstood way. Here, so that the task achieving is utilized as much as possible, we will introduce the main points of things we want you to take care and the don'ts of it and we hope you will make them as a help for understanding.

## Theme Selection

> Do Select a Theme that is Appropriate to Task Achieving Type

Among the circles, there we such cases that think "Because we are tackling task, we will approach with task achieving type", or "Because we are tackling with the theme that is given by the boss we will do the activity with task achieving type." On the others, we see the case examples that clearly seems it could have been better tackled with problem solving type.

The task achieving type is, as it is explained in the Chapter 1, the procedures appropriate when we tackle with:

① the cases of new works that is not experienced so far
② the cases where the introduction of new ways of doing is needed
③ the cases where problem solving is insufficient with partial change of the old way of doing.

Don't be caught with the term "task" only and judge surely whether it is a theme that is the task achieving is applicable or not, using "Improvement Procedures Selection Method."

## To Utilize "Task Achieving" Effectively

> Don't think "Make it to task achieving type because we don't have to pursue causes"
> Don't confuse between task achieving type and measures implementing type.

It is a wrong thinking to apply the task achieving type to a simple theme that does not needs cause analysis because there is no step of "factors analysis (cause pursuing)" in the steps of the procedures of task achieving type. As to the problem solving type, the most important procedures is the analytical approach that pursue the causes by exploring the problems and defective phenomena, and analyzing/ verifying.

On the other hand, the task achieving type is featured by the design approach that work out the countermeasures by expanding ideas, making import of idea generation free from current situation.

The measures implementing type is to be applied in the cases where the direction of factors and countermeasures are known on the problems and defectives, and the idea of countermeasures almost known, and the approach is basically different from task achieving even though it doesn't do "cause analysis."

Do understand these three types of problems/ tasks solving procedures, and don't mix them and let's select the most appropriate solving procedures to the theme utilizing the "Improvement Procedures Selection Method".

## Clarification of the Attack Points and Setting of Targets

> Don't omit "current level" (present state) even "the tasks that are not experienced so far.

215

# Chapter 7

Even to the "tasks that are not experienced so far", there is necessary be the "current level" that is shown in the implementation step of "Clarification of the Attack Points". For example, you can use the similar things (way of doing, works, products/ goods, etc.) or information and data of related things as the "Current Level". In the case you cannot find any, information/ data, "none" can be thought of as the "current level." If the "current level" is not grasped without investigation, the gap from the "desired level" is not made clear and there is a possibility of the shift of the attack points.

To check whether there is any omission of grasping the "desired level" and "current level," it is recommended to use the "Attack Points Selection Sheet."

> Do grasp the "Attack Points Candidates" widely.

The "Attach Points Candidates" is not the measures themselves, but because they indicate the scope, area, and points of view of generating measures that realize the achievement level of the theme characteristic, it is necessary to grasp them widely.

If you grasp them in detailed manner when grasping the "desired level" and "current level," the "attack point candidates" also becomes of concrete things of narrow scope, and it become difficult to generate many ideas and measures at "planning of measures" and it might not able to attain the objectives. Because the practical measures are examined at the following "Planning of Measures," the "Candidates of Attack Points" do good at the level to judge the directions and scopes of the measures (Refer to Table 7.6). In the tree diagram, expressions of secondary level against tertiary level, primary level against the secondary level, are the expression grasped in the larger sense.

## To Utilize "Task Achieving" Effectively

Table 7.6  Case Examples of Attack Point Candidates Expression

| Example of gap | Example of attack point candidates ||
| --- | --- | --- |
| | narrowly grased attack point | Widely grasped attack point |
| Necessity to halve the number of days that required in endurance test | Increase number of endurance line | Provide endurance test method that can be done in shot time |
| | Explanation: Not sticking to the costly number of lines, make it an attack point with wide view ||
| Dissatisfaction waiting time by patients | Introduce a reservation system | Introduce a method that does not give dissatisfaction to waiting time |
| | Explanation: Reservation system only save time and it can't eliminate dissatisfaction during waiting ||

> **Don't evaluate the narrowing down of the "attack points candidates" with feasibility.**

In the implementation step of "Deciding the Attack Points," the purpose is to narrow down the "Attack Points" that can set the effective directions to realize the achievement level (target) of the characteristics.

When narrowing down these "candidates of the attack points", if the feasibility is evaluated/ judged only with past experiences and knowledge/ technologies, it might happen that the breakthrough idea thoughts with efforts are not adopted and the target is not attained. Even it might be difficult to realize with the capability of the workshop to cope with, there might be a possibility to realize with other methodologies like education and training or getting help.

Therefore, to evaluate the "candidates of attack points," let's evaluate the evaluation items with "possibility of elimination of the gaps" and "largeness of expected effects", rather than the "feasibility." Or depending on the position or the situation of circles, it is possible to include "Effects to the desires of customers", "newness", "ability of the workshop to cope with" into the "evaluation items"

# Chapter 7

## Planning of Measures

> Don't be satisfied with a few ideas by out deciding the "measures"

At the "Planning of Measures," it is the point to generate novel ideas along with the "attack points" fully mobilizing the inherent technologies and knowledge referring to the Chapter 4. If thinking is tied with stereotype or the scope is limited to what can be done by oneselves, only measures with narrow band will be hit and change in thinking will not be made.

As it is said that "He who shoots often, hits at last", novel ideas are really hidden among many ideas. But even that said, it is not easy to generate good measures, and it is important to do previous preparation and training, and devise meetings. We introduce main devises/ methods.

① **Level up of Inherent Technology/Collecting Related Information**

Because many of the ideas are generated applying the original ideas such as the past experience, technology/ knowledge currently owned, or the combination or repeated development of them, it is necessary to make vigilant efforts to do self development consciously, to accumulate experience/ exposures, and to collect related information on regular basis.

② **Utilization of Creativity Techniques and QC 7 Tools**

There are creativity techniques as the most effective things for idea generation. Main techniques are "Brainstorming Method", "Brain-writing Method", "Wish Points Listing Method", "Defects Listing Method", "Checklist Method", "Focusing object Method" and please use them referring to the Chapter 4 for the details. In addition, "Cause and Effect Diagram" in QC 7 tools and "Affinity Diagram" in New QC 7 Tools etc. are also effective.

③ **Regular training of Idea Generation**

As to idea generation, one can generate many ideas when necessary if one undergoes exercises/ training and make the ideas to generate easier on regular basis. Also, if one can overcome the three barriers (of recognition/ of culture/of feeling) that inhibit ideas consciously, many ideas could be generated.

④ **Idea Generating in a Group**

It is easier to generate many good ideas when the intelligence are gathered in a group rather than it is left to an individual. Furthermore, it is said that the change in thinking is easier when heterogeneous people (other workshops/jobs) join as members rather than that of homogeneous people.

## Don't tied up with feasibility in the evaluation of "measures plan", too

The themes that are tackled with the task achieving type are the cases where new works first tackled with, those not experienced so much so far, or it has been tackled many times but could not solve and a breakthrough is necessary. To cope with these, the solution is difficult by the customary measures, and ideas from drastic change in thinking are needed. The measures that do not confined to known technology or framework may involve risks or it may be difficult to realize, but it is the feature of task achieving type to make the success scenarios successful overcoming such obstacles and side effects (effects to others).

If the evaluation is done easily with such as "feasibility" and "ability of circle" like the evaluation of the countermeasures in problem solving type procedures, many of the good ideas will be thrown out that are difficult from experiences, and as the result it might be end up with nonattainment of the target.

Therefore, in the task achieving type, measures are arranged in the "matrix diagram" and so forth and evaluate only with expected effects (predicted effects) and pursue the success scenarios. It is no problem to evaluate with feasibility when narrowing down the scenarios or judging totally in the next step of "Success Scenarios"

Depending on the theme, the expected effects are not limited to one. For example, other than the characteristics targeted, other characteristic effects such as QCDPSME are aimed at the same time. In the Fig. 7.25, expected effects and promptness, economy are evaluated at the same time.

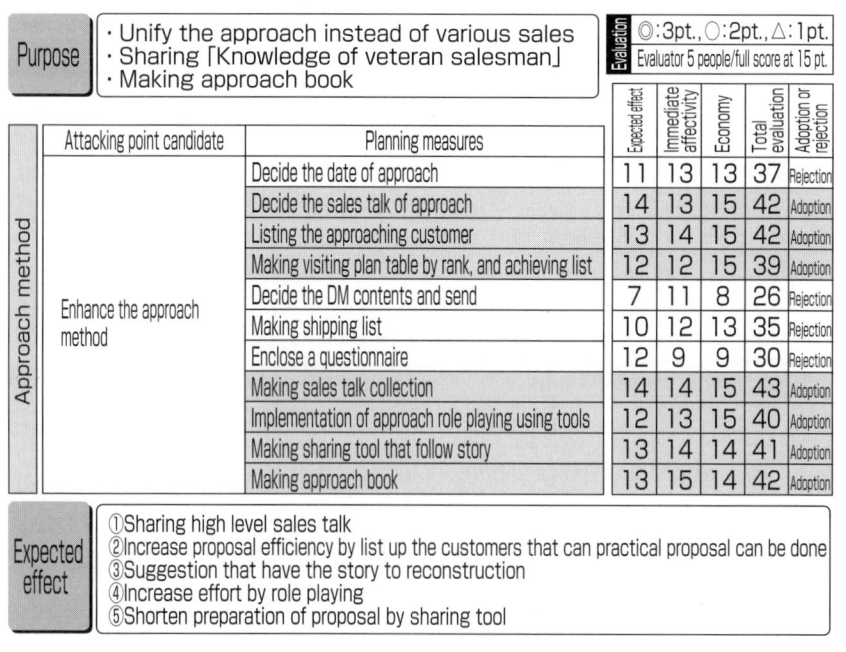

| Purpose | · Unify the approach instead of various sales<br>· Sharing「Knowledge of veteran salesman」<br>· Making approach book | | | | | | |
|---|---|---|---|---|---|---|---|

Evaluation: ◎:3pt., ○:2pt., △:1pt.
Evaluator 5 people/full score at 15 pt.

| | Attacking point candidate | Planning measures | Expected effect | Immediate affectivity | Economy | Total evaluation | Adoption or rejection |
|---|---|---|---|---|---|---|---|
| Approach method | Enhance the approach method | Decide the date of approach | 11 | 13 | 13 | 37 | Rejection |
| | | Decide the sales talk of approach | 14 | 13 | 15 | 42 | Adoption |
| | | Listing the approaching customer | 13 | 14 | 15 | 42 | Adoption |
| | | Making visiting plan table by rank, and achieving list | 12 | 12 | 15 | 39 | Adoption |
| | | Decide the DM contents and send | 7 | 11 | 8 | 26 | Rejection |
| | | Making shipping list | 10 | 12 | 13 | 35 | Rejection |
| | | Enclose a questionnaire | 12 | 9 | 9 | 30 | Rejection |
| | | Making sales talk collection | 14 | 14 | 15 | 43 | Adoption |
| | | Implementation of approach role playing using tools | 12 | 13 | 15 | 40 | Adoption |
| | | Making sharing tool that follow story | 13 | 14 | 14 | 41 | Adoption |
| | | Making approach book | 13 | 15 | 14 | 42 | Adoption |

| Expected effect | ①Sharing high level sales talk<br>②Increase proposal efficiency by list up the customers that can practical proposal can be done<br>③Suggestion that have the story to reconstruction<br>④Increase effort by role playing<br>⑤Shorten preparation of proposal by sharing tool |
|---|---|

Fig.7.25 Planning and Evaluation of Measures

(Source : Polus Grand Tec Co., Ltd., "Oshare (dress up) Shisanzei (assets tax) Circle", *QC Circle Magazine*, April2006, Case Example 3, JUSE.)

# To Utilize "Task Achieving" Effectively

## Pursuit of Success Scenarios

Don't forget to check the obstacles and side effects (bad effects) of the "Success Scenarios"

The success scenarios that is based on the measures (ideas) obtained changing thinking has big effects, or the higher the newness, it is necessary to think that there are many obstacles or side effects. How to understand obstacles and side effects and prediction/ examination methods are shown in the Table 7.7. If these examinations are omitted or do with only narrow area of examination, problems might occur during implementation or hit against walls and it may become difficult to realize. Depending on the success

Table 7.7 Examination Methods of Obstacles/Side Effect

| Classify | How to grasp | Prediction/ examination methods | Example |
|---|---|---|---|
| Obstacles | The things that prevent and cause difficultly to implementation of measures and scenarios | Think existance of obstacles disability in your head, or ferret out using such a tree diagram and PDPC the merit/demerit table and consider countermeasures. Utilizing FTA (Fault Tree Analysis) and FMEA (Failure Mode and Effect Analysis) for technical analysis If it is not enough to exame only to think in head and the simulation, confirm with the trials and experiments practically. | Install new method of production ↓ Develop new carrying machine ↓ The department budget shortfall ↓ Make original machine instead of outsourcing |
| Side effect | Bad effect to others that can happen by implementing measures and scenarios | Predict and examine utilizing the way and of thinking method, like above Simulation is effective because it is effects examination for others | Significant decline of waiting time ↓ Install reservation system ↓ Request public announcement to public relations department |

## Chapter 7

scenarios, utilizing the "Obstacles/ side effects examination table" and by asking for the help of boss, by receiving support of related peoples, or by doing research of documents and materials, let's examine/ address obstacles/ side effects.

> **Don't mix up the "Planning of Measures" and the "Pursuit of Success Scenarios" and implement at the same time**

It is ultimately the short cut to implement along with the implementation procedures of each step, to evaluate many measures (ideas) generated at "Planning of Measures" and to narrow down the measures of large expected effects, then in the next "Pursuit of Success Scenarios" to summarize into the success scenarios of large effects. Combining the both steps into one, and if the success scenario is examined each time from the many attack points and measures, it become inefficient by pursuing success scenarios of measures of small effects that do not need examination, and it might be delayed to reach to the optimum success scenarios. Also, it become impossible to foster success scenarios combining some of the narrowed down measures.

However, in the case of tackling with the theme of relatively narrow area of examination, and the number of the attack points and measures are small, it might be good to examine the success scenarios consecutively without evaluating the measures generated at "Planning of Measures," and after that to evaluate the scenario candidates of large effects. In such a case, by utilizing the "Measures Planning/ Success Scenario Pursuit Table" like Fig. 7.26, it could be possible to tackle with the both step understanding the connection/ relationship between the "Planning of Measures" and "Pursuit of Success Scenarios".

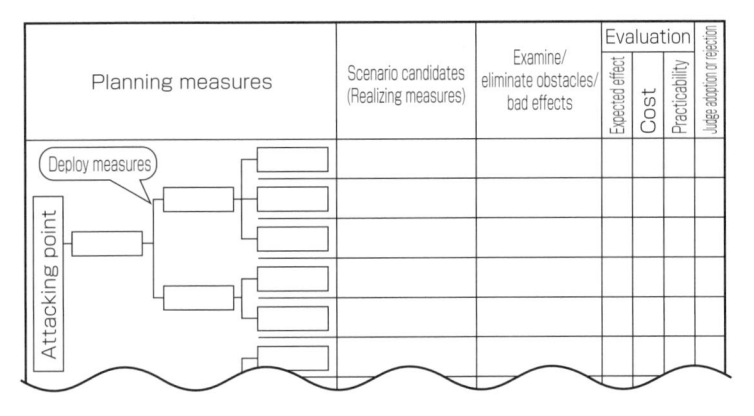

Fig.7.26 Example of "Measures Planning/ Success Scenario Pursuit Table"

## Confirmation of Effects

> Do Return and Re-do in Case of the "Effects" didn't Reach to the Target

In case of failure to achieve the target, to go back and re-do is important. Reflecting back where problems existed and return to the corresponding step and re-examine.

First, if there are omission of implementation within the implementation plan, do the non-implemented items. When all are implemented without omission, return to the "Pursuit of Success Scenarios" or the "Planning of Measures," and add/ examine success scenarios and measures, and implement the new success scenarios. When even after that the target is not achieved, return to the "Clarification of Attack Points and Setting Target", and re-do them.

If cases investigation of complex non-achievement came to be necessary, or when unexpected problem were hit in the middle, there would be cases of using "Problem Solving Type"

# Chapter 7

## Standardization and Fixing of Control

> Do implement the "Standardization and Fixing of Control" surely in Task Achieving Type

The "Standardization and Fixing of Control" should basically be done in any problem solving procedure surely using "5W1H Matrix Diagram" and so forth.

In the case of task achieving type, it is necessary to conduct standardization carefully, for new work and improvement related to breakthrough is the main, measures/ scenario varies widely, high in novelty in contents, in many cases they influence system or mechanisms. Furthermore, it is difficult to fix them by one deployment, it is important to follow up until they are completely fixed while also reviewing.

**References**

1) Ayano, Katsutoshi, ed, *QC Circle Kanagawa District Task Achieving Study Group ed., Kadai Tassei Jissen Manual, 2nd revision* (Task Achieving Practice Manual 2nd revision), JUSE Press, Ltd., 2001.

2) Hosotani, Katsuya, ed, *Suguwakaru Mondai Kaiketsu ho* (Quickly Understandable Problem Solving Method), JUSE Press, Ltd., 2000.

3) New QC 7 Tools Study Group *Yasashii Shin QC Nanatsudougu* (Introductory New QC 7 Tools), JUSE Press, Ltd., 1984.

4) Kano, Noriaki, ed, Nitta, Mitsuru, *QC Circle no tameno Kadai Tassei Gata QC Story* (Task Achieving QC Story for QC Circles), JUSE Press, Ltd., 1999.

5) Ishikawa, Kaoru, *Kanri Gijutsu Pocket Jiten* (Management Techniques Pocket Dictionary), JUSE Press, Ltd., 1981.

6) Onodera, Katsushige, *FMEA Shuho to Jissen Jirei* (FMEA Technique and Practice Cases), JUSE Press, Ltd., 2006.

7) Sugiura, Tadashi, *Konnani Yasashii Aidea Hasso ho* (Such a Easy Idea Generating Method), JUSE Press, Ltd., 1999.

8) Ohfuji, Tadashi/ Ono, Mitsuteru/ Akao, Yoji, *Hinshitsu Kinou Tenkai ho (1)* (Quality Function Deployment (1)), JUSE Press, Ltd, 2006, p.75.

9) Akao, Yoji, ed., *Hinshitsu Tenkai Katsuyo no Jissai* (Practice of Quality Deployment Use), JSA, 1988.

10) Makoto Takahashi, *Shinpen Souzoryoku Jiten* (New Edition Creativity Dictionary), JUSE Press, Ltd., 2002.

11) "Rensai: Ikita Data no Torikata, Tsukaikata (Series: How to Take and Use Lively)", *QC Circle Magazine*, June, 2000, JUSE.

12) Nissan Motor Co., Ltd., "PB Circle", *QC Circle Magazine*, Sept. 2001, Case Example 1, JUSE.

13) Konica Co. Ltd., "AP-50 Joint Circle", *QC Circle Magazine*, Jan. 2002 Case Example 1, JUSE.

14) Nissan Motor Co., Ltd., "Denshiman (Electron Man) Circle", *QC Circle Magazine*, Feb, 2002, Case Example 1, JUSE.

15) Kansai Electric Power Co., Ltd., "Challenge Up Circle", *QC Circle Magazine*, Feb., 2003, Case Example 1, JUSE.

16) Kansai Electric Power Co., Ltd., "Chameleon Circle", *QC Circle Magazine*, Sept. 2003, Case Example 1, JUSE.

17) Nissan Motor Co., Ltd., "Climb Circle", *QC Circle Magazine*, April 2004, Case Example 1, JUSE.

18) Honda Co., Ltd., "Kamataki (Boiler) man Circle", *QC Circle Magazine*, May 2004, Special Feature Case Example, JUSE.

19) Kobe Steel Co. Ltd., "Active Power Circle", *QC Circle Magazine*, July 2004, Case Example 3, JUSE.

20) Nissan Motor Co. Ltd., "Clean World Circle", *QC Circle Magazine*, June, 2005, Case Example 2, JUSE.

21) Takano Co., Ltd., "Hitohito (man-man) Circle", *QC Circle Magazine*, March 2006, Case Example 3, JUSE.

22) Polus Grand Tec Co., Ltd., "Oshare (dress up) Shisanzei (assets tax) Circle", *QC Circle Magazine*, April 2006, Case Example 3, JUSE.

23) 2nd Air Wing, Air Defense Command, "Key Point Circle", *QC Circle Magazine*, May 2006, Special Issue Case Example, JUSE.

24) East Japan Railway Company, "Sweet Potato Circle", *QC Circle Magazine*, April 2007, One Point Case Example, JUSE.

25) Nagano Electronics Industrial Co., Ltd, "Ohizamoto (Home turf) Circle", *QC Circle Magazine*, May 2007, Case Example 3, JUSE.

26) Konica Minolta Medical & Graphic, Inc., "Chienowa (Puzzle Ring) Circle", *QC Circle Magazine*, Dec. 2007, One Point Case Example, JUSE.

27) ONDA TECHNO Intl. Patent Attys., "3D Squadron CAD Ranger Circle", *QC Circle Magazine*, Dec. 2007, JUSE.

28) Nissan Motor Co. Ltd., "Wakakusa (Young Grass) Circle", *QC Circle Magazine*, April 2008, Case Example 3, JUSE.

29) Bohsei Pharmacy, "Ayaka 3 Months Circle", *QC Circle Magazine*, Aug. 2008, Case Example 1, JUSE.

30) Hitachi Global Storage Technologies, "25TEST Circle", *QC Circle Magazine*, March 2009, Case Example 1, JUSE.

31) Komatsu Ltd., "TM series checkerman zero accident circle", *QC Circle Magazine*, April 2010, JUSE.

32) Isuzu Motors Ltd., Hokkaido Plant (Current Isuzu Engine Manufacturing Hokkaido, Ltd.), "Dreamer Circle" Presentation Materials at the 3139th QC Circle Convention held by the QC Circle Hokkaido Branch.

33) Hokushin Industry Inc., "EDP Circle" Presentation Materials, at the 3573th QC Circle Convention held by the QC Circle Kanto Branch, Kanagawa District.

34) Nissan Motor Co. Ltd., "Performance Circle" Presentation Materials at the 3780th QC Circle Convention held by the QC Circle Kanto Branch, Kanagawa District.

35) Nissan Motor Co., Ltd., "COOLS Circle" Presentation Materials at the 3940th QC Circle Convention held by the QC Circle Kanto Branch, Kanagawa District.

36) Ichiko Industries, Ltd., "Aun Circle" Presentation Materials at the 4100th QC Circle Convention held by the QC Circle Kanto Branch, Kanagawa District.

37) Kansai Electric Power Co. Ltd., "Hino kuruma (Wheel of Fire) Circle" Presentation Materials at the 4970th held by the QC Circle Headquarter.

38) HAKUTSURU SAKE Brewing Co. Ltd., "Yatto Deta (Finally Emergeg) Circle" Presentation Materials at the 5064th QC Circle Convention held by the QC Circle Kinki chapter, Hyogo District.

39) Nissan Motor Co. Ltd., "Powerful/ Adventure Circle" Presentation Materials, at the 5090th QC Circle Convention held by the QC Circle Headquarter.

## 執筆担当

綾 野 克 俊 … まえがき，第 1 章，第 2 章
　　　　　　　　東海大学 政治経済学部 経営学科 教授

飯 田 庄 三 … 第 4 章
　　　　　　　　元 NTT データ東京 SMS

井 上 喜 義 … 第 5 章
　　　　　　　　井上 KAIZEN 研究所代表，元 出光興産

下 田 敏 文 … 第 3 章（ツール 5 ～ 7）
　　　　　　　　日産自動車㈱生産事業本部 生産人事部 シニアエンジニア

福 島 光 彦 … 第 3 章（ツール 1 ～ 4）
　　　　　　　　光彦問題解決研究所 所長

山 上 隆 男 … 第 1 章，第 6 章，第 7 章
　　　　　　　　総合学園ヒューマンアカデミー 原宿校・渋谷校 校長

---

### （英語版）課題達成に役立つツール

日本語版
　2010 年 6 月 30 日　第 1 刷発行
英語版
　2011 年 9 月 19 日　第 1 刷発行
　2019 年 8 月 23 日　第 2 刷発行

訳・編著　綾　野　克　俊
著　者　　飯　田　庄　三
　　　　　井　上　喜　義
　　　　　下　田　敏　文
　　　　　福　島　光　彦
　　　　　山　上　隆　男
発 行 人　戸　羽　節　文

検印省略

発行所　株式会社 日科技連出版社
〒 151-0051　東京都渋谷区千駄ヶ谷 5-15-5
　　　　　　DS ビル
電　話　出版　03-5379-1244
　　　　営業　03-5379-1238

印刷・製本　河北印刷株式会社

Printed in Japan

© Katsutoshi Ayano 2011　　ISBN978-4-8171-9415-2
URL http://www.juse-p.co.jp/

＜本書の全部または一部を無断で複写複製（コピー）することは，著作権法上での例外を除き，禁じられています．＞